Third Edition

Soccer

STEPS TO SUCCESS

Joseph A. Luxbacher, PhD
University of Pittsburgh

Human Kinetics

Library of Congress Cataloging-in-Publication Data

Luxbacher, Joe.
  Soccer : steps to success / Joseph A. Luxbacher.-- 3rd. ed.
    p. cm.
  ISBN 0-7360-5435-9 (soft cover)
  1. Soccer. I. Title.
  GV943.L87 2005
  796.334--dc22   2004018570

ISBN: 0-7360-5435-9

The Web addresses cited in this text were current as of December 22, 2004, unless otherwise noted.

Acquisitions Editor: Jana Hunter
Developmental Editor: Cynthia McEntire
Assistant Editor: Scott Hawkins
Copyeditor: Jan Feeney
Proofreader: Darlene Rake
Graphic Designer: Nancy Rasmus
Graphic Artist: Kim McFarland
Cover Designer: Keith Blomberg
Photographer (cover): © Peter Parks/Getty Images
Art Manager: Kareema McLendon
Illustrator: Roberto Sabas
Printer: Versa Press

Human Kinetics books are available at special discounts for bulk purchase. Special editions or book excerpts can also be created to specification. For details, contact the Special Sales Manager at Human Kinetics.

Printed in the United States of America   10 9 8 7 6 5 4 3 2 1

Human Kinetics
Web site: www.HumanKinetics.com

United States: Human Kinetics
P.O. Box 5076
Champaign, IL 61825-5076
800-747-4457
e-mail: humank@hkusa.com

Canada: Human Kinetics
475 Devonshire Road Unit 100
Windsor, ON N8Y 2L5
800-465-7301 (in Canada only)
e-mail: orders@hkcanada.com

Europe: Human Kinetics
107 Bradford Road
Stanningley
Leeds LS28 6AT, United Kingdom
+44 (0) 113 255 5665
e-mail: hk@hkeurope.com

Australia: Human Kinetics
57A Price Avenue
Lower Mitcham, South Australia 5062
08 8277 1555
e-mail: liaw@hkaustralia.com

New Zealand: Human Kinetics
Division of Sports Distributors NZ Ltd.
P.O. Box 300 226 Albany
North Shore City
Auckland
0064 9 448 1207
e-mail: blairc@hknewz.com

This book is dedicated to my father, Francis Luxbacher,
my first and finest coach, and to his father,
my grandpap, Joseph Luxbacher Sr.
Together they introduced me to the world's most popular
game, taught me its subtleties, and instilled in me
a lifelong respect and passion for the sport.
Their presence will forever be with me.

◪ Contents

◪ Climbing the Steps to Soccer Success

The fact that you are reading this book suggests that you have been bitten by the bug—the soccer bug—and you are definitely not alone. Soccer is far and away the most popular pastime on the planet. It is a game that evokes passion and emotion unparalleled within the realm of competitive sport. More than 150 million registered athletes, including more than 10 million women, play the sport on an official basis. Millions more kick the ball around on an unofficial basis, on sandlots, in playgrounds, and on the back streets of small towns and large cities. Legions of rabid fans follow their favorite teams and players by attending games or viewing the action on television and through other media. Upward of 35 billion television viewers tuned in to watch the 2002 World Cup games played in South Korea and Japan. Approximately 2 billion people watched live as Brazil downed Germany in the final, a number that dwarfs the television audiences of our own NFL Super Bowl and baseball World Series. These numbers reinforce the fact that soccer is deserving of its unofficial title of "the World Game."

The immense popularity of soccer does not mean that it is an easy game to play success-

fully. In reality, soccer poses several physical and mental challenges for participants. With the exception of the goalkeeper, there are no specialists on the soccer field. As in the sport of hockey, in soccer each player must be able to defend as well as attack. They must control the ball using a variety of foot skills, and they do so under the pressures of restricted space, limited time, physical fatigue, and the determined challenge of opponents. Decision-making abilities are constantly tested as players respond to rapidly changing situations during play. Players face many challenges. Individual performance and ultimately team success depend on each player's ability to meet these challenges. Such ability will not occur by chance—it must be developed. *Soccer: Steps to Success* is written with that goal in mind.

Whether you're at the purely recreational or highly competitive level, you will improve your performance and enjoy the game more as you develop greater competency in the skills and strategies required for successful play. The third edition of *Soccer: Steps to Success* provides a progressive plan for developing soccer skills and gaining a more thorough understanding of individual and group strategies underlying team play. Follow the same sequence each step of the way:

1. Read the explanation of the skill covered in the step, why the step is important, and how to execute the step.

2. Study the illustrations, which show exactly how to position your body to execute each skill successfully.

3. Read the instructions for each drill. Practice the drill and record your score.

4. Have a qualified observer—a teacher, coach, or trained partner—evaluate your basic skill technique once you've completed each set of drills. The observer can use the success checks with each drill to evaluate your execution of the skill.

5. At the end of the step, review your performance and total up your scores from the drills. Once you've achieved the indicated level of success with the step, move on to the next step.

This updated and expanded version is organized into 12 clearly defined steps that enable you to advance at your own pace. Each step provides an easy and logical transition to the next step. You cannot leap to the top of the staircase! You get to the top by climbing one step at a time. The first few steps provide a foundation for basic skills and concepts. As you progress through the book, you will learn how to use those skills to execute tactics and work with teammates. Numerous illustrations further clarify the proper execution of soccer skills and tactics, including those used by the goalkeeper. Drills are sprinkled throughout each step so that you can practice and master fundamental skills and tactical concepts before engaging in more pressure-packed simulated game situations. At the completion of all 12 steps you will become a more experienced and accomplished soccer player.

Acknowledgments

The writing and publishing of a book are truly a team effort. In that regard, I am deeply indebted to several people for their help and support with this project. Although it is not possible to mention everyone by name, I would like to express my appreciation to the staff at Human Kinetics, particularly Dean Miller and Cynthia McEntire, for their assistance in the development of the book; to my coaching colleagues at the University of Pittsburgh and Shoot to Score Soccer Academy for their willingness to share thoughts and ideas; and last, but certainly not least, to my lovely wife, Gail, and children, Eliza and Travis, for their constant love and support.

◨ The Sport of Soccer

Without question, soccer is the most popular team game in the world, played and watched by millions of people each year. In a global society divided by physical and ideological barriers, soccer's popularity is not limited by age or sex or by political, religious, cultural, or ethnic boundaries. Known internationally as football, soccer is the major sport of nearly every country in Asia, Africa, Europe, and South America. The game provides a common language among people of diverse backgrounds and heritages.

Soccer is popular for many reasons. First and foremost is the fact that soccer players come in all shapes and sizes, so virtually everyone is a potential player. Pele, considered by most to be the greatest soccer player ever, is only average in height and weight. While physical attributes such as speed, strength, and stamina are essential for high-level performance, so too are a player's technical ability, tactical knowledge, anticipation, savvy, and overall game sense. And while team success ultimately depends on the coordinated efforts of teammates, each player is afforded the opportunity to express his or her individuality within the team structure. Soccer offers something for everyone. The fact that soccer is considered a player's game as opposed to a game dominated by coaches is probably the overriding reason for the sport's universal appeal.

The Federation Internationale de Football Association (FIFA) is the governing body of world soccer. Founded in 1904, FIFA is arguably the most prestigious sport organization in the world with more than 200 member nations. In 1913 the United States Soccer Football Association (USSFA) was founded and approved as a member of FIFA. The name was later changed to the United States Soccer Federation (USSF). The various professional and amateur associations in the United States are organized under the auspices of the USSF. In 1974 the United States Youth Soccer Association (USYSA) was established as an affiliate of the USSF to administer and promote the sport for players under 19 years of age.

A soccer game, generally referred to as the match, is played between two teams of 11 players each; one of the players on each team is designated as the goalkeeper. Each team defends a goal and can score by kicking or heading the ball through the opponent's goal. The goalkeeper's primary job is to protect the team's goal, although he or she also plays an important role in initiating team attack. The goalkeeper is the only player allowed to control the ball with the hands and can do so only within the penalty area, which is 44 yards wide and 18 yards out from the end line of the field. Field ("out") players may not use their hands or arms to control the ball. Instead they must use their feet, legs, bodies, or heads. Each goal counts as one point, and the team that scores the most goals wins the match.

Soccer is played on a field area, commonly called a *pitch,* that is both longer and wider than an American football field. A regulation game consists of two 45-minute periods with a 15-minute halftime intermission. A coin toss generally determines which team kicks off to start the game. Once play begins, the action is virtually continuous. The clock stops only after a goal is scored, on a penalty kick, or at the discretion of the referee. There are no official time-outs, and substitutions are limited. Field players often cover more than five miles during a regulation match, much of that distance at sprinting pace. It is not surprising that soccer players are among the most highly conditioned of all athletes.

The organization of the 10 field players is generally referred to as a system of play, or formation. Formations can vary from one team to another and even from one game to the next,

depending on the strengths and weaknesses of the individual players, the roles and responsibilities assigned to each player, and the personal philosophy of the coach. Most systems deploy three or four defenders, four or five midfielders, and two or three forwards. Field players are not restricted in their movement, although each has specific responsibilities within the system of play employed by the team. (See step 12, page 187, for more information on team organization.)

The strategies of team play have undergone modifications during the evolution of the sport. The goalkeeper is considered the one true specialist on the soccer team, the final barrier between the team's goal and an opponent's score. The keeper is the only player allowed to use the hands to control the ball. In the not-so-distant past the field players fulfilled more specialized roles than they do today. Forwards were expected to stay up front and score goals. Defenders were expected to "stay home" and do whatever was necessary to keep the ball out of their goal. They rarely ventured forward into the attack. But over the past couple of decades all that has changed, for the better, I might add. The modern game places greater emphasis on the complete soccer player, the individual who can defend as well as attack. With the exception of the goalkeeper, the days of the soccer specialist are history.

THE SOCCER FIELD

The official field of play must be 100 to 130 yards long and 50 to 100 yards wide. The length must always exceed the width. For international matches, the length must be 110 to 120 yards and the width 70 to 80 yards. Distinctive lines no more than 5 inches wide mark the *field area.* As shown in figure 1, the end boundaries of the field are called the *goal lines* and the side boundaries are called the *touchlines.* The *halfway line* divides the playing area into two equal halves, and the *center spot* marks the center of the field. A *center circle* with a radius of 10 yards surrounds the center spot.

A *goal* is positioned at each end of the field on the center of the goal line. The dimensions of each goal are 8 feet high and 24 feet wide.

The *goal area* is a rectangular box drawn along each goal line. The goal area is formed by two lines drawn at right angles to the goal line, 6 yards from each goalpost. These lines extend 6 yards onto the field of play and are joined by a line drawn parallel to the goal line.

The *penalty area* is a rectangular box drawn along each goal line formed by two lines drawn at right angles to the goal line 18 yards from each goalpost. The lines extend 18 yards onto the field of play and are joined by a line drawn parallel with the goal line. The goal area is enclosed within the penalty area. Located within the penalty area is the *penalty spot.* The penalty spot is marked 12 yards front and center of the midpoint of the goal line. Penalty kicks are

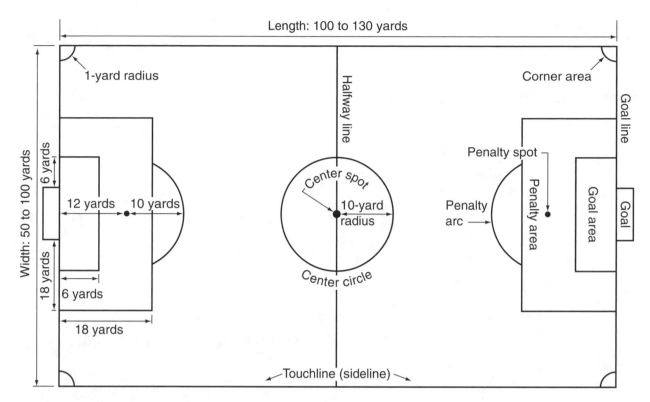

Figure 1 The soccer field.

taken from the penalty spot. The *penalty arc,* with a radius of 10 yards from the penalty spot, is drawn outside the penalty area.

A *corner area,* with a radius of 1 yard, is marked at each corner of the field. Corner kicks are taken from within the corner area.

EQUIPMENT

The soccer ball is spherical and made of leather or other approved materials. The regulation-size adult soccer ball is designated internationally as the size #5 ball. The official FIFA #5 ball is 27 to 28 inches in circumference and weighs between 14 and 16 ounces. Smaller balls (size #4 and size #3) are sometimes used for youth games.

The required uniform for field players consists of a jersey or shirt, shorts, and socks that match those of their teammates and contrast with those of their opponents. Shin guards are worn underneath the socks. The goalkeeper often wears a long-sleeve jersey and shorts with padding at the elbows and hips. The colors should distinguish him or her from the field players and the referee. All players must wear some type of soccer shoes during play. Players are not permitted to wear any article of clothing that the referee determines to be a potential danger to another player. For example, watches, chains, or other forms of jewelry are usually forbidden.

RULES OF THE GAME

Soccer is a simple game with only 17 fundamental rules. The official FIFA Laws of the Game are standard throughout the world and pertain to all international competition. Minor modifications of the FIFA laws are permissible for youth and school-sponsored programs in the United States. These modifications may involve the field size, size and weight of the ball, size of the goals, number of substitutes allowed, and duration of the game. The following is an abbreviated discussion of the rules governing play.

Start of Play

The match begins with a placekick from the center spot of the field. Every player on the kicking team must be in his or her own half of the field. Opponents must position themselves outside the center circle and within their own half of the field. The ball is considered in play when it travels into the opponent's half of the field the distance of its own circumference. The initial kicker is not permitted to play the ball a second time until another player touches it. A similar placekick restarts the game after a goal has been scored and also begins the second half of play. A goal may be scored directly from the kickoff.

Ball In and Out of Play

The ball is considered out of play when it completely crosses a touchline or goal line (whether on the ground or in the air) or when the referee stops the game. The ball is in play at all other times, including

- rebounds from a goalpost, crossbar, or corner flag onto the field of play;
- rebounds off the referee or linesmen when they are in the field of play; and
- intervals while a decision is pending on a supposed infringement of the laws (for example, the "play-on" situation).

When the referee is unsure of who last touched a ball that traveled out of the field area, or when a temporary stoppage occurs during the run of play (because of a severe injury to a player, for example), play is restarted with a *drop ball* at the spot where the ball was last in play. The referee drops the ball between two opposing players, who cannot kick the ball until it contacts the ground.

When the ball travels out of play over a sideline, either on the ground or in the air, it is returned into play by a *throw-in* from the spot where it left the playing field. A player from the team opposite that of the player who last touched the ball takes the throw-in. The thrower must hold the ball with both hands and deliver it from behind and over the head. The player must face the field of play with each foot touching the sideline or the ground outside the sideline at the moment the ball is released. The ball is considered in play immediately after it crosses the touchline onto the field of play. The thrower may not touch the ball a second time until it has been touched by another player. A throw-in is awarded to the opposing team if the ball is improperly released onto the field of play. A goal cannot be scored directly from a throw-in.

A ball last touched by a member of the attacking team that passes over the goal line, excluding the portion of the line between the goalposts and under the crossbar, is returned to play by a *goal kick* awarded to the defending team. The goal kick is spotted within that half of the goal area nearest to where the ball crossed the goal line. The ball is considered in play once it has traveled outside the penalty area. The kicker cannot play the ball a second time until a teammate or an opponent touches it. A goal kick cannot be played directly to the goalkeeper within the penalty area. All opposing players must position themselves outside the penalty area when a goal kick is taken. A goal cannot be scored directly off a goal kick.

A ball last touched by a member of the defending team that passes over the goal line, excluding the portion of the line between the goalposts and under the crossbar, is returned to play by a *corner kick* awarded to the attacking team. The corner kick is taken from within the quarter circle of the corner nearest the spot where the ball left the playing area. Defending players must position themselves at least 10 yards from the ball until it is played. The kicker is not permitted to play the ball a second time until another player touches it. A goal may be scored directly from a corner kick.

Scoring

A goal is scored when the whole ball passes completely over the goal line, between the goalposts, and under the crossbar, provided it has not been intentionally thrown, carried, or propelled by an arm or hand of a player of the attacking team. Each goal counts as one point. The team scoring the most goals during a contest wins the game. The game is termed a *draw* if both teams score an equal number of goals during regulation time.

RULE VIOLATIONS AND SANCTIONS

An appointed *referee* officiates at each game and has ultimate authority on the field. The referee enforces the rules and decides on any disputed point. The referee is assisted by two *assistant referees* who take positions along opposite touchlines. Assistant referees indicate when the ball is out of play (subject to the decision of the referee) and determine which team is entitled to the throw-in, goal kick, or corner kick. Assistant referees also assist the referee in determining when offside violations have occurred, and they alert the referee when a substitute wishes to enter the game.

Players need to be aware of the potential rule violations and penalties that may be called. A penalty at the wrong time can be devastating for a team, resulting in loss of momentum, a turnover, or even a goal for the other team. Learn the following rule violations and penalties, and work to avoid them during play.

Offside

All players should be familiar with the offside law. A player is in an *offside position* if he or she is nearer the opponent's goal line than the ball is at the *moment the ball is played* unless

- the player is in his or her own half of the field, or
- the player is not nearer to the opponent's goal line than at least two opponents.

Just because a player is in an offside position does not mean that he or she must be whistled offside by the referee. A player is declared offside and penalized for being in an offside position only if, at the moment the ball touches or is played by a teammate, the referee judges the player to be interfering with play or with an opponent or gaining an advantage by being in an offside position. A player is not offside merely because he or she is in an offside position or if the player receives the ball directly from a goal kick, corner kick, or throw-in.

The punishment for infringement of the offside law is an indirect free kick awarded to the opposing team at the spot where the offside occurred. The referee shall judge offside at the instant the ball is played and not at the moment the player receives the ball (see figure 2). For example, a player who is in an onside position at the moment the ball is played does not become offside if he or she moves forward into an offside position to receive the pass while the ball is in flight.

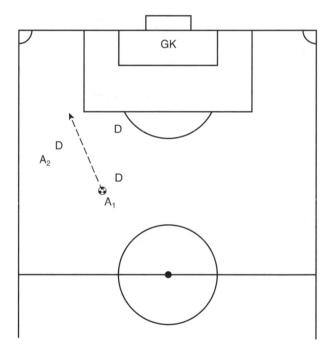

Figure 2 Player is not offside.

Free Kicks

The two classifications of free kicks are direct and indirect. A goal can be scored directly by the kicker from a *direct free kick*. To score from an *indirect free kick*, a second player other than the kicker (who can be a member of either team) must play or touch the ball before it passes over the goal line. Defending players must position themselves at least 10 yards from the ball for both direct and indirect free kicks. The only instance in which defending players can get in position closer than 10 yards to the ball is when the attacking team has been awarded an indirect free kick spotted within 10 yards of the defending team's goal. In that situation, defending players can stand on their goal line between the goalposts in an attempt to prevent the ball from entering the goal.

When a player takes a free kick from within his or her penalty area, all opposing players must remain outside the area and be in position at least 10 yards from the ball. The ball must be stationary when the kick is taken and is considered in play once it has traveled the distance of its circumference and beyond the penalty area. The goalkeeper may not receive the ball into his or her hands and then kick it into play. If the ball is not kicked directly into play beyond the penalty area, the kick must be retaken. If the kicker touches the ball a second time before another player touches it, then the opposing team is awarded an indirect free kick.

Fouls and Misconduct

Fouls are either *direct* or *indirect*. A player who intentionally commits any of the following offenses will be penalized by the award of a direct free kick to the opposing team at the spot where the foul occurred:

- Spitting at an opponent
- Kicking or attempting to kick an opponent
- Tripping an opponent
- Jumping at an opponent
- Charging an opponent in a violent or dangerous manner
- Charging an opponent from behind unless the opponent is obstructing the player from the ball
- Striking or attempting to strike an opponent
- Holding an opponent
- Pushing an opponent
- Carrying, striking, or propelling the ball with a hand or arm (this violation does not apply to the goalkeeper within his or her penalty area)

When a player on the defending team intentionally commits an offense of a direct free kick within his or her own penalty area, he or she is penalized by the award of a *penalty kick* to the opposing team.

Indirect free kicks result from the following rule infractions:

- Playing in a manner the referee considers dangerous to you or another player, referred to as "dangerous play"
- Charging an opponent with your shoulder when the ball is not within playing distance of the players involved (charging with the shoulder is legal if you are attempting to play the ball)
- Intentionally impeding the progress of an opponent when you are not attempting to play the ball, commonly referred to as "obstruction"
- Intentionally preventing the goalkeeper from releasing the ball
- Violating the offside rule
- Charging the goalkeeper except when he or she has possession of the ball or has moved outside of the goal area

An indirect free kick is awarded to the attacking team if the goalkeeper engages in any of the following:

- Violating the six-second rule, in which the goalkeeper, while in possession of the ball, fails to release it into play within six seconds
- Indulging in tactics that the referee rules are designed to waste time, delay the game, and give an unfair advantage to the goalkeeper's own team
- Violating the goalkeeper back-pass rule (see the next section)

Goalkeeper Back-Pass Rule

The *Laws of the Game* state that the goalkeeper is not permitted to receive the ball in his or her hands after it has been deliberately kicked to him or her by a teammate. The kick must be a deliberate pass for this rule to take effect; a deflection, for example, is not penalized. Violation of the back-pass rule results in the award of an indirect free kick to the opposing team at the spot of the infraction.

Players may use the head, chest, or knees to intentionally pass the ball to their goalkeeper. However, if a player deliberately attempts to circumvent the rule (such as using the feet to flip the ball in the air to head it to the goalkeeper), then the player will be guilty of unsporting conduct and will be officially cautioned. In that situation, the opposing team is awarded an indirect free kick from the place where the foul was committed.

Cautions and Ejections

It is at the referee's discretion to reprimand a player who continually commits flagrant violations of the laws. The referee issues a *yellow card* to officially caution a player. A yellow card violation conveys a warning to the player that he or she will be ejected from the game if similar violations continue. The referee issues a *red card* to signal that a player has been ejected from the game. A player can be sent off the field and shown the red card if, in the opinion of the referee, the player

- is guilty of violent conduct,
- is guilty of serious foul play,
- spits at an opponent or any other person,
- uses foul or abusive language,
- receives a second caution in the same match,
- denies the opposing team a goal or an obvious goal-scoring opportunity by

deliberately handling the ball (this does not apply to the goalkeeper within his or her own penalty area), or

- denies an obvious goal-scoring opportunity to an opponent moving toward the player's goal by an offense punishable by a free kick or penalty kick.

The player who receives a red card cannot return to the game and may not be replaced by a substitute.

Penalty Kick

The most severe sanction for a direct foul, other than ejection from the game, is the penalty kick. A penalty kick results when a player commits a direct foul offense within his or her team's penalty area. (Note: A penalty kick can be awarded irrespective of the position of the ball.) The kick is taken from the penalty spot 12 yards front and center of the goal. All players except the kicker and the goalkeeper must position themselves outside the penalty area at least 10 yards from the penalty spot. The goalkeeper must stand between the goalposts with feet touching the goal line. The keeper is permitted to move sideways along the line before the kick but may not move forward off the line until the ball has been played. The player taking a penalty kick must kick the ball forward and cannot touch it a second time until it has been played by another player (the second player can be the goalkeeper). The ball is in play once it has traveled the distance of its circumference. A goal can be scored directly from a penalty kick. Time should be extended at halftime or the end of regulation time to allow a penalty kick to be taken.

WARM-UP AND COOL DOWN

Before every practice session or game, perform a warm-up to prepare yourself both physically and mentally for the more strenuous training to follow. *Warm-up* activities elevate muscle temperature, stimulate increased blood flow to the muscles, and stretch the major muscle groups. A thorough warm-up will improve muscular contraction and reflex time, increase muscle supple-

ness, prevent next-day soreness, and reduce the likelihood of muscle and joint injuries.

The intensity and duration of the warm-up can vary from one situation to another and from one person to the next. Environmental conditions, such as ambient temperature and humidity, should be taken into account. For example, you probably will not have to warm up as long or as hard on a hot, humid afternoon in June as you would on a cold, blustery day in November. As a general rule, you should warm up for 15 to 20 minutes at sufficient intensity to break a sweat. Sweating indicates an elevation in muscle temperature.

Before stretching, begin your warm-up by increasing the blood flow to the muscles. Any form of aerobic activity that involves the large muscle groups will suffice, although from a practical standpoint it is to your advantage to use soccer-specific movements and activities whenever possible. Skill-related drills that involve dribbling maneuvers combined with sudden changes of speed and direction, or passing the ball among teammates who are moving throughout the field area, are a great means of getting the blood moving. For example, many of the dribbling drills described in step 1 are appropriate as soccer-specific warm-up activities.

Once your muscles are sufficiently warmed, perform a series of stretching exercises that target all the major muscle groups used in soccer. Don't bounce or jerk! Slowly extend the muscle or group of muscles to its greatest possible length without discomfort. A slow, steady extension of the muscle will inhibit firing of the stretch reflex, the body's built-in safeguard against overstretching. Hold the stretch for 30 seconds, relax, and then move gently into a deeper stretch for another 30 seconds. Stretch each muscle group twice, focusing on the hamstrings, quadriceps, back, groin, calves and Achilles tendons, and neck.

At the end of every practice and game, take a few minutes to allow your heart rate and body functions to gradually return to their normal resting state. The *cool-down* can include light aerobic exercise, such as a slow jog with or without the ball, combined with stretching exercises that target the most-used muscle groups. Stretching after a hard training session may actually be more beneficial than prepractice stretching in preventing next-day soreness.

INTERNATIONAL AND NATIONAL ORGANIZATIONS

The following organizations are under the auspices of FIFA and administer soccer competition in the United States. The United States Soccer Federation (US Soccer) directs amateur and professional soccer competition. The National Collegiate Athletic Association (NCAA), the National Association for Intercollegiate Athletes (NAIA), and the National Junior College Athletic Association (NJCAA) administrate collegiate competition for both men and women. Questions or requests for information should be directed to the appropriate organization.

International Organizations

Federation Internationale de Football Association (FIFA)

FIFA House, Hitzigweg 11

8030 Zurich, Switzerland

Phone 41-1-384-9595

Fax 41-1-384-9696

www.fifa.com

Confederation of North, Central American and Caribbean Association Football (CONCACAF)

725 Fifth Avenue, 17th Floor

New York, NY 10022

Phone 212-308-0044

Fax 212-308-1851

www.footballconfederation.com

National Organizations

American Youth Soccer Organization (AYSO)

12501 S. Isis Avenue

Hawthorne, CA 90250

Phone 310-643-6455

Fax 310-643-5310

National Soccer Coaches Association of America (NSCAA)

6770 Squibb Road, Suite 215

Mission, KS 66202

Phone 800-458-0678

Fax 913-362-3439

www.nscaa.com

National Soccer Hall of Fame

18 Stadium Circle

Oneonta, NY 13820

Phone 607-432-3351

Fax 607-432-8429

Soccer Association for Youth (SAY)

4050 Executive Park Drive, Suite 100

Cincinnati, OH 45241

Phone 800-233-7291

Fax 513-769-0500

www.saysoccer.org

United States Soccer Federation (US Soccer)

U.S. Soccer House

1801 South Prairie Avenue

Chicago, IL 60616

Phone 312-808-1300

Fax 312-808-9535

www.ussoccer.com

US Youth Soccer

1717 Firman Drive, Suite 900

Richardson, TX 75081

Phone 972-235-4499

Fax 972-235-4480

www.youthsoccer.org

Scholastic Organizations

National Association of Intercollegiate Athletics (NAIA)

23500 W. 105th Street

P.O. Box 1325

Olathe, KS 66061

Phone 913-791-0044

Fax 913-791-9555

National Collegiate Athletic Association (NCAA)

P.O. Box 6222

Indianapolis, IN 46206-6222

Phone 317-917-6222

Fax 317-917-6800

National Intercollegiate Soccer Officials Association (NISOA)

541 Woodview Drive

Longwood, FL 32779

Phone 407-862-3305

Fax 407-862-8545

National Junior College Athletic Association (NJCAA)

1825 Austin Bluffs Parkway, Suite 100

Colorado Springs, CO 80918

Phone 719-590-9788

Fax 719-590-7324

www.njcaa.org

U.S. Professional Leagues

Major League Soccer (MLS)

110 E. 42nd Street, 10th Floor

New York, NY 10017

Phone 212-450-1200

Fax 212-450-1300

www.MLSnet.com

United Soccer Leagues

14497 North Dale Mabry Highway, Suite 201

Tampa, FL 33618

Phone 813-963-3909

Fax 813-963-3807

www.USLsoccer.com

Major Indoor Soccer League (MISL)

1175 Post Road East

Westport, CT 06880

Phone 203-222-4900

Fax 203-221-7300

www.misl.net

☐ Key to Diagrams

GK   Goalkeeper

D   Defender

A   Attacker

X   Player

⚽   Soccer ball

〜〜〜▶   Dribble

———▶   Run

- - - ▶   Pass

Dribbling, Shielding, and Tackling

The soccer ball is a very precious commodity. Every player on the pitch wants a piece of it, and without it your team cannot score goals. The fact remains, however, that there is only one ball to be shared among 22 players. For that reason, it is essential that once you are in possession of the ball you be able to evade, or ward off, the challenge of opponents attempting to steal the ball.

Dribbling and shielding are the fundamental techniques used for maintaining possession of the ball. *Dribbling* skills enable you to run with the ball past opponents and to advance the ball at speed when moving in open space. Depending on the situation, you will use different surfaces of the foot (inside, outside, instep, and sole) to control the ball.

Three different dribbling styles are commonly observed in game situations: dribbling to penetrate (bypass) opponents, dribbling for close control when in tight spaces, and dribbling for speed when advancing with the ball in open space. *Shielding* skills are used in conjunction with dribbling skills to protect, or hide, the ball from opponents attempting to steal it. Shield the ball by positioning your body between the ball

and the opponent. This technique is sometimes referred to as *screening* the ball.

Though dribbling skills are an essential part of every team's attacking arsenal, players must never lose sight of the fact that excessive dribbling serves no useful purpose and can actually undermine the team's efforts. Refrain from taking on opponents (attempting to dribble past them) in the defending third of the field nearest your own goal; in this area, the reward for beating an opponent on the dribble is not worth the potential consequences associated with loss of possession. Dribbling skills are used to best advantage in the attacking third of the field near the opponent's goal; in this area, the potential reward for beating an opponent outweighs the risk of getting stripped of the ball. If you can beat an opponent on the dribble in the attacking third, there is a good chance that you've created a scoring opportunity for your team.

Soccer players must be able to defend as well as attack. When your team does not have the ball you must do your part to win it back. You can do this in two ways: by intercepting an opponent's pass or by tackling the ball away from the player in possession. *Tackling* is the defensive technique used to strip, or steal, the ball from an opponent. The term *tackle* has a different meaning in soccer than it has in American football. Soccer players tackle the ball, not the opposing player. Three different techniques—*block tackle, poke tackle,* and *slide tackle*—are used to dispossess an opponent depending on the defender's angle of approach. In most situations the block tackle is preferred because it allows for greater body control and puts the defender in a position to counterattack quickly once he or she gains possession of the ball.

DRIBBLING SKILLS

Dribbling in soccer serves the same basic function as dribbling in basketball—it enables the player to maintain control of the ball while running past opponents or accelerating into open space. Dribbling is sometimes referred to as an art rather than a skill because different people express themselves in different ways. Players are free to develop their own style, or dribbling

personality so to speak, so long as it achieves the desired objectives. Some players dribble using long, fluid strides, while others prefer short, choppy steps. Others rely on deceptive foot movements and sudden changes of speed and direction to beat opponents. Whatever works for you is right for you.

Dribbling to beat an opponent (figure 1.1) is the first fundamental dribbling situation we will cover. Creative dribbling skills used in appropriate situations can wreck havoc on an opposing defense. World-class dribblers such as Ryan Giggs (Wales, Manchester United) and Ronaldinho (Brazil), players who have the ability to weave through opposing defenses with the ball seemingly glued to their feet, are extremely valuable to their respective teams. Single-handedly they can break down even the most compact defenses with bursts of dribbling brilliance to create scoring opportunities where none existed. Most great dribblers have perfected two or three different moves that are virtually impossible to stop, and you can do the same. It simply takes practice—and lots of it.

Figure 1.1 Dribbling to Beat an Opponent

APPROACH

1. Face the defender
2. Maintain balance and body control
3. Keep the ball close to your feet
4. Keep the head up with vision on opponent

EXECUTION

1. Attack (dribble at) the defender at speed
2. Use deceptive body and foot movements to unbalance the defender
3. Push the ball past the defender

FOLLOW-THROUGH

1. Accelerate past the defender
2. Take the most direct route to goal

Misstep

The ball gets tangled between your feet as you prepare to take on the defender.

Correction

Don't be too fancy or attempt too many deceptive body movements. Become proficient with a few dribbling maneuvers and rely on those to beat opponents.

Beat an Opponent
Dribbling Drill 1.   Slalom Dribble

Partner with a teammate. Set up a line of 6 to 8 cones spaced 2 yards apart. One player works while the other rests. Begin at the first cone and dribble in and out of the cones until you get to the last one, then turn and dribble in and out of the cones back to the starting line. Keep the ball in close control at all times and complete the slalom as quickly as possible. Exchange the ball with your partner and rest while he or she dribbles the circuit. Repeat the slalom dribble course 20 times each. Knocking down a cone is considered a dribbling error. Award yourself 1 point for each complete circuit without error.

To Increase Difficulty

- Position cones 1 yard apart.
- Place the cones in a random pattern.

To Decrease Difficulty

- Increase distance between cones.

- Reduce number of cones.
- Slow the pace.

Success Check

- Maintain balance and body control.
- Use inside and outside surfaces of the foot to cut the ball sharply as you weave in and out of the cones.
- Maintain close ball control.
- Keep the head up with vision on field as much as possible.

Score Your Success

0 to 12 points = 0 points

12 to 14 points = 1 point

15 to 17 points = 3 points

18 to 20 points = 5 points

Your score ___

Beat an Opponent
Dribbling Drill 2. Take on a Passive Defender

Within the penalty area of the field, 12 to 20 players set up, 1 ball for every 2 players. On the coach's command, all players begin moving within the area. Those with a ball dribble and those without a ball act as passive defenders. As dribblers move throughout the area, they take on passive defenders at every opportunity, rehearsing the foot and body movements used to beat an opponent on the dribble. Dribblers perform at game speed. Passive defenders are just that—passive—and do not attempt to win the ball from the dribblers. Play for 5 minutes, after which dribblers exchange possession of the ball with defenders and repeat.

To Increase Difficulty

- Reduce size of area to restrict available space in which to dribble.
- Allow defenders to tackle ball.

To Decrease Difficulty

- Increase size of area.

- Reduce dribbling pace.

Success Check

- Keep close control of the ball.
- Attack the defender at speed.
- Use deceptive body movements to unbalance the opponent.
- Accelerate past the defender.

Score Your Success

Lose control of your ball 6 times or more = 1 point

Lose control of your ball 3 to 5 times = 3 points

Lose control of your ball 0 to 2 times = 5 points

Your score ___

Beat an Opponent
Dribbling Drill 3. Line-to-Line Game

Compete one-on-one with a partner within a 15-by 20-yard grid. Position on opposite end lines of the grid; your opponent has the ball. To begin, he or she serves (kicks) the ball to you and immediately moves forward as the defender. You receive and control the ball, then attempt to dribble past your opponent and beyond his or her end line. Award yourself 1 point for successfully dribbling past the defender and over the end line. After each attempt, return to your respective end lines and repeat. Partners alternate playing as dribbler and defender. Continue the exercise until each player has attempted to take on his or her opponent 20 times. The player scoring more points wins.

To Increase Difficulty for Attacker

- Decrease width of field so that the dribbler has less space in which to maneuver.
- Add a second defender to the drill, creating a one-on-two situation in which the dribbler must beat two opponents on the dribble.

To Decrease Difficulty for Attacker

- Increase width of field to increase available space for dribbler.

Success Check

- Use deceptive body feints.
- Attack the defender at speed.
- Employ sudden changes of speed and direction.
- Accelerate past the defender.

Score Your Success

0 to 7 points scored = 0 points

8 to 11 points scored = 1 point

12 to 14 points scored = 3 points

15 points or more scored = 5 points

Your score ___

Beat an Opponent
Dribbling Drill 4.   Score by Dribbling Only

Form two equal teams of four to six players each. Play on a field area approximately 50 by 35 yards. Regular soccer rules apply except for the method of scoring. Goals are scored by dribbling the ball over the opponent's end line rather than by shooting. The entire length of the end line is considered the goal line. Award 1 team point each time a player dribbles the ball over the opponent's end line. Play for 20 minutes and keep track of points. The team scoring more points wins.

To Increase Difficulty for the Attacking Team

- Decrease width of field to limit available space.
- Add two neutral players who always play with the defending team to give that team a two-player numerical advantage.

To Decrease Difficulty for the Attacking Team

- Increase width of field to provide more space in which to maneuver.
- Add two neutral players who always play with the attacking team to give that team a two-player advantage.

Success Check

- Use dribbling skills in appropriate situations.
- Maintain close control of the ball.
- Attack the defender at speed.
- Employ sudden changes of speed and direction.

Score Your Success

Each player on the winning team is awarded 1 point for each goal scored, up to a maximum of 6. Each player on the losing team is awarded 1 point for each goal scored, up to a maximum of 3.

Your score ___

Beat an Opponent
Dribbling Drill 5.   Tactical Dribbling

Divide into two equal teams of 4 to 6 players. Use markers to outline a 60- by 40-yard field with a regulation goal on each end line. Divide the field lengthwise into three 20- by 40-yard zones. Designate one player from each team as a goalkeeper who positions in the goal. Begin with a kickoff from the center of the field. Teams score 1 point for kicking the ball through the opponent's goal and 1 point each time an attacker penetrates past a defender on the dribble in their attacking third of the field. Regular soccer rules apply except for the following zone restrictions:

- Players may use only one- and two-touch passes in the zone nearest their goal.
- In the middle zone, players may dribble to advance the ball into open space but may not take on and beat opponents.
- Dribbling to take on an opponent is mandatory in the attacking third of the field, an area in which players must beat an opponent on the dribble before passing to a teammate or shooting on goal.

Violation of a zone restriction is penalized by loss of possession to the opponents. Play for 20 minutes. The team scoring more points wins the game.

To Increase Difficulty for the Attacking Team

- Reduce field size to restrict space and time available.
- Add one neutral player to the game who plays with the defending team to give that team a one-player numerical advantage.

To Decrease Difficulty for the Attacking Team

- Increase field size to provide dribblers more space in which to maneuver.
- Add one neutral player to the game who plays with the attacking team to give that team a one-player numerical advantage.

Success Check

- Maintain close control of the ball at all times.
- Employ sudden changes of speed and direction to unbalance the opponent.
- Keep the head up to see available options.
- Dribble in appropriate situations and in appropriate areas of the field.

Score Your Success

Each player on the winning team gets 2 points for the win and 1 additional point for each time he or she successfully dribbles past an opponent in the attacking third of the field. Each player on the losing team gets 0 team points but is awarded 1 point each time he or she successfully dribbles past an opponent in the attacking third of the field.

Your score ___

There will be times when you find yourself with very little room to maneuver, as when being pressured by two or even three opposing players. In this situation, your immediate concern becomes possession rather than penetration. You must be able to retain control of the ball by dribbling out of trouble so that you can pass the ball to an available teammate. By combining sudden changes of speed and direction with deceptive foot and body movements, you can unbalance opponents and create space in which to dribble and maneuver with the ball. It is imperative that you keep the ball under very close control at all times (see figure 1.2).

Figure 1.2   Dribbling for Close Control

PREPARATION	**EXECUTION**	**FOLLOW-THROUGH**
1. Keep in crouched position with knees bent	1. Respond to pressure of opponents	1. Maintain close control of the ball
2. Keep a low center of gravity	2. Use body feints and deceptive foot movements	2. Move away from pressure
3. Maintain balance and body control	3. Control ball with appropriate surface of foot	3. Release the ball to a teammate
4. Be aware of options	4. Change speed, direction, or both	

Misstep

The ball rolls away from your feet and into the path of a defending opponent.

Correction

Keep the ball beneath your body as you dribble, as close to your feet as possible. From that position you can change direction quickly, and the ball is always within your immediate control.

Misstep

You fail to recognize pressure and dribble directly into an opponent.

Correction

This error can occur when vision is focused entirely on the ball and you are not aware of your immediate surroundings. Keep your head up as much as possible when dribbling. Maintaining good field vision is just as important as maintaining close control of the ball.

Control Dribbling Drill 1.   Unopposed Dribble

Randomly position 15 to 20 cones to represent stationary defenders within a 20- by 20-yard area. Dribble unopposed within the area, using various surfaces of your foot to control the ball as you quickly move between and around the imaginary defenders. Incorporate sudden changes of direction into your dribbling pattern. For example, quickly change direction by cutting the ball around a cone with the instep of your right foot, then accelerate into open space by pushing the ball with the outside of your left foot. Begin slowly and gradually increase the pace to game speed. Dribble at pace for 5 minutes continuously, rest for 60 seconds, and repeat. Keep track of the number of cones you knock over while dribbling.

To Increase Difficulty

- Place the cones closer together to reduce the available space.
- Change both speed and direction with each touch of the ball.
- Increase dribbling speed.

To Decrease Difficulty

- Position the cones farther apart.
- Reduce dribbling speed.

Success Check

- Maintain close control of the ball.
- Keep knees bent and a low center of gravity.
- Combine sudden changes of speed and direction.

Score Your Success

Knock down 11 cones or more in 5 minutes = 1 point

Knock down 6 to 10 cones in 5 minutes = 3 points

Knock down 0 to 5 cones in 5 minutes = 5 points

Your score ___

Control Dribbling Drill 2.   Cone-to-Cone Drill

Pair with a partner. Position 2 cones approximately 10 yards apart along a sideline or end line of the field. Position yourself with a ball midway between the cones on one side of the line. Your partner (the defender) faces you without a ball on the opposite side of the line. Your objective is to dribble the ball laterally to one cone or the other before the defender can position there.

Use body feints, deceptive foot movements, and sudden changes of direction to unbalance your opponent. Neither player is permitted to cross the line during the exercise. You score 1 point each time that you dribble to a cone before the defender can establish position there. Play for 2 minutes, rest, switch roles, and repeat the game. Play a total of 10 games, 5 as the dribbler and 5 as the defender.

To Increase Difficulty

- Increase distance between cones to 15 yards.

To Decrease Difficulty

- Decrease distance between cones to 5 yards.

Success Check

- Keep the ball under close control.
- Use sudden changes of speed and direction.
- Employ deceptive body feints to catch the defender flat-footed.

Score Your Success

Score 1 or 2 points in a 2-minute game when playing as the dribbler = 1 point

Score 3 to 5 points in a 2-minute game when playing as the dribbler = 3 points

Score 6 points or more in a 2-minute game when playing as the dribbler = 5 points

Your score ____

Control Dribbling Drill 3.   Evade the Challenge

Play this game with several teammates. All players but two station within the center circle of the soccer field, each with a ball. The two players without balls station outside of the circle to play as "chasers." On the command "go" the chasers enter the area and attempt to kick the dribblers' balls out of the circle. Dribblers use sudden changes of speed and direction coupled with close control of the ball to keep possession. A dribbler whose ball is kicked out of the circle should quickly retrieve it and return to play. Play for 5 minutes continuously. Keep track of how many times your ball is kicked out of the circle.

To Increase Difficulty

- Reduce size of area.
- Add additional chasers to the game to reduce available space.

To Decrease Difficulty

- Increase size of circle so that dribblers have more space in which to maneuver.

Success Check

- Keep the ball under close control.
- Shield the ball from chasers.
- Employ sudden changes of speed and direction.
- Keep the head up with vision on field.
- Maintain balance and body control.

Score Your Success

Ball kicked out of circle 6 times or more = 1 point

Ball kicked out of circle 3 to 5 times = 3 points

Ball kicked out of circle 0 to 2 times = 5 points

Your score ____

In some situations dribbling speed takes priority over close control of the ball, as when you find yourself behind the opponent's defense in a breakaway situation. In this case your primary objective is to get to the goal as fast as possible. Use either the outside surface of your instep or your full instep to push the ball ahead into the open space, sprint to it, and then push it again (see figure 1.3).

Figure 1.3 — Dribbling for Speed

PREPARATION

1. Keep the head up with vision on the field
2. Maintain upright posture
3. Keep the ball within range of control

EXECUTION

1. Use outside surface of instep to push the ball forward
2. Accelerate forward

FOLLOW-THROUGH

1. Push the ball toward goal
2. Sprint to the ball and push again

Misstep

You use short, choppy steps to advance the ball, which slows your pace.

Correction

Push the ball out ahead and away from your feet. Stride to the ball and push it again. Do not touch the ball every step or two as you would when dribbling for close control.

Speed Dribbling Drill 1. Speed Dribble Relay

Partner with two teammates. You and one teammate station on the goal line while the third player positions on the edge of the penalty area (18-yard line) facing you. You have the ball. Begin the relay by dribbling as quickly as possible to the top edge of the penalty area. Exchange possession of the ball with the player positioned there. Remain at that spot while he or she dribbles to the goal line and exchanges possession with the player there. That player completes the cycle by dribbling the ball back to you. Continue the relay until each player has dribbled 20 lengths of the penalty area. Award yourself 1 point each time you dribble the 18-yard distance at top speed and exchange pos-session of the ball without error. An error occurs if the ball bounces out of your range of control as you dribble or as you exchange possession with a teammate.

To Increase Difficulty

- Increase dribbling distance to 30 yards.
- Increase number of repetitions performed.
- Add an extra player to the drill. The new player chases dribbler from behind.

To Decrease Difficulty

- Reduce dribbling distance.

- Dribble at half speed.

Success Check

- Maintain upright posture.
- Push the ball several steps ahead with outside surface of the instep.
- Accelerate to the ball.
- Slow down when exchanging possession.

Speed Dribbling Drill 2.   First to the Penalty Area

Players partner with a teammate. Both players position within the center circle of the soccer field, one with a ball and one without. The player with possession pushes the ball toward one of the goals and attempts to dribble at top speed into the penalty area. The other player, the chaser, pauses for a count of 1 and then tries to catch the dribbler and kick the ball away before the dribbler can reach the penalty area. The chaser must stay on his or her feet at all times; sliding from behind to dislodge the ball is prohibited. The dribbler is awarded 1 point for entering the penalty area with possession of the ball. Players return to the halfway line, switch roles, and repeat the drill. Continue the drill until each partner has taken 10 turns as the dribbler.

To Increase Difficulty

- Do not require the chaser to pause for a count of 1 before leaving the center circle.
- Require dribbler to reach the goal line to score a point.

To Decrease Difficulty

- Shorten distance to be dribbled.

Success Check

- Maintain upright dribbling posture.
- Push the ball several feet ahead and accelerate to it.
- Push the ball forward with the outside surface of the instep.
- Take the most direct route to the goal.
- Reposition your body to cut off the defender's path to the ball.

Speed Dribbling Drill 3.   Attack or Defend

Form two equal teams of four to six players each. Use markers to outline a 30- by 40-yard playing area bisected by a midline. Position a supply of soccer balls, one ball for every two players, evenly spaced along the midline. Teams station on opposite end lines with players spread an equal distance apart. On the command "go," players from both teams sprint to the midline and compete for possession of a ball. Players who win a ball attempt to return it over their own end line by dribbling. Players who fail to gain possession of a ball can prevent scores by chasing the dribblers and kicking their ball away before they can return it over the end line. Dribblers score 1 point for dribbling a ball over their end line. The round ends when all balls have been returned over an end line or kicked out of the area. Play 10 rounds with a short rest between each. Individual players keep totals of their points scored.

To Increase Difficulty

- Increase length of field.
- Add two extra defenders to the game to chase the dribblers.

To Decrease Difficulty

- Place two balls for every three players on the midline to decrease the number of chasing defenders.

Success Check

- Be first to a ball.
- Quickly turn and begin dribbling back to the end line.

- Push the ball out from your feet and accelerate forward.
- Position your body between the ball and challenging defenders.
- Follow the most direct route to the end line.

Score Your Success

Return 0 to 2 balls over the end line = 1 point

Return 3 to 5 balls over the end line = 2 points

Return 6 balls or more over the end line = 3 points

Your score ___

SHIELDING SKILLS

There will be times when you simply can't dribble fast enough to lose an opponent who is chasing you down. Or possibly you are being tightly marked in an area where there is no available space in which to dribble away from pressure. In these situations, you must be able to fend off the challenge and maintain possession of the ball until an available passing option presents itself. To do so will require proper positioning of your body between the ball and the opponent, a technique commonly referred to as *shielding the ball* (figure 1.4).

Position sideways to the opponent and assume a slightly crouched posture with knees bent and a low center of gravity. In this position, you can establish a wide base of support and create greater distance between the opponent and the ball. Control the ball with the foot farthest from the opponent, and use body feints, deceptive foot movements, and sudden changes of direction to unbalance the defender. Keep the ball under close control at all times.

Figure 1.4 Shielding the Ball

PREPARATION

1. Position sideways to the defender
2. Assume a crouched posture with knees bent
3. Extend arm nearer to the defender to make yourself wider
4. Keep the head up for maximum field vision

Figure 1.4 (continued)

EXECUTION

1. Control ball with the foot farthest from opponent
2. Manipulate the ball with outside, inside, or sole of foot
3. Maintain a wide base of support
4. React to the opponent's pressure
5. Use body feints to unbalance opponent

FOLLOW-THROUGH

1. Readjust body position in response to pressure from opponent
2. Use sudden changes of direction to maintain maximum space between the ball and defender
3. Release the ball to a teammate to alleviate pressure

Misstep

You expose the ball and the defender pokes it away.

Correction

Keep the ball as far from the defender as possible but within your range of control. Constantly reposition your body between the ball and the defender to hide the ball.

Misstep

You are knocked off balance by an opponent's legal shoulder charge and lose possession of the ball.

Correction

Poor balance can result from standing too upright with feet too close together. Maintain a crouched posture with feet approximately shoulder-width apart (that is, a wide base of support) and weight evenly distributed. Proper balance leads to increased strength on the ball.

Shielding Drill 1. One-on-One Possession

Partner with a teammate. Play within a 12- by 12-yard area. You are the attacker; your partner plays the defender. Attempt to shield the ball from the defender while moving within the field area. He or she marks tightly but applies only passive pressure and does not actually try to win the ball. Play for 90 seconds. Penalize yourself 1 point each time the ball leaves the field area or each time it rolls outside of your range of control where the defender could poke it away. Play five 90-second rounds with a short rest between each, then switch roles and play five more rounds. Keep a tally of your penalty points.

To Increase Difficulty

- Decrease size of playing area.
- Increase duration of a round to 2 minutes.
- Permit defender to apply maximum pressure in an attempt to win the ball.

To Decrease Difficulty

- Increase size of playing area.
- Shorten rounds to 60 seconds.

Success Check

- Position yourself sideways to the opponent with your body between the ball and the opponent.
- Control the ball with the foot farthest from the opponent.
- Employ quick changes of speed and direction.
- Move away from defensive pressure.

Score Your Success

16 penalty points or more in 5 games = 1 point

11 to 15 penalty points in 5 games = 3 points

0 to 10 penalty points in 5 games = 5 points

Your score ___

Shielding Drill 2. Evade the Double Team

Form groups of three. Each player has a ball. Use markers to outline a 25- by 25-yard playing area. Designate one player as "it"; the others are chasers. The player who is it dribbles into the field area. The chasers closely follow, dribbling their balls, and attempt to pass and contact the it player's ball with their own. The it player uses sudden changes of speed and direction to elude the chasers, and positions his or her body to shield the ball from the chasers. Play for 90 seconds. The it player is assessed 1 penalty point each time his or her ball is contacted by one of the chaser's balls. Play three 90-second rounds, with a different player designated as it for each round.

To Increase Difficulty

- Decrease size of playing area to restrict available space.
- Add a third chaser to the game.

To Decrease Difficulty

- Shorten the duration of the rounds to 60 seconds.

Success Check

- Maintain close control of the ball at all times.
- Use sudden changes of speed and direction to lose the chasers.
- Shield the ball with your body.
- Feel the pressure and move away from it.

Score Your Success

6 penalty points or more per round = 1 point

3 to 5 penalty points per round = 3 points

0 to 2 penalty points per round = 5 points

Your score ___

Shielding Drill 3. All Versus All

Use markers to outline a 30- by 30-yard playing area. Sixteen to 20 players, each with a ball, dribble within the playing area. On a signal from the coach, the game becomes "all versus all." Each player must protect his or her ball while attempting to kick the other players' balls out of the field area. A player whose ball leaves the area is eliminated from the game. This exercise emphasizes proper execution of shielding and dribbling skills. The game continues until only one player remains in possession of his or her ball. Eliminated players should immediately retrieve their balls and practice ball juggling outside of the field area until the game ends. Repeat for several rounds.

To Increase Difficulty

- Reduce size of playing area to limit available space.
- Add additional chasers who are not dribbling a ball.

To Decrease Difficulty

- Increase size of playing area.

Success Check

- Keep the head up with vision on opponents.
- Feel the pressure and react accordingly.
- Control the ball with the foot farthest from the challenging opponent.
- Shield the ball with your body.
- Use dribbling skills to create additional space and time in which to maneuver.

Score Your Success

One of final 8 players eliminated = 1 point
One of final 6 players eliminated = 2 points
One of final 4 players eliminated = 3 points
Last player standing = 5 points
Your score ___

TACKLING SKILLS

It is obvious that your team can't score goals if the other team has possession of the ball. You can regain possession for the team by intercepting passes or by tackling the ball from an opponent. Three basic skills are used for tackling the ball: the block, the poke, and the slide tackle. Successful execution of each technique requires balance and body control, proper timing of the challenge, sound judgment, and confidence.

In my 30-plus years as a player, coach, and camp director it has been my observation that few players demonstrate adequate tackling skills. This is because these important defensive skills are somewhat difficult to execute and also because players simply do not practice them as often as they should. Granted, it is probably more fun to practice shooting or dribbling skills, but you won't get a chance to use either of those skills in actual match situations unless you first gain possession of the ball.

Use the block tackle (figure 1.5) to win the ball from an opponent who is dribbling directly at you. Quickly close the distance to the ball. Position your feet in a staggered stance with one foot slightly ahead of the other. Assume a slightly crouched posture with knees bent and arms out to the sides for balance. From this position you will be able to react quickly to the dribbler's sudden movements or changes of direction. Tackle the ball by contacting it with the inside surface of your blocking foot. Position the blocking foot sideways with toes pointed slightly upward. Keep the foot firm as you lean forward and drive it powerfully through the center of the ball.

Once you've made the decision to challenge for the ball, you must commit yourself to the tackle with your full body weight. You must play the ball, not the opponent. If the referee judges that you are intentionally contacting the opponent before contacting the ball, you will be signaled for a rule violation.

Figure 1.5	Block Tackle

APPROACH

1. Close distance to dribbler
2. Maintain a staggered stance with weight balanced over balls of feet
3. Maintain a crouched posture with a low center of gravity
4. Keep shoulders square to dribbler

EXECUTION

1. Position blocking foot sideways with toes pointed slightly upward
2. Keep blocking foot firm
3. Drive foot through center of ball
4. Shift momentum forward

FOLLOW-THROUGH

1. Use full body weight through point of contact
2. Win the ball
3. Initiate counterattack

Misstep

The opponent dribbles the ball through your block and races past you.

Correction

Keep your body compact with a low center of gravity. Block the ball with a short, powerful snap of your leg. Transfer your full body weight forward through the point of contact.

Use the poke tackle technique (figure 1.6) when approaching from the side or slightly behind the dribbler. Close the distance, extend the leg and foot nearest to the ball, and poke the ball away with your toes. Be sure to play the ball, not the opponent. Kicking the opponent while trying to set the ball free is a foul.

Figure 1.6 Poke Tackle

APPROACH

1. Close distance to dribbler
2. Maintain balance and body control
3. Focus on the ball

EXECUTION

1. Extend nearest leg or foot toward ball
2. Bend balance leg
3. Poke ball with toes
4. Avoid physical contact with dribbler before tackle

FOLLOW-THROUGH

1. Maintain balance and body control
2. Chase after and collect the ball

Misstep

You physically contact the dribbler before tackling the ball.

Correction

Maintain body control at all times. Close the distance to the dribbler, keep a clear view of the ball, and extend your leg and foot to poke the ball away. Focus on the ball.

The slide tackle technique (figure 1.7) is generally used to dispossess an opponent when you are approaching from the side. The body action looks similar to that of a baseball player sliding into a base. Quickly close the distance to the dribbler. Leave your feet as you near the ball and slide on your side to a position slightly ahead of the dribbler. At the same time, snap your lower (sliding) leg straight and kick the ball away using the instep of your foot.

Figure 1.7 Slide Tackle

APPROACH

1. Approach dribbler from the side or from behind
2. Maintain balance and body control
3. Focus on the ball

EXECUTION

1. Leave feet and slide on your side
2. Place arms to sides for balance
3. Extend sliding (lower) leg ahead of the ball with foot extended
4. Bend opposite leg at knee
5. Snap sliding leg or foot into ball
6. Contact ball on instep

Misstep

You foul the dribbler when attempting to win the ball.

Correction

Do not initiate the slide tackle from directly behind the dribbler. Angle your approach from one side or the other before leaving your feet to slide ahead of the ball. Hook your leg around from the side to kick the ball away.

The hook slide (see figure 1.8) is a slight variation of the standard slide tackle. The hook slide technique is typically used to dispossess an opponent when approaching from behind. As you get near the dribbler, slide on your side past him or her. Snap your blocking (upper) foot on a slightly downward plane with ankle locked. Contact the ball with the instep of the upper foot. Time your challenge to tackle the ball when it separates from the dribbler's feet so that you avoid contact with the opponent before contacting the ball. After executing the tackle, jump quickly to your feet and initiate a counterattack.

Figure 1.8 Hook slide tackle.

In most instances the standard slide tackle and the hook tackle variation are not the preferred options. These techniques are appropriate in situations where the block tackle is not possible, such as when an opponent has beaten you on the dribble and there is little hope of catching him or her or when an opponent is dribbling past you along a touchline and you leave your feet to kick the ball out of bounds. Because you must go to the ground to challenge for the ball, you are in a poor position to recover should you fail to execute the tackle successfully.

Tackling Drill 1.   Block Tackle

Face a teammate who stands 3 yards away with a ball at his or her feet. Practice the block tackle technique as your partner walks the ball toward you. Close the distance to the ball, position the blocking foot sideways, and tackle the ball with the inside surface of your foot. Maintain a low center of gravity and keep your foot firm as it contacts the ball. Execute 25 block tackles with your favorite foot. Award yourself 1 point for each correct repetition of the technique.

To Increase Difficulty

- Increase number of repetitions.
- Attempt to tackle the ball from a player who is dribbling at you.

To Decrease Difficulty

- Practice the block tackle on a stationary target.

Success Check

- Maintain crouched posture with knees bent.
- Maintain balance and body control.
- Position blocking foot firmly sideways.
- Tackle with power and commitment.

Score Your Success

Fewer than 20 correct repetitions = 0 points

20 to 24 correct repetitions = 1 point

25 correct repetitions = 3 points

Your score ___

Tackling Drill 2.   Deny Penetration

Use markers to outline a 5- by 10-yard playing area. You and a partner get in position at opposite ends of the area; your partner has the ball. On command, he or she dribbles at you from a distance of 10 yards. Move forward to close the distance to the dribbler and attempt to block tackle or poke tackle the ball. You may tackle with either foot, depending on the dribbler's angle of approach. Repeat 20 times, after which you switch roles with the dribbler and repeat. Award yourself 1 point for each successful tackle that prevents the opponent from dribbling the ball over your end line.

To Increase Difficulty for Defender

- Increase width of area.

To Decrease Difficulty for Defender

- Decrease width of area.
- Require dribbler to advance at half speed.

Success Check

- Maintain a crouched posture with a low center of gravity.
- Maintain balance and body control.
- Keep blocking foot firm.
- Contact center of ball.
- Avoid contact with opponent before contacting the ball.

Score Your Success

0 to 8 points scored = 0 points

9 to 11 points scored = 1 point

12 to 15 points scored = 3 points

16 to 20 points scored = 5 points

Your score ___

Tackling Drill 3.   Tackle All

Position markers to outline a field area approximately 30 by 30 yards. Divide the group into two teams of equal numbers. Members of one team play as defenders; members of the other team are attackers. Each attacker has possession of a ball. To begin, the attackers dribble in random fashion within the field area. On the coach's command, the defenders sprint into the area and attempt to tackle a dribbler's ball. Defenders may use either the block or poke tackle technique. Slide tackles are prohibited in this drill because of the restricted space. If a defender successfully tackles a ball, he or she kicks it out of the area and immediately tries to dispossess another dribbler. Defenders are awarded 1 point for each ball that they kick out of the area. A dribbler who loses his or her ball should retrieve it immediately and reenter the game. Play for 3 minutes, then switch roles. Defenders keep track of points scored.

To Increase Difficulty for Defenders

- Increase size of playing area.
- Increase number of dribblers.

To Decrease Difficulty for Defenders

- Reduce size of playing area.
- Reduce number of dribblers.

Success Check

- Maintain balance and body control.
- Maintain a low center of gravity.
- Avoid contact with dribbler before tackling the ball.
- Commit to the tackle with power and determination.

Score Your Success

0 to 4 points scored as defender = 1 point

5 points or more scored as defender = 3 points

Your score ____

Tackling Drill 4.   Slide Tackle Drill

Partner with a teammate. Play on one end of a regulation field. You position at the top edge of the penalty area, 18 yards from goal, facing the end line. Your partner (server) positions directly behind you, about 20 yards from the goal, with a supply of balls. The server kicks a rolling ball toward the end line. You immediately sprint after the ball and execute a slide tackle to prevent the ball from rolling over the end line. Attempt to slide and kick the ball out over the touchline for a throw-in. Perform 10 repetitions. Award yourself 1 point for each successful execution of the slide tackle technique.

To Increase Difficulty

- Server dribbles the ball toward the end line and you attempt to slide tackle the ball.

To Decrease Difficulty

- Reduce distance of recovery run.

Success Check

- Slide ahead of the ball.
- Place arms at sides for balance and body control.
- Snap lower leg and contact ball on instep.

Score Your Success

0 to 3 points scored = 1 point

4 to 6 points scored = 2 points

7 to 10 points scored = 3 points

Your score ____

SUCCESS SUMMARY OF DRIBBLING, SHIELDING, AND TACKLING

Players who can consistently take on and beat opponents on the dribble play a vital role in team attack. Although some players are by nature better dribblers than others, everyone can develop effective dribbling skills. It simply takes practice. All you need is a ball and a patch of open ground. Keep in mind that dribbling is an individual art that can be expressed in different ways. Rehearse your moves against stationary cones, imaginary defenders, or live defenders when training with teammates. Pay particular attention to how quickly you can change speed and direction, how effective your body feints and foot movements are, and how you position your body to protect the ball from an opponent challenging for possession. Review the illustrations and the success checks in the drills to evaluate your overall performance and get helpful hints for improvement.

It's also important to develop individual defensive skills. Practice the block, poke, and slide tackle techniques in both practice and actual game situations. If possible, watch a videotape of yourself in training or actual game competition to evaluate your ability to execute the various tackling techniques.

Each of the drills described in this step has been assigned a "score your success" point value so that you can evaluate your performance and chart progress. Enter your score in the following table and total the points to get an estimate of your total success.

Beat an Opponent Dribbling Drills

1. Slalom Dribble _____ out of 5

2. Take On a Passive Defender _____ out of 5

3. Line-to-Line Game _____ out of 5

4. Score by Dribbling Only _____ out of 6

5. Tactical Dribbling _____ (varies)

Control Dribbling Drills

1. Unopposed Dribble _____ out of 5

2. Cone-to-Cone Drill _____ out of 5

3. Evade the Challenge _____ out of 5

Speed Dribbling Drills

1. Speed Dribble Relay _____ out of 5

2. First to the Penalty Area _____ out of 5

3. Attack or Defend _____ out of 3

(continued)

(continued)

Shielding Drills

1. One-on-One Possession   _____ out of 5

2. Evade the Double Team   _____ out of 5

3. All Versus All   _____ out of 5

Tackling Drills

1. Block Tackle   _____ out of 3

2. Deny Penetration   _____ out of 5

3. Tackle All   _____ out of 3

4. Slide Tackle Drill   _____ out of 3

Total   **_____ out of 78**

A combined score of 70 or greater indicates that you are prepared to move on to meet the challenges presented in step 2. A score in the range of 50 to 69 is considered adequate. You can move on to step 2 after additional practice of the dribbling, shielding, and tackling skills described in step 1. If you scored 49 or fewer points, you have not sufficiently mastered the skills covered in step 1. Review, practice, and improve your performance of all of these skills before moving on to the next step.

Passing and Receiving Rolling Balls

Although players need to master the individual dribbling skills discussed in step 1, it is important to realize that the soccer team is much more than a group of individuals all running in the same direction doing their own thing. While flashes of individual brilliance can and sometimes do decide the outcome of a game, at the end of the day team success ultimately depends on players' working in combination. Even the most talented players can't do it alone!

To maximize team performance, players must mesh individual talents to create a smooth, functioning whole. Passing and receiving skills form the vital thread that allows 11 individuals to play as one—that is, the whole to perform greater than the sum of its parts.

To perform successfully at higher levels of competition, players must be able to pass and receive the ball accurately under the game pressures of limited time and space, physical fatigue, and challenging opponents. Passing and receiving skills are generally grouped together for the simple reason that they complement one another. Each passed ball should, in theory, be received and controlled by a teammate. Mastery of passing and receiving skills will enable teammates to maintain possession of the ball, dictate

the tempo of the game, and ultimately create scoring opportunities.

Successful passing combinations are characterized by passes that are accurate, correctly paced, and properly timed. The team will not be able to generate the teamwork required to score goals if its players cannot pass the ball accurately over distance. Correct pace deals with the speed, or weight, of the pass. The pass should be at a speed that allows the receiving player to easily control and prepare the ball for the next action. Timing deals with the moment of release. The pass should arrive at a teammate's feet so that he or she does not have to break stride. Passes that arrive too early or too late often result in loss of possession.

Once the passer does his or her job, it is up to the receiving player to follow suit. Players must become adept at controlling balls arriving on the ground and through the air. Ground balls are most often controlled with the inside or outside surface of the foot. In rare instances, the sole of the foot can also be used to receive a rolling ball. In all cases, the receiving player must present a "soft target." By withdrawing the receiving surface as the ball arrives, you can cushion the impact and control the ball in proximity of your feet. When receiving the ball, do not stop it completely. Soccer is a fluid game; as such, the ball should rarely be stopped dead during a match. In most instances you should receive and control the ball in the direction of your next movement or into the space away from a challenging opponent.

PASSING GROUND BALLS

A variety of passing techniques can be observed during a soccer game. Some passes travel along the ground while others are driven through the air. In most situations, ground passes are preferred because they are easier to control and usually can be played with greater accuracy. Three fundamental techniques—the push pass, the outside-of-the-foot pass, and the instep pass—are used to pass the ball along the ground. Your choice of technique will depend on the situation.

The most basic type of pass and the first that you should become comfortable with is the *push pass* (figure 2.1). The push pass is used for playing the ball over distances of 5 to 15 yards and can also be used for slipping the ball past an opposing goalkeeper when a close-in shot requires accuracy rather than power.

As you approach the ball, face the target with shoulders square. Plant your balance (nonkicking) foot beside the ball with the knee bent and toes pointed toward the target. Position the passing foot square to the target with toes pointed slightly up and away from the midline of your body. Contact the center of the ball with the inside surface of your foot. Keep the ankle locked and foot firmly positioned. Follow through with a short, powerful kicking motion.

| **Figure 2.1** | **Push Pass** |

APPROACH	EXECUTION	FOLLOW-THROUGH
1. Face the target	1. Position body square to target	1. Transfer weight forward
2. Plant the balance foot beside the ball and pointed toward target	2. Swing kicking leg forward	2. Generate momentum through ball
3. Keep shoulders and hips square	3. Keep ankle locked and kicking foot firm	3. Perform a short and smooth follow-through
4. Position kicking foot sideways	4. Contact center of ball with inside surface of foot	
5. Keep arms out to sides for balance		
6. Keep the head steady with vision on ball		

Misstep

Ball leaves the ground.

Correction

You have leaned back and contacted the ball too far forward on your foot, near the toes. Wedging your toes beneath the ball will cause it to pop up into the air. Strike the center of the ball with the large inside surface of your kicking foot between the ankle and toes.

Misstep

Accuracy is poor.

Correction

Plant your balance foot beside the ball and pointed toward the target. Square your hips and shoulders. Keep your head steady as you contact the ball. Follow through directly toward the target.

Soccer players are rarely still for any length of time during a match. This fact necessitates being able to release accurate passes while running with the ball. For these situations, the *outside-of-the-foot pass* (figure 2.2) is usually your best choice. The passing technique can be used for both short- and medium-distance passes.

Plant your balance foot slightly behind and to the side of the ball. Draw back the kicking leg with the foot extended and rotated slightly inward. Use an inside-out kicking motion to contact the inside half of the ball with the outside surface of your instep. Keep the kicking foot firmly positioned and arms out to the sides for balance. Use a snaplike kicking motion of the lower leg (from the knee) for short-range passes. Use a more complete follow-through to generate greater distance on the pass.

Figure 2.2   Outside-of-the-Foot Pass

APPROACH

1. Plant supporting foot slightly behind and to the side of ball
2. Bend balance leg at knee
3. Draw kicking leg back behind balance leg
4. Position kicking foot down and rotated inward
5. Keep the head steady with vision on ball

EXECUTION

1. Keep knee of kicking leg over ball
2. Snap kicking leg forward at the knee
3. Keep foot extended and firm
4. Contact inside half of ball on outside surface of instep

FOLLOW-THROUGH

1. Transfer weight forward
2. Use an inside-out kicking motion
3. Use a snaplike follow-through of the kicking leg

Misstep

Ball leaves the ground.

Correction

Position the knee of the kicking leg over the ball at the moment of contact. Position the kicking foot down and keep it rotated inward. Lean forward as you kick the ball.

Misstep

The pass lacks pace.

Correction

Contact the ball with as much foot surface as possible just left or right of the ball's vertical midline. Keep the kicking foot firm and use a short, powerful kicking motion.

The *instep* of the foot provides a hard, flat surface that you can use to pass the ball over longer distances, both on the ground and through the air. The technique used to pass the ball along the ground (figure 2.3) is as follows: Approach the ball from behind at a slight angle. Plant your balance (nonkicking) foot beside the ball with the leg slightly bent at the knee and toes pointed toward the target. Draw back the kicking leg with foot extended and firmly positioned. Keep your head steady with vision on the ball. Square hips and shoulders to the target as you drive the instep through the ball. The kicking foot is pointed down at the moment of contact. The kicking mechanics are very similar to those used when shooting the ball at goal.

Figure 2.3   Instep Pass

APPROACH

1. Approach ball from behind at a slight angle
2. Plant balance foot beside ball with knee bent
3. Square shoulders and hips to target
4. Draw back kicking leg with foot extended and firm
5. Keep knee of kicking leg over ball
6. Keep arms out to sides for balance

EXECUTION

1. Keep the head steady with vision on ball
2. Transfer weight forward
3. Initiate kicking motion
4. Keep foot extended and firm
5. Contact the center of the ball with instep

FOLLOW-THROUGH

1. Generate momentum forward through the ball
2. Keep body weight centered over ball of balance foot
3. Follow-through motion of kicking goes to waist level or higher

---

Misstep

Ball travels upward into air.

Correction

This will occur when you plant your nonkicking foot behind the ball. To pass the ball along the ground, you must place your balance foot beside the ball as you kick it. This will enable you to position the knee of your kicking leg over the ball with the foot fully extended and toes pointed down as the foot contacts the ball.

Misstep

Poor accuracy.

Correction

Square shoulders and hips with the target as you kick the ball. Keep the kicking foot firm. Strike the ball directly through its center with the large flat surface of the instep. Use a complete follow-through motion to generate distance on the pass.

Passing on the Ground Drill 1. Off the Wall and Back

Get in position with a ball 5 yards from a wall or kickboard. Use the inside-of-the-foot (push pass) technique to pass the ball off the wall so that it rebounds back to you. As the ball rolls toward you, pass it off the wall again. This is commonly referred to as one-touch passing. Repeat for 50 consecutive passes. When possible, alternate passes with the right and left foot.

To Increase Difficulty

- Move 10 yards from the wall.
- Increase speed of repetition.
- Perform all passes with your weaker (non-dominant) foot.

To Decrease Difficulty

- Move closer to the wall.
- Stop the ball before passing it.
- Make all passes with your stronger (dominant) foot.

Success Check

- Plant nonkicking foot beside ball and point it toward target.
- Keep passing foot firmly positioned.
- Square shoulders and hips to target.
- Contact center of ball with inside surface of foot.
- Follow through toward target.

Score Your Success

Fewer than 25 one-touch passes off the wall without error = 0 points

25 to 34 one-touch passes off the wall without error = 1 point

35 to 44 one-touch passes off the wall without error = 3 points

45 or more one-touch passes off the wall without error = 5 points

Your score ___

Passing on the Ground Drill 2. Rapid Fire

Two players (servers A and B), each with a ball, face one another at a distance of 20 yards. Markers are set up to represent a two-yard-wide goal directly in front of each server. Player C gets in position midway between the servers. Server A begins the drill by passing the ball to player C, who uses the inside-of-the-foot passing technique to return the ball through the goal to server A. Player C immediately turns to play a ball arriving from server B and returns the ball in the same manner. Player C executes a total of 40 one-touch push passes before switching positions with one of the servers. Continue the drill until each player has taken a turn in the middle.

To Increase Difficulty

- Increase distance between servers to 30 yards.
- Increase the number of repetitions.
- Reduce width of goal to 1 yard.

To Decrease Difficulty

- Decrease distance between servers to 15 yards.
- Allow the central player two touches to receive and pass the ball.
- Increase width of goal to 3 yards.

Success Check

- Square shoulders and hips to target.
- Firmly position the passing foot sideways.
- Contact the center of the ball.
- Follow through toward the target.

Score Your Success

Fewer than 25 one-touch passes through goals = 0 points

25 to 29 one-touch push passes through goals = 1 point

30 to 34 one-touch push passes through goals = 3 points

35 or more one-touch push passes through goals = 5 points

Your score ___

Passing on the Ground Drill 3.   Pass and Follow

Form two groups of 4 to 6 players each. Groups line up in single file facing each other at a distance of 10 yards. The first player in group 1 passes the ball to the first player in group 2 and immediately sprints to the end of line 2. The first player in line 2 moves forward to meet the ball, passes to the next player in line 1, and immediately sprints to the end of line 1. Use one-touch push passes only. Continue the drill until each player has passed 30 balls.

To Increase Difficulty

- Increase passing distance to 15 yards.
- Pass with weaker foot only.
- Increase speed of repetition.

To Decrease Difficulty

- Reduce passing distance.
- Allow two touches to control and pass ball.

Success Check

- Move forward to meet the ball.
- Square shoulders and hips to target.
- Contact the center of the ball.
- Follow through toward the target.

Score Your Success

Fewer than 15 passes accurately played to the opposite line = 0 points

15 to 19 passes accurately played to the opposite line = 1 point

20 to 24 passes accurately played to the opposite line = 3 points

25 or more passes accurately played to the opposite line = 5 points

Your score ___

Passing on the Ground Drill 4.   Six-on-One Keep-Away

Use markers to outline a 12- by 12-yard playing area. Designate six players as attackers and one as the defender. The defender takes a position in the center of the square. Attackers spread apart along the perimeter of the square; one has possession of the ball. The six attackers attempt to keep the ball away from the defender within the playing area. Attackers may use inside-of-the-foot or outside-of-the-foot techniques to pass the ball. All passes must be one-touch passes. If the defender steals the ball or the ball is played out of the field area, the attacker who committed the error becomes the defender, and the defender becomes an attacker. Play for 15 minutes continuously.

To Increase Difficulty for Attackers

- Decrease size of playing area.
- Add a second defender to the drill.

To Decrease Difficulty for Attackers

- Increase size of playing area.

Success Check

- Square shoulders and hips to target.
- Keep passing foot firm and in correct position.
- Play the ball firmly to the target.
- Get in position to make yourself available to receive passes.

Score Your Success

9 errors or more in 15 minutes = 1 point

6 to 8 errors in 15 minutes = 3 points

0 to 5 errors in 15 minutes = 5 points

Your score ___

Passing on the Ground Drill 5.   Passing the Circuit

Play with five to seven teammates within a 40-by 40-yard area. Assign each player a number, beginning with one and continuing up through the number of players in the group. Two players each have possession of a ball. All players begin to jog randomly within the area; those with a ball dribble. Dribblers locate the teammate numbered directly above them and pass to him or her. The player with the highest number passes to player 1 to complete the circuit. All passes must be made with the outside surface of the instep. Once play begins, players move continuously as they pass to the teammate numbered above them and receive passes from the teammate numbered below them. Keep tally of inaccurate passes (for example, a ball that is played behind or too far ahead of the intended target). Play for 15 minutes.

To Increase Difficulty

- Require players to pass the ball with their weaker foot only.
- Require all passes to be 20 yards or longer.

- Add an additional ball to the drill.
- Add a defender to the drill who tries to intercept passes.

To Decrease Difficulty

- Perform the drill at half speed.

Success Check

- Properly position the kicking foot.
- Contact ball on outside surface of instep.
- Use an inside-out kicking motion.
- Play the ball with accuracy and correct pace.

Score Your Success

11 inaccurate passes or more = 1 point

6 to 10 inaccurate passes = 3 points

0 to 5 inaccurate passes = 5 points

Your score ___

Passing on the Ground Drill 6.   One–Two Combination in the Box

The entire team can participate in this drill. Each player pairs with a partner and takes position within a penalty area of the field. One ball is required per pair. All players jog randomly within the penalty area; those with a ball dribble. Dribblers look to execute a give-and-go (wall) pass with any player who does not have a ball. The dribbler makes eye contact with his or her intended target, who checks toward the dribbler to receive a short, crisp pass. The dribbler immediately sprints forward to collect a one-touch pass from the receiver, controls the ball, and then continues to dribble while looking for another free player with whom to execute a one–two (wall) pass. The dribbler's initial pass must be made with the outside of the foot, the most appropriate passing surface for executing a wall pass. Continue for 5 minutes, after which players switch roles and play for another 5 minutes. Keep tally of inaccurate passes, such as passes that disrupt the one–two combination.

To Increase Difficulty

- Reduce size of area.
- Add a defender to pressure the dribblers.

To Decrease Difficulty

- Increase size of area.
- Perform drill at half speed.

Success Check

- Dribble toward the target.
- Pass the ball with outside surface of the foot.
- Sprint forward to collect the return pass.

Score Your Success

7 or more inaccurate passes = 1 point

4 to 6 inaccurate passes = 3 points

0 to 3 inaccurate passes = 5 points

Your score ___

Passing on the Ground Drill 7.   Multiple Gates Game

Form two teams of four to six players each. Use markers to outline a playing area 40 by 40 yards. Position cones or flags to represent six small goals randomly spaced throughout the area. Each goal is 2 yards wide. Teams can score in all six goals and must defend all six goals. To score, a player must complete a pass through a goal to a teammate positioned on the opposite side. Each goal scored earns the passer 1 point. Players may pass the ball through either side of a goal, but not twice consecutively through the same goal. Regular soccer rules apply except that teams do not change possession of the ball after a goal, and the offside law is waived. All scores must be made with the outside- or inside-of-the-foot techniques. Play for 15 minutes. Keep track of your points.

To Increase Difficulty

- Decrease size of playing area.
- Reduce width of goal to 1 yard.
- Add one neutral player to the game who always joins with the defending team, providing the defenders an advantage over the attackers.

To Decrease Difficulty

- Make the goals larger.
- Increase the number of goals.
- Add one neutral player to the game who always plays with the team in possession, giving the attackers a one-player advantage over the defenders.

Success Check

- Combine with teammates to maintain possession.
- Strive for accuracy and correct pace of passes.
- Attack the goal least defended.

Score Your Success

1 or 0 points = 0 points

2 to 5 points = 2 points

6 points or more = 4 points

Your score ___

Passing on the Ground Drill 8.   Partner Pass

Position cones to represent a goal 4 yards wide. Two players (A and B) face each other on opposite sides of the goal at a distance of 30 yards (15 yards to each side). Player A has the ball to begin. Player A pushes the ball forward a couple of feet with his or her first touch and passes the ball through the goal with his or her second touch to player B, who is positioned on the other side. Player B controls the ball, touches it forward, and returns the ball to player A in the same manner. Partners continue passing back and forth for a total of 40 passes each. All passes must be made with the instep technique and must be played along the ground. Award 1 point for each pass traveling through the goal. Keep track of points scored.

To Increase Difficulty

- Reduce size of goal to 3 yards.
- Increase passing distance.

To Decrease Difficulty

- Increase size of goal to 6 yards.
- Decrease passing distance.

Success Check

- Square shoulders and hips to target.
- Extend and firmly position the kicking foot.
- Keep the knee over ball with toes pointed down at moment of contact.
- Complete the follow-through toward target.

Score Your Success

24 points or fewer scored = 1 point

25 to 29 points scored = 3 points

30 to 34 points scored = 5 points

35 to 40 points scored = 7 points

Your score ___

Passing on the Ground Drill 9.   Hunt the Foxes

Play this game with 12 to 15 teammates. Use markers to outline a playing area of approximately 30 by 30 yards. Designate five players as hunters who get in position outside the area, each with a ball. The remaining players (the foxes), without balls, get in position within the area. On command, the hunters dribble into the area to hunt the foxes. The objective is to contact a fox below the knees with a passed ball. Foxes use sudden changes of speed and direction to avoid being "shot" by a hunter. Any fox contacted with a passed ball immediately locates a loose ball and becomes a hunter; the original hunter becomes a fox. A hunter is awarded 1 point for each opponent he or she contacts below the knees with a passed ball. Play for 10 minutes continuously. Use any of the passing techniques discussed thus far. Keep a tally of points you score as a hunter.

To Increase Difficulty for Hunters

- Enlarge playing area.
- Require hunters to pass with their non-dominant foot.

To Decrease Difficulty for Hunters

- Reduce size of playing area.

Success Check

- Choose the appropriate passing technique.
- Keep passing foot properly positioned.
- Follow through toward target.

Score Your Success

0 to 2 points = 1 point

3 to 4 points = 3 points

5 points or more = 5 points

Your score ___

Passing on the Ground Drill 10.   Combine With Moving Targets

A group of three players stations within an area approximately 40 by 40 yards. One player has the ball to begin; the remaining players get in position 20 yards or more from the ball. On command, all players begin moving randomly within the field area. The player with the ball passes to either of the other players using the instep pass technique. The passer immediately sprints to a position near the player to whom he or she passed the ball, receives a short return pass, turns, locates the third player, and passes the ball to that player. All passes should be 20 yards or greater and must be played along the ground. All players, with and without the ball, move constantly throughout the exercise. The player with the ball executes 25 passes before switching roles with one of the other players who does not have a ball. Repeat the exercise until each player has performed 25 passes. An accurate pass is defined as one that arrives within 2 yards of the receiving player's feet. Award yourself 1 point for each accurate

pass. Players should perform the drill at near-game speed.

To Increase Difficulty

- Increase the passing distance.
- Require all passes to be with the nondominant foot.

To Decrease Difficulty

- Reduce the passing distance to 15 yards.
- Perform drill at half speed.

Success Check

- Keep the passing foot firm and properly positioned.
- Square shoulders and hips to target.
- Follow through the kicking motion toward target.
- Pass the ball so that a teammate can receive it without breaking stride.

RECEIVING GROUND BALLS

Rolling balls are usually received and controlled with the inside or outside surface of the foot, and on occasion with the sole of the foot. I have observed the sole-of-the-foot technique used more often in indoor soccer, where the space is restricted and players are almost always under challenge of an opponent as they receive the ball.

For the inside-of-the-foot reception (figure 2.4), use the inside surface of the foot to receive and control the ball in situations when you are not under immediate pressure from an opponent. Move forward to meet the ball as it arrives. Extend the receiving leg and position the receiving foot sideways with toes pointed up and away from the midline of the body. To cushion the impact of the ball, withdraw the foot as the ball arrives. Do not stop (trap) the ball completely. Receive and control the ball in the direction of your next movement or into the space away from a nearby opponent.

Figure 2.4   Inside-of-the-Foot Reception

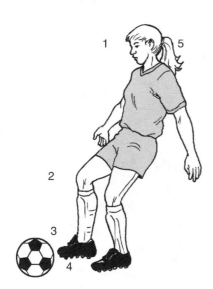  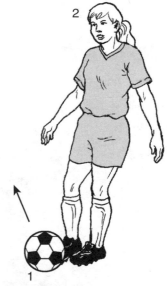

PREPARATION

1. Move toward ball.
2. Extend receiving leg to meet ball.
3. Position receiving foot sideways.
4. Keep ankle locked and receiving foot firm.
5. Keep the head steady with vision on ball.

RECEPTION

1. Receive ball on inside surface of foot.
2. Withdraw foot to cushion impact.
3. Control ball into the space away from nearby opponent.

FOLLOW-THROUGH

1. Push ball in direction of next movement.
2. Keep the head up with vision on the field.

Misstep

The ball bounces off your foot and out of your range of control.

Correction

You must provide a soft receiving surface for the ball. To cushion the impact, withdraw your foot as the ball arrives, and control the ball in the direction of your next movement.

Misstep

The ball rolls under your foot.

Correction

This can occur because of improper positioning of the receiving foot or if you take your eyes off the ball. Keep your head steady and focus on the ball. Raise your receiving foot only about an inch or so off the ground, and contact the center of the ball with the inside surface of your foot.

There are times during a match when you will receive the ball while tightly marked by an opponent. In this situation, the inside-of-the-foot technique is not the most appropriate choice because the defending player may be able to reach in with a foot to kick the ball free. You can use your body to protect the ball from a challenging opponent by receiving it with the outside surface of your foot (figure 2.5). Position yourself sideways and control the ball with the foot farthest from the opponent. Rotate your receiving foot inward and downward and receive the ball on the outside surface of your instep. Turn the ball into the space away from the opponent, an action that will afford you additional time to pass the ball or dribble away from pressure.

| Figure 2.5 | **Outside-of-the-Foot Reception** |

PREPARATION

1. Move toward the ball
2. Position sideways between ball and opponent
3. Maintain semicrouched posture with low center of gravity
4. Control ball with foot farthest from opponent
5. Keep the head steady with vision on the ball

RECEPTION

1. Extend the receiving foot down and rotate inward
2. Receive ball on outside surface of instep
3. Withdraw receiving leg to cushion impact
4. Turn ball into space away from nearby opponent

FOLLOW-THROUGH

1. Readjust body position as needed to shield ball from opponent
2. Keep the head up and watch the field
3. Push ball in direction of next movement

Misstep

You fail to protect the ball as you receive it, and an opponent reaches in with his or her foot and kicks the ball away from you.

Correction

Position sideways and control the ball with the foot farthest from the defender. Readjust position in response to the opponent's movement.

Misstep

The defender steps in front of you to intercept the pass.

Correction

Always move toward the ball as you prepare to receive it. The first player to the ball will always win the prize.

You can use the sole-of-the-foot reception (figure 2.6) effectively to control the ball in situations where an opponent is challenging for the ball from behind. You can maintain maximum distance between the ball and the opponent by leaning back into him or her, extending the receiving leg to meet the ball, and controlling the ball with the sole of the foot. Square your hips and shoulders to the ball, angle the receiving foot upward, and pin the ball to the ground with the sole of the foot. In that position you can manipulate the ball by rolling it forward or sideways with the sole of the foot to evade the opponent's challenge.

Figure 2.6   Sole-of-the-Foot Reception

PREPARATION

1. Move toward the ball
2. Keep hands out to sides for balance
3. Extend the receiving leg toward ball
4. Receiving foot is angled upward

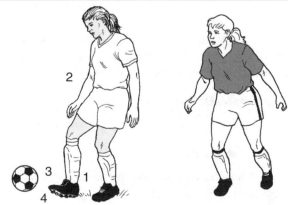

Figure 2.6 (continued)

RECEPTION

1. Lean back into defender
2. Pin ball between sole of foot and ground
3. Maintain distance between ball and defender

FOLLOW-THROUGH

1. Manipulate ball by rolling with foot
2. React to pressure of opponent
3. Relieve pressure by moving away from opponent

Misstep

You feel awkward and lack mobility when receiving the ball with the sole of your foot.

Correction

Keep your supporting leg bent at the knee with arms out to the sides for balance. This will enhance your mobility and enable you to react more quickly to the movements of the opponent.

Receiving Ground Balls Drill 1. Dancing Feet

Partners face one another at a distance of 5 yards. One player has the ball to begin. On command, partners pass the ball back and forth along the ground as many times as possible in 60 seconds. Use the inside- or outside-of-the-foot reception to control and prepare the ball. Players must use two touches to control and return the ball. You are assessed 1 penalty point for each time you use more than two touches. Keep track of your penalty points. Perform five 60-second rounds with a short break between each.

To Increase Difficulty

- Increase the duration to 90 seconds.

To Decrease Difficulty

- Allow three touches to receive, control, and return the ball.

Success Check

- Choose proper receiving technique.
- Provide a soft receiving surface.
- Receive and control the ball in one fluid movement.
- Use the first touch to prepare the ball for your next action.

Score Your Success

7 penalty points or more in 5 rounds = 2 points

3 to 5 penalty points in 5 rounds = 3 points

0 to 2 penalty points in 5 rounds = 4 points

Your score ___

Receiving Ground Balls Drill 2.   Turn and Play On

In one half of a regulation field, 15 to 20 players get in position with one ball for every two players. On command, all players begin moving throughout the area. Those with a ball dribble for a few yards before passing the ball to a player who is moving without a ball. The player receiving the ball must turn it left or right with his or her first touch, then dribble for a few yards in that direction before passing to a player who does not have a ball. Passes can be controlled with either the inside or outside surface of the foot. Players must receive and turn with the ball with their first touch. A player who requires more than one touch to turn with the ball is penalized 1 point. Play for 10 minutes continuously, keeping tally of your penalty points.

To Increase Difficulty

- Add several defenders to the drill who challenge receiving players for the ball.

To Decrease Difficulty

- Allow two touches to receive, control, and turn the ball.

Success Check

- Turn left or right with the ball in one fluid movement.
- Provide a soft receiving surface.
- Keep the ball in close control.

Score Your Success

10 penalty points or more = 1 point

6 to 9 penalty points = 3 points

0 to 5 penalty points = 5 points

Your score ___

Receiving Ground Balls Drill 3.   Two-Touch Possession Game

Use markers to outline a 12- by 12-yard playing area. Four players form an attacking team and try to keep the ball away from a fifth player (defender) within the square. Use the receiving technique most appropriate for the situation. The attacking team scores 1 point for each time it makes 8 consecutive passes without loss of possession to the defender. Attacking players are allowed only two touches to receive and pass the ball. The passing sequence is broken if the defender steals the ball, the ball is played outside of the square, or an attacker uses more than two touches to receive and pass the ball. The attacker who commits the error becomes the defender, and the defender becomes an attacker. Play for 5 minutes.

To Increase Difficulty for Attackers

- Reduce playing area to 10 by 10 yards.
- Require 10 consecutive passes for 1 point.

To Decrease Difficulty for Attackers

- Enlarge playing area to 15 by 15 yards to give attackers more space and time.

- Allow attackers three touches to pass and receive the ball.
- Add a fifth attacker.
- Award 1 point for five consecutive passes.

Success Check

- Choose appropriate receiving technique.
- Provide a soft receiving surface.
- Control ball into space away from defender.
- Keep the play fluid—do not stop the ball.

Score Your Success

10 errors or more committed in a 5-minute game = 1 point

6 to 9 errors committed in a 5-minute game = 3 points

0 to 5 errors committed in a 5-minute game = 5 points

Your score ___

Receiving Ground Balls Drill 4. Control Under Pressure

Six players participate in this drill. Two players, without balls, get in position within the center circle of a regulation field. One player is designated as the attacker, the other the defender. Four servers, each with a ball, take position an equal distance apart on the perimeter of the circle. To begin, the attacker uses sudden changes of speed and direction in an attempt to lose the marking defender while looking to receive a ball from a server. At an opportune moment, a server plays the ball to the feet of the attacker, who must control it using the appropriate technique and maintain possession for 5 seconds before returning it to the same server. The attacker uses dribbling or shielding skills to maintain possession of the ball. After releasing the ball, the attacker immediately looks to receive a ball from a different server. Play for 90 seconds. After a brief rest, the defender and attacker switch roles and repeat. Continue the drill until all players have taken a turn as a defender and attacker. An attacker is assessed 1 penalty point each time he or she fails to maintain possession of the ball for 5 seconds.

To Increase Difficulty for Attacker

- Add a second defender.

- Require the attacker to turn with the ball and play it to a different server.

To Decrease Difficulty for Attacker

- Increase size of playing area.
- Require attacker to maintain possession for only 3 seconds before returning ball to server.

Success Check

- Protect the ball with your body as you receive it.
- Maintain balance and body control at all times.
- Use sudden changes of direction with the ball to evade defensive pressure.

Score Your Success

4 penalty points or more in 90-second round = 1 point

1 to 3 penalty points = 3 points

0 penalty points = 5 points

Your score ___

Receiving Ground Balls Drill 5. Find the Open Player

Three players (servers) get in position side-by-side 3 yards apart. A fourth player (target) faces the servers at a distance of 6 yards. Servers 1 and 2 each have a ball; server 3 does not have a ball to begin. Server 1 starts play by passing a ball to the target, who receives and prepares the ball with the first touch, then passes to server 3 (who is without a ball) with the second touch. Server 2 then passes a ball to the target, who receives and prepares the ball with the first touch, then returns it to server 1 (who is without a ball) with the second touch. Continue the drill at maximum speed for 2 minutes, after which one of the servers switches positions with the target player. Repeat until each player has taken a turn as the target. The target player is assessed 1 penalty point each time he or she fails to receive and return the ball with two touches to the server who does not have a ball. Keep track of penalty points.

To Increase Difficulty for Target

- Increase the speed of repetition.

- Increase duration of drill.
- Add two additional servers.

To Decrease Difficulty for Target

- Allow the target player three touches to receive and return the ball.

Success Check

- Provide a soft receiving surface.
- Prepare the ball with the first touch.
- Receive and return the ball as quickly as possible.

Score Your Success

5 penalty points or more = 1 point

3 to 4 penalty points = 3 points

0 to 2 penalty points = 5 points

Your score ___

Receiving Ground Balls
Drill 6.   Three-on-Three-on-Three

Organize three groups of three players each. Assign each group different-colored vests to differentiate the teams. Play within the penalty area (44 by 18 yards). To begin, designate one group as defenders; the two remaining groups join to form a six-player attacking team. The attacking team attempts to keep the ball from the defenders within the penalty area. Attackers must use two or fewer touches to receive and pass the ball to one another. Loss of possession occurs when a defending player steals the ball, when an attacker plays the ball outside of the area, or when an attacker uses more than two touches to receive and pass the ball. The group of three whose error causes the loss of possession immediately becomes the defending team, and the original defending team joins the remaining attackers. Play continuously for 15 minutes as teams alternate from attack to defense. A player who uses more than two touches to receive and pass the ball is assessed 1 penalty point. Individual players should keep track of their penalty points throughout the game.

To Increase Difficulty for Attackers

- Add two neutral players who always join the defending team, creating a six-on-five advantage for the attacking team.
- Reduce size of area to 15 by 35 yards to

further reduce the time and space available to receive and pass the ball.

To Decrease Difficulty for Attackers

- Add two neutral players to the game who always join the attacking team, creating an eight-on-three player advantage for the attack.
- Allow the attackers three touches to receive, control, and pass the ball.

Success Check

- Receive and control the ball in the direction of your next movement.
- Withdraw the receiving surface as the ball arrives.
- Keep your head up so that you're aware of passing options.
- Move the ball quickly from one player to another.

Score Your Success

9 penalty points or more = 1 point

5 to 8 penalty points = 3 points

0 to 4 penalty points = 5 points

Your score ___

SUCCESS SUMMARY OF PASSING AND RECEIVING ROLLING BALLS

Effective passing and receiving skills are the foundation of successful team play, the thread that ties the 10 field players into one cohesive unit. As you master the skills described in step 2, you will gain confidence and become a better all-round soccer player. The game itself will become more enjoyable as you improve your ability to combine with your teammates.

As the saying goes, "perfect practice makes perfect." Begin by rehearsing the correct tech-

nique for each skill under minimal pressure. Gradually add the game pressures of restricted space, limited time, and challenging opponents so that the drills more closely simulate the actual conditions you will face in the match.

Each of the drills described in this step has been assigned a "score your success" point value to help you evaluate performance and chart your progress. Enter your score and total the points to get an estimate of your total success.

Passing on the Ground Drills

1. Off the Wall and Back _____ out of 5
2. Rapid Fire _____ out of 5
3. Pass and Follow _____ out of 5
4. Six-on-One Keep-Away _____ out of 5
5. Passing the Circuit _____ out of 5
6. One-Two Combination in the Box _____ out of 5
7. Multiple Gates Game _____ out of 4
8. Partner Pass _____ out of 7
9. Hunt the Foxes _____ out of 5
10. Combine With Moving Targets _____ out of 5

Receiving Ground Balls Drills

1. Dancing Feet _____ out of 4
2. Turn and Play On _____ out of 5
3. Two-Touch Possession Game _____ out of 5
4. Control Under Pressure _____ out of 5
5. Find the Open Player _____ out of 5
6. Three-on-Three-on-Three _____ out of 5

Total _____ *out of 80*

A combined score of 65 points or greater suggests that you have sufficiently mastered the skills and are prepared to move on to step 3. A score in the range of 45 to 64 is considered adequate. You can move on to step 3 after additional practice on the passing and receiving skills that you find most difficult to perform. A score of 44 or fewer points suggests a lack of sufficient competency in the various passing and receiving techniques. You should review and practice all of the skills discussed in step 2 again before moving on to step 3.

Passing and Receiving Flighted Balls

In most situations, it is to your advantage to pass the ball along the ground. Rolling balls are easier to control and can generally be played with greater accuracy. There will be times, however, when going airborne is your best option. For example, an opponent may be positioned to block the passing lane between you and a teammate who is stationed in a dangerous attacking position, or you may decide to serve the ball into the open space behind the defense for a teammate to run to. On rare occasions, you can even score a goal by chipping an opposing goalkeeper who has drifted too far forward of the goal line.

To take advantage of these special situations, you must become competent at passing the ball through the air. Two basic techniques, the *chip pass* and the *flighted instep pass,* are commonly used. The choice of technique depends in large part on how far the ball must travel and how quickly it must achieve height to clear a defending player. Likewise, you must be able to skillfully receive and control balls dropping from above. Step 3 is designed to develop your competence and confidence in passing and receiving balls through the air.

EXECUTING FLIGHTED PASSES

To make the ball airborne, lean back and drive your foot through the lower third of the ball. It is essential that the ball achieve sufficient height to clear any opponents positioned between you and your target. In general, the chip pass technique is used for short- to medium-distance passes. The flighted instep pass is your best choice for sending the ball over longer distances, as when changing the point of attack from one side of the field to the other.

Chip Pass

The chip pass technique is used to loft, or pop, the ball up and over an opponent who is blocking the passing lane to a teammate. This situation can occur during the general run of play and when opponents have formed a wall of players to defend against a free kick. In either case, a properly executed chip pass enables you to exploit the open space behind the defending players.

To execute the chip pass (figure 3.1), begin your approach from behind the ball and at a slight angle. Plant your supporting (nonkicking) foot beside the ball. Draw back the kicking leg with foot extended and firm. Square shoulders and hips with the target as you drive (wedge) the kicking foot beneath the ball. Use a short, powerful kicking motion with minimal follow-through. Wedging your foot beneath the ball will impart slight backspin, which makes for a softer pass that is easier to control.

Figure 3.1   Chip Pass

  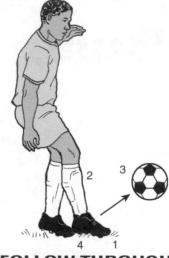

APPROACH	EXECUTION	FOLLOW-THROUGH
1. Approach the ball from behind and at a slight angle	1. Position knee of kicking leg over ball	1. Use forward momentum through point of impact
2. Plant the supporting foot beside the ball with the knee bent	2. Lean forward with hips and shoulders square to target	2. Snap the kicking leg straight
3. Draw back kicking leg with foot extended and firm	3. Drive inside surface of instep beneath ball	3. Impart slight backspin on ball
4. Keep arms out to sides for balance	4. Kicking foot is extended and firm	4. Use minimal follow-through
5. Keep the head steady with vision on ball	5. Use a short, powerful kicking motion	

Misstep

Pass does not achieve sufficient height to clear the defender.

Correction

Use a short, powerful, snaplike motion of the kicking leg to impart immediate lift on the ball. Wedge the instep underneath the ball to send it over an opponent.

Misstep

The pass travels right or left of the intended target.

Correction

Square your shoulders and hips to the target. Keep the kicking foot firm and contact the ball on the inner surface of the instep.

Flighted Instep Pass

The instep surface of the foot is used to drive the ball over longer distances. The kicking mechanics are similar to those used for the instep ground pass.

For the flighted instep pass (figure 3.2), begin your approach from behind the ball at a slight angle. Plant the supporting foot slightly behind and to the side of the ball. Placement of the supporting foot behind the ball will allow a greater follow-through motion of the kicking leg and will enable you to lean back slightly as you kick the ball. In this position you will be able to generate loft and distance on the pass. Extend and firmly position your kicking foot as the instep is driven through the lower third of the ball. Use a complete follow-through motion.

Figure 3.2   Flighted Instep Pass

APPROACH

1. Approach from behind the ball at a slight angle
2. Plant your supporting foot to the side and slightly behind the ball
3. Draw back the kicking leg
4. Keep kicking foot extended and firm
5. Keep arms out to the sides for balance
6. Keep the head steady with vision on ball

EXECUTION

1. Position knee of kicking leg slightly behind ball
2. Lean back and square shoulders with target
3. Drive instep of kicking foot through lower third of ball
4. Keep kicking foot firm throughout

FOLLOW-THROUGH

1. Kicking leg snaps straight
2. Weight moves forward over ball of the supporting foot
3. Arms move forward
4. Follow-through motion goes to waist level or higher

Misstep

The pass fails to travel the desired distance.

Correction

Keep the kicking foot firmly positioned and use a complete follow-through motion of the kicking leg. Generate momentum forward through the point of contact.

Misstep

Pass is off target.

Correction

Square shoulders and hips to the target. Lean back and contact the lower third of the ball with the full instep. Keep your kicking foot firm. Follow through toward the target.

Passing Through the Air Drill 1. Chip to Chest

Face a partner (server) at a distance of 5 yards. The server rolls the ball slowly toward you. Return the ball by chipping to the server's chest. The server catches the ball and repeats the sequence. Perform 40 repetitions, then switch roles. Score 1 point each time you chip the ball accurately to the server's chest. Keep track of points scored.

To Increase Difficulty

- Decrease distance to 4 yards (ball must achieve sufficient height more quickly).
- Increase pace of serve.

To Decrease Difficulty

- Chip a stationary ball.

Success Check

- Square shoulders and hips to target.
- Drive instep beneath ball.
- Keep kicking foot extended and firm.
- Use minimal follow-through.

Score Your Success

9 points or fewer = 0 points
10 to 19 points = 2 points
20 to 29 points = 3 points
30 to 34 points = 4 points
35 to 40 points = 5 points
Your score ___

Passing Through the Air Drill 2. Pass Under and Chip Over

Partner with a teammate. Get in position as the server 10 yards front and center of a regulation goal. Your partner faces you from the opposite side of the goal, also 10 yards from the goal. Raise the goal net off the ground so that a ball can be rolled back and forth through the goal. Begin by rolling the ball through the goal to your partner, who returns the ball to you by chipping it over the 8-foot-high crossbar. Control the ball out of the air and repeat the sequence. Award the kicker 1 point for each ball chipped over the goal that drops within 3 feet of the server. Perform 30 repetitions, then switch roles and repeat.

To Increase Difficulty

- Get in position 7 yards to each side of the goal (chip pass must achieve sufficient height more quickly to clear the bar).

- Pass the ball with your weaker (nondominant) foot.

To Decrease Difficulty

- Stop the ball before chipping over the goal.
- Use a smaller goal (6 feet high).

Success Check

- Square shoulders and hips to target.
- Drive instep underneath ball.
- Use a short, powerful leg snap.

Score Your Success

0 to 14 points = 0 points
15 to 19 points = 1 point
20 to 24 points = 3 points
25 to 30 points = 5 points
Your score ___

Passing Through the Air Drill 3.   Chip the Middle Man

Face a teammate at a distance of 20 yards. A third player (the server) gets in position with the ball midway between the two end players. The server begins the drill by passing a slowly rolling ball toward you. Step forward and chip the rolling ball over the server's head so that it lands at the feet of the third player. Players rotate positions after each chip pass. You follow the ball to the opposite end of the line. The server moves to your original position, and the player who received the ball dribbles it to the server (middle) position. Continue the drill until each player has executed 30 chip passes. Score 1 point for each pass that clears the middle player and lands within 3 feet of the receiving player. Players are permitted to chip the ball with their favorite (stronger) foot.

To Increase Difficulty

- Increase pace of serve.

- Require players to chip the ball with the weaker foot.

To Decrease Difficulty

- Reduce passing distance.
- Allow players to stop the ball before chipping over the middle player.

Success Check

- Square shoulders and hips to target.
- Drive instep beneath ball.
- Use a short, powerful kicking motion.

Score Your Success

0 to 14 points = 0 points
15 to 19 points = 1 point
20 to 24 points = 3 points
25 to 30 points = 5 points
Your score ____

Passing Through the Air Drill 4.   Flighted Balls Only

Organize two equal teams of six to eight players, each with a goalkeeper. Use colored scrimmage vests to differentiate teams. Play on a 75- by 50-yard field area. Position cones or flags to mark an 8- by 8-yard goal box at each end of the area. Station a goalkeeper in each goal box. Begin with a kickoff from the center of the field. Teams defend the goal box on their end of the field and score points by flighting the ball into the opponent's goal box so that the goalkeeper can receive the ball directly out of the air. Keepers are not permitted to leave the goal box to receive the ball in their hands, although they can move outside the box to use their feet to control a rolling ball. A ball received directly out of the air is distributed immediately to a teammate, and play continues. Award the attacking team 1 point for each ball flighted into a goal box that the opposing goalkeeper receives out of the air. Regular soccer rules are in effect, other than the method of scoring. Play for 25 minutes. The team scoring more points wins.

To Increase Difficulty

- Make the goal box smaller.

To Decrease Difficulty

- Make the goal box larger.
- Allow the goalkeeper to field the ball after one bounce.

Success Check

- Quickly change the location of the ball to create passing lanes to the goal.
- Square shoulders and hips to target.
- Drive instep through lower third of the ball.
- Use a complete follow-through motion toward target.

Score Your Success

Member of losing team = 3 points
Member of winning team = 5 points
Your score ____

Passing Through the Air
Drill 5.   Change the Point of Attack

Form groups of four players, one ball per group. Players pass among themselves within an area 30 by 50 yards. Passing combinations must be executed in a short-short-long sequence. For example, players must combine for two consecutive short passes (5 to 10 yards) followed by a long flighted ball to the most distant player. Another short-short-long sequence follows immediately. Short passes should be played along the ground while the long pass must be flighted through the air. Perform the drill at game speed, even though there are no opponents to apply pressure on the passer. Players are penalized 1 point for each flighted pass that does not drop to the ground within 5 yards of the intended target. Play for 10 minutes and keep track of penalty points.

To Increase Difficulty

- Place a touch restriction on players (such as a two-touch maximum, three-touch maximum).

To Decrease Difficulty

- Require the flighted ball to drop within 10 yards of the intended target.

Success Check

- Square shoulders and hips to target.
- Drive instep though lower third of the ball.
- Use a complete follow-through toward target.

Score Your Success

10 penalty points or more = 0 points.
6 to 9 penalty points = 3 points.
0 to 5 penalty points = 5 points.
Your score ___

RECEIVING FLIGHTED BALLS

Four body surfaces—the instep, thigh, chest, and head—are commonly used for collecting and controlling balls arriving through the air. The choice of surface depends on the flight trajectory of the ball and the position of nearby opponents. In all situations you must be able to receive and control the ball skillfully and, if an opponent is nearby, protect the ball as you do so. As is the case when receiving ground passes, your first touch of the ball is most important. You can put yourself at an immediate disadvantage with a poor first touch or gain a decided edge on your opponent with a great first touch.

Receiving With the Instep

A ball dropping from above can be collected on the instep surface of the foot (figure 3.3). Imagine that your shoe is a baseball glove and that you are going to catch the ball on the instep (shoelaces) of the foot. Anticipate where the ball will drop and move quickly to that spot. Square your shoulders and hips to the ball and raise the receiving foot approximately 12 inches off the ground. At the same time extend and position the receiving foot parallel to the ground. As the ball arrives, withdraw your foot downward. This action will cushion the impact and drop the ball at your feet.

Figure 3.3   Receiving With the Instep

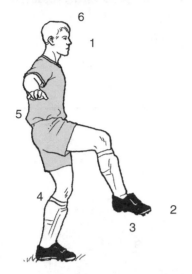

PREPARATION	RECEPTION	FOLLOW-THROUGH
1. Move into position to receive the ball	1. Collect ball on flat surface of instep	1. Maintain close control
2. Raise the receiving foot approximately 12 inches off the ground	2. Withdraw receiving foot downward	2. Push ball into open space
3. Position the receiving foot parallel to the ground	3. Drop ball to ground	3. Position your head up with vision on the field
4. Bend knee of the supporting leg		
5. Keep arms out to sides for balance		
6. Keep the head steady with vision on ball		

Misstep

The ball bounces up and out of your control.

Correction

Raise the receiving foot early, position it parallel to the ground, and then withdraw it downward the instant the ball contacts the instep. This action will cushion the impact and drop the ball within range of control.

Misstep

The ball spins back into your body.

Correction

This occurs because the receiving foot is angled back and improperly positioned. Extend the receiving foot so that it is parallel to the ground as the ball arrives. Receive the ball on the full instep.

Receiving With the Thigh

The mid-thigh can also be used for receiving and controlling a ball dropping from above or a ball traveling directly at you at approximately waist height (figure 3.4). Anticipate the flight path of the ball and move to intercept it. If you are tightly marked by an opponent, position your body between the defender and the ball as the ball arrives. Raise the receiving leg so that the thigh is nearly parallel to the ground. Bend the supporting leg at the knee with arms out to the sides for balance. Receive the ball on the large surface of the mid-thigh. To soften the impact, withdraw the receiving surface downward as the ball arrives. This action will drop the ball to the ground within your range of control.

Figure 3.4 — Receiving With the Thigh

PREPARATION

1. Move into position to intercept the ball's flight path
2. Raise the receiving leg with thigh almost parallel to ground
3. Bend the supporting leg at the knee
4. Keep arms out to sides for balance
5. Watch the ball
6. Receive the ball on mid-thigh

RECEPTION

1. Withdraw thigh downward
2. Drop ball at feet

FOLLOW-THROUGH

1. Control the ball into space away from challenging opponent
2. Pick head up for good field vision

Misstep

The ball bounces upward off the thigh.

Correction

Raise the receiving leg and thigh into the proper receiving position before the arrival of the ball. Withdraw leg downward as the ball contacts the thigh.

Misstep

An opponent kicks the ball away from you as it drops to the ground.

Correction

Position your body to protect the ball as it arrives. Your first touch should guide the ball into the space away from a challenging defender.

Receiving With the Chest

The central chest area provides an excellent surface with which to control a ball arriving through the air. Two different receiving techniques are used depending on the situation: one to control a ball that is bouncing upward off the ground, and the other to control a ball that is descending out of the air. In both cases, you should position your body between the ball and a challenging opponent.

To collect a ball that is dropping directly out of the air, arch back at the waist and receive the ball on the central area of your chest (figure 3.5). As the ball arrives, withdraw your upper body slightly to soften the impact. Control the ball into the space away from a challenging opponent by turning your upper trunk just before the ball contacts your chest.

Female players usually are permitted to cross their arms against the chest and receive the ball on the arms, although most high school and college players use the same technique as the men.

| Figure 3.5 | Receiving a Flighted Ball With the Chest |

PREPARATION

1. Get in position to intercept the oncoming ball
2. Arch your upper body back from the waist
3. Center weight over balls of feet with knees bent slightly
4. Keep arms out to sides for balance
5. Keep the head steady with vision on the ball

RECEPTION

1. Receive ball on upper-chest area
2. Withdraw slightly to cushion impact
3. Turn upper torso to control ball into space away from opponent

FOLLOW-THROUGH

1. Position your body to protect the ball from a challenging opponent
2. Push ball in direction of next movement

Misstep

The ball rebounds off your chest and away from your range of control.

Correction

Receive the ball slightly right or left of the center chest where fleshy tissue provides a softer receiving surface. Withdraw your upper torso as the ball makes contact.

Misstep

The ball skims off your chest and over your shoulder.

Correction

This will occur if you angle your upper body too far back from the vertical. Lean back slightly from the vertical as the ball arrives.

Controlling a high-bouncing ball with the chest requires a slightly different technique. Move toward the ball so that you can meet it as it rebounds up off the ground. Lean forward from the waist, arms extended out to the sides (figure 3.6). Allow the ball to contact your chest as it rebounds up off the ground. This action will direct the ball downward within your range of control.

Figure 3.6 Receiving a bouncing ball with the chest.

Misstep

Ball skips up off chest.

Correction

Make sure your upper torso is angled forward over the ball as the ball bounces up off the ground. With your chest in this position, the ball will be directed down to your feet.

Receiving With the Forehead

Usually you will use your head to pass the ball to a teammate, make a shot on goal, or possibly clear a flighted ball from the area in front and center of your goal. On rare occasions, you can also use the flat surface of your forehead to control a ball that is dropping from above (figure 3.7). This is a difficult skill to master. Successful execution requires proper technique coupled with precise timing of the jump.

Quickly move into the path of the descending ball. Use a two-foot takeoff to jump up. Leave the ground early, before the ball's arrival. Angle your forehead back slightly from the vertical, focus on the ball, and allow the ball to contact the flat surface of your forehead. If you've timed the jump properly, you should begin to descend to the ground as the ball arrives. To further cushion the impact, withdraw your head slightly as the ball contacts the forehead. The ball should bounce up off your forehead only a few inches before dropping to the ground at your feet.

Figure 3.7   **Receiving With the Forehead**

PREPARATION

1. Move into path of descending ball
2. Bend knees with weight centered over balls of feet
3. Extend arms back and to sides
4. Focus on the ball

RECEPTION

1. Jump upward before the ball arrives
2. Square shoulders and hips with the ball
3. Angle forehead back slightly with chin tucked
4. Keep eyes open and mouth closed
5. Meet ball at highest point of jump
6. Contact ball on forehead

FOLLOW-THROUGH

1. Withdraw head slightly on contact
2. Drop ball to ground within range of control
3. Push ball in direction of next movement

Misstep

The ball rebounds up off your forehead and out of your range of control.

Correction

This occurs because your body is too rigid or because you jumped too late and were still moving up as the ball contacted your forehead. Timing is everything. Leave the ground early so that your body begins to descend as the ball arrives. To further soften the impact, withdraw your head slightly as the ball contacts the forehead.

Misstep

The ball glances sideways off your head.

Correction

Allow the ball to contact the large, flat surface of the forehead just above the eyebrows. Keep your neck firm and your head steady, and focus on the ball at all times.

Receiving Flighted Passes
Drill 1. Individual Ball Juggle

Use your instep, thigh, chest, and head to keep the ball airborne while jogging slowly throughout a large field area. Try to keep the ball in the air for as many touches as possible. Beginners can toss the ball up to get started; experienced players must use their feet to lift the ball. Count consecutive touches of the ball without letting it drop to the ground. Perform a total of 10 trials. Count your highest total of touches as your best score.

To Increase Difficulty

- Require a specific order of touches (for example, instep to thigh to head to thigh to instep).

To Decrease Difficulty

- Juggle the ball while stationary.

Success Check

- Select receiving surface early.
- Withdraw receiving surface to cushion impact.
- Keep ball within range of control.

Score Your Success

0 to 14 consecutive touches = 1 point
15 to 19 consecutive touches = 3 points
20 consecutive touches or more = 5 points
Your score ___

Receiving Flighted Passes
Drill 2. Two-Touch Collect and Return

Stand facing a teammate at a distance of 3 yards. Pass (juggle) the ball back and forth through the air with your partner using only two touches—one touch to receive and control the ball, the second touch to return it. A player is penalized 1 point each time he or she causes the ball to drop to the ground. Play 20 rounds, keeping track of penalty points.

To Increase Difficulty

- Require partners to move throughout a field area while juggling.

To Decrease Difficulty

- Permit three touches to control and return the ball.

Success Check

- Select the receiving surface early.
- Provide a soft target.
- Prepare the ball with your first touch.
- Return the ball with your second touch.

Score Your Success

11 penalty points or more = 3 points
7 to 10 penalty points = 4 points
0 to 6 penalty points = 5 points
Your score ___

Receiving Flighted Passes
Drill 3. Rapid-Fire Receive and Return

Two players (servers A and B), each with a ball, face each other at a distance of 10 yards. The third player gets in position midway between the servers. Server A begins the drill by tossing the ball to the middle player. The middle player controls the ball out of the air with the first touch and returns it to the server with the second touch. The ball can be controlled with the instep, thigh, chest, or head. The middle player immediately turns to receive a ball tossed from server B, and then repeats the sequence. After the middle player has received 50 tosses, the players rotate positions and repeat. Continue the drill until each player has taken a turn in the middle. Award the middle player 1 point for each ball received and returned to the server using only two touches. Keep track of individual points.

To Increase Difficulty

- Increase height or velocity of serves.
- Add a third server.

To Decrease Difficulty

- Allow three touches to receive and return the ball to the server.

Success Check

- Align body with ball.
- Prepare the receiving surface early.
- Withdraw receiving surface as ball arrives.

Score Your Success

0 to 20 points = 0 points
21 to 34 points = 1 point
35 to 44 points = 3 points
45 to 50 points = 5 points
Your score ___

Receiving Flighted Passes
Drill 4.   Toss, Receive, and Catch to Score

Organize two equal teams of four to six players and play within an area approximately 30 by 40 yards. Award one team the ball to begin. The team with the ball attempts to play keep-away from the other team. There is one restriction: Teammates must pass to one another by using throwing rather than kicking. The receiving player must control the ball out of the air with the instep, thigh, chest, or head, and then catch the ball in the hands before it drops to the ground. Players are permitted only two touches to control the ball: one touch to receive and control it, the second touch to catch it. A player may take up to five steps while in possession of the ball before tossing to a teammate. Loss of possession occurs when an opponent intercepts a pass or when a receiving player fails to control the ball with two touches before it drops to the ground. Defending players are not permitted to wrestle the ball from opponents, but they can intercept passes with their hands. Individual players score 1 point for each ball they receive and control without error, and they are penalized 1 point for each ball they fail to receive and control with two touches. Individual players keep a running total of points scored minus points deducted. Play for 15 minutes.

To Increase Difficulty

- Require all passes to be 10 yards or greater.
- Require players to control the ball with a specific body part (for example, thigh only, head only).

To Decrease Difficulty

- Add two neutral players to the game who play with the team in possession of the ball.

Success Check

- Align body with oncoming ball.
- Select receiving surface early.
- Withdraw receiving surface slightly as ball arrives.

Score Your Success

0 to 5 points = 1 point
6 to 9 points = 3 points
10 points or more = 5 points
Your score ___

Receiving Flighted Passes Drill 5.   Team Volleyball

Play on a regulation volleyball court or an area of similar size. Form two teams of four to six players each. Teams get in position on opposite sides of the net. One team has the serve to begin. To serve, a player must chip a stationary ball over the net from behind the end line. The receiving team must control the ball directly out of the air or after it bounces once. This applies to all plays, not only service returns. If the ball bounces two or more times in the receiving team's court, or if the receiving team fails to return the serve over the net, the serving team scores 1 point and retains service. A player receiving the ball is allowed three touches to control it and play it back over the net or to play it to a teammate who then plays it over the net. Once the ball has been received out of the air, however, it must be returned over the net before it drops to the ground. A fault occurs when

- the serve or return fails to clear the net,
- the serve or return lands out of bounds,
- the ball is allowed to bounce more than once, or
- a player uses his or her arms or hands to pass or control the ball.

When a member of the serving team commits a fault, the team loses the serve. When the receiving team commits a fault, the serving team scores 1 point. The first team to score 30 points wins the game.

To Increase Difficulty

- Require the server to chip a rolling ball.
- Do not allow the ball to bounce before returning it over the net.
- Allow players only two touches to receive and return the ball.

To Decrease Difficulty

- Permit the server to volley the ball out of the hands.
- Permit the ball to bounce twice before returning it over the net.

Success Check

- Position in line with the descending ball.
- Prepare the receiving surface early.
- Withdraw the receiving surface to cushion impact of ball.

Score Your Success

Member of losing team = 3 points
Member of winning team = 5 points
Your score ___

SUCCESS SUMMARY OF PASSING AND RECEIVING FLIGHTED BALLS

Successfully executing the skills in passing and receiving flighted balls requires correct technique coupled with confidence in your ability. You can acquire these important assets only through hours of dedicated practice. There are no shortcuts to success. You simply must be willing to put in the time and effort if you want to become an elite player.

Beginners should practice passing and receiving skills in a relatively pressure-free setting. Focus on performing the correct technique without the pressure of opponents' trying to steal the ball from you. Gradually progress to more game-simulated practice situations as your skill level improves and you gain confidence in your abilities. Eventually you can add the pressure of challenging opponents to your exercises. Your ultimate goal should be to execute all of the fundamental passing and receiving skills under match conditions.

Each of the drills described in this step has been assigned a point value to enable you to evaluate your performance and chart progress. Enter your scores in the following chart and then total the points to get an estimate of your overall level of competence.

Passing Through the Air Drills

1. Chip to Chest ____ out of 5

2. Pass Under and Chip Over ____ out of 5

3. Chip the Middle Man ____ out of 5

4. Flighted Balls Only ____ out of 5

5. Change the Point of Attack ____ out of 5

Receiving Flighted Passes Drills

1. Individual Ball Juggle ____ out of 5

2. Two-Touch Collect and Return ____ out of 5

3. Rapid-Fire Receive and Return ____ out of 5

4. Toss, Receive, and Catch to Score ____ out of 5

5. Team Volleyball ____ out of 5

Total ____ *out of 50*

A combined score of 45 or more of 50 possible points indicates that you have mastered the techniques and are ready to move on to step 4. A score in the range of 35 to 44 is considered adequate. Move ahead to step 4 after reviewing and practicing the techniques for passing and receiving balls out of the air. A score of 34 or fewer points indicates that you have not sufficiently mastered the skills described in step 3. Review and rehearse the techniques a few more times before moving on to step 4.

Dominating the Air Game

Using the head to propel the ball is unique to the game of soccer. Mastery of heading skills is essential because they are used for both attacking and defending purposes. Three heading techniques are commonly used; each is featured in a specific situation and for a slightly different purpose.

The *jump header* technique is used for passing the ball, for striking on goal, and for the defensive purpose of clearing a flighted ball from the goal area. To execute the jump header, use a two-foot takeoff to jump upward, arch back from the waist, and then snap forward to contact the ball with the flat surface of your forehead.

The *dive header* is an exciting and acrobatic skill used only in special situations, such as to score a spectacular goal off a low cross or to clear low-driven balls out of the goal area. To execute the dive header, dive parallel to the ground with your head tilted back and neck firm. Contact the ball on the flat surface of the forehead. Extend your arms down to break your fall to the ground. Use good judgment when executing the dive header. It's not an appropriate choice when in the midst of a crowd of players; an opponent (or even a teammate) may try to kick the ball away and, in doing so, inadvertently kick you in the head.

The *flicked header* is designed to alter the flight path of the ball while allowing it to continue in the same direction. This skill is generally used in attacking situations to deflect a flighted ball into the path of a rushing teammate. To execute the flicked header, you must move into a position to intercept the ball's flight path, angle your forehead back, and allow the ball to glance off the top of the forehead. This action will create a sudden change in the ball's flight trajectory, which can pose problems for defending players.

Some teams rely on heading skills much more than others. For example, the national teams from Norway, Ireland, and to a lesser extent England have traditionally based their attacking games on their forwards' ability to go up and win air balls. From a tactical point of view, these teams have traditionally favored a style of play that emphasizes long-driven balls played through the air direct from the defenders to the forwards. In contrast, most South American and Central American teams have traditionally embraced a shorter-pass, ball-control style of play with the ball on the ground much of the time.

Regardless of the team's philosophy of play, it is inevitable that the ball will be airborne at various times during a game. Goal kicks, corner kicks, free kicks, flighted passes, throw-ins, and defensive clearances must in many cases be played directly out of the air with the head. To become a complete soccer player, you must develop competence in performing the various heading skills.

JUMP HEADER

Face the ball with shoulders square (figure 4.1). Judge the ball's flight, bend the knees slightly, and prepare to go airborne to meet it. Use a two-foot takeoff to jump straight up. While airborne, arch back from the waist and tuck your chin to your chest. Keep your neck and upper body firm. As the ball arrives, snap your upper trunk forward from the waist and contact the ball on the flat surface of your forehead at the highest point of the jump.

Timing your takeoff is probably the most difficult element of the jump header. Beginners have a tendency to jump either too late or too early. If you jump late, you will still be moving up as the ball arrives. If you jump too early, you will descend as the ball sails over your head. The key is to jump at the correct time, hang suspended in the air for a moment or two, and then snap your upper trunk and head forward to meet the oncoming ball.

You must attack the ball; do not simply allow the ball to hit your head and bounce off. When attempting to score, strike through the top half of the ball to send it on a downward plane toward the goal line. The same form applies when passing to a teammate's feet.

Conversely, for defensive clearances you should contact the lower half of the ball to send it high, far, and wide, preferably toward the flank area of the field. In all cases, keep your eyes open and mouth closed as the ball contacts your forehead. Heading with the mouth open is inviting injury because you may inadvertently bite your tongue if an opponent who is also jumping for the ball collides with you.

Figure 4.1   Jump Header

PREPARATION

1. Face the ball with shoulders square
2. Bend knees with weight centered over balls of feet
3. Draw arms back, preparing to jump
4. Focus on the ball

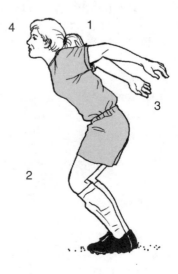

EXECUTION

1. Use two-foot takeoff to jump up
2. Simultaneously raise arms for upward momentum
3. Arch upper trunk back from vertical with chin tucked
4. Keep the neck firm and upper body rigid
5. Snap upper trunk forward to meet ball
6. Contact ball on forehead
7. Keep eyes open and mouth closed

FOLLOW-THROUGH

1. Drive forehead through point of contact with ball
2. Keep arms out to sides for balance
3. Descend to ground

Misstep

The header lacks power.

Correction

Attack the ball. Maintain the arched position until the last possible moment before snapping your upper trunk forward. Keep the head steady and neck firm. Proper timing and correct technique are essential.

Misstep

The ball hits you in the face or nose.

Correction

Keep your eyes open with vision on the ball as it contacts your forehead. Do not be distracted by nearby opponents.

Jump Header Drill 1. Head Juggle With Partner

Stand with a ball facing a partner at a distance of 3 yards. To begin, toss a head-high ball toward your partner. Head the ball back and forth with your partner, keeping the ball airborne for as many touches as possible using only your head to contact the ball. Keep track of the number of combined headers with your partner before the ball drops to the ground. Take the best of 10 trials.

To Increase Difficulty

- Require two-touch heading (receive with first touch, return ball with second touch).
- Do the head juggle with partner while jogging slowly around a large field area.

To Decrease Difficulty

- Keep the ball airborne on your own (individual head juggle).

Success Check

- Bend knees for balance and body control.
- Contact ball on upper forehead.
- Keep arms out to the sides for balance.

Score Your Success

0 to 19 consecutive headers = 1 point

20 to 29 consecutive headers = 3 points

30 consecutive headers or more = 5 points

Your score ___

Jump Header Drill 2.   Jump and Head a Stationary Ball

Face a teammate who holds the ball about 12 inches above and to the front of his or her head. Step forward, jump straight up, and snap forward from the waist to contact the ball on your forehead. Combine all elements of the jump-header technique. Repeat 30 times, then switch roles with your partner.

To Increase Difficulty

- Increase number of repetitions.
- Increase speed of repetition.
- Require partner to hold the ball higher.

To Decrease Difficulty

- Reduce number of repetitions.

Success Check

- Jump straight up.
- Arch upper body back from vertical.
- Tuck chin with neck rigid.
- Keep eyes open and mouth closed.
- Thrust forward from waist.
- Contact ball on forehead.

Score Your Success

0 to 14 correct jump headers = 0 points

15 to 19 correct jump headers = 1 point

20 to 24 correct jump headers = 3 points

25 to 30 correct jump headers = 5 points

Your score ___

Jump Header Drill 3.   Heading in Pairs

Face a teammate (server) standing 5 yards away. The server tosses a ball to a spot 12 to 18 inches above your head. Use a two-foot takeoff to jump up and head the ball back to the server. Contact the ball on your forehead at the highest point of the jump and direct it on a downward plane toward the server's chest. Execute 30 jump headers, then switch roles with your partner and repeat.

To Increase Difficulty

- Increase distance from server.
- Perform headers at maximum speed.

- Increase number of repetitions.

To Decrease Difficulty

- Reduce distance to server.
- Slow the speed of repetition.

Success Check

- Use a two-foot takeoff.
- Arch upper trunk back from waist.
- Keep eyes open and mouth closed.
- Snap forward to meet the ball.

Score Your Success

0 to 14 headers directed to server's chest =
  0 points

15 to 19 headers directed to server's chest =
  1 points

20 to 24 headers directed to server's chest =
  3 points

25 to 30 headers directed to server's chest =
  5 points

Your score ___

Jump Header Drill 4.   Repetition Headers

Two players (servers), each with a ball, face one another at a distance of 8 yards. A third player stands midway between the servers. The servers alternate turns tossing a ball up toward the middle player, who jumps up and heads the ball directly back to the server. After each header the middle player immediately turns 180 degrees to head a ball tossed by the opposite server. Continue heading for a total of 40 jump headers. Award 1 point for each ball headed back to the server so that he or she can catch it directly out of the air. Each player takes a turn as the middle player.

To Increase Difficulty

- Increase distance between servers to 12 yards.
- Increase number of repetitions.
- Increase speed of repetitions.

To Decrease Difficulty

- Head the ball without jumping.
- Decrease number of repetitions.

Success Check

- Square shoulders to target.
- Use a two-foot takeoff.
- Snap upper trunk forward.
- Contact ball on forehead.
- Keep head steady and neck firm.

Score Your Success

0 to 19 points = 0 points

20 to 27 points = 1 point

28 to 34 points = 3 points

35 to 40 points = 5 points

Your score ___

Jump Header Drill 5.   Toss, Head, and Catch to Score

Three teammates form a triangle with about 10 yards between players. One player (A) has the ball to begin. Player A tosses the ball to player B, who jumps up and heads the ball to player C. Player C catches the ball and tosses it to player A, who jumps up and heads the ball to player B, who catches and tosses it to player C. Continue the toss-head-catch routine until each player has executed 30 jump headers. Award 1 point for each ball headed directly to a teammate so that it does not bounce to the ground.

To Increase Difficulty

- Increase distance between players to 12 yards.

- Perform drill with all three players moving slowly through field area.

To Decrease Difficulty

- Reduce distance between players to 6 yards.
- Execute headers without jumping.

Success Check

- Use a two-foot takeoff to jump up.
- Square shoulders to target.
- Contact ball on forehead.
- Keep eyes open and mouth closed.

0 to 14 tosses headed directly to teammate = 0 points

15 to 19 tosses headed directly to teammate = 1 point

20 to 24 tosses headed directly to teammate = 3 points

25 to 30 tosses headed directly to teammate = 5 points

Your score ___

Jump Header
Drill 6.   Heading Race Front to Back to Front

Divide the group into equal-sized teams of three to five players. Teams stand side by side in single file with 3 yards between teams. One player from each team functions as the server who holds a ball and faces the first person in his or her line at a distance of 3 yards. On the signal "go," the server tosses a ball up to the first player in line. That player jumps up and heads the ball back to the server and then drops to his or her knees. The server immediately tosses to the next player in line, who also heads the ball and then kneels. Servers continue through their lines until they reach the last player, at which point all team members have headed the ball and are kneeling. The last player in line heads two consecutive tosses to the server. The next to the last in line immediately stands to jump up and head a ball back to the server, then the player in front of him or her stands to head, and so on. The race continues, from front to back to front, until all players are again standing and the server has control of the ball.

Individual players are assessed 1 penalty point each time they fail to head the ball directly back to the server so that the server can catch it directly out of the air. The team whose server goes through the entire line of players, front to back to front, in the shortest time wins the race. Repeat with a different player as server. The first team to win five races wins the competition.

To Increase Difficulty

• Add more players to each team.

To Decrease Difficulty

• Do not require players to jump.

Success Check

• Jump up with shoulders square.
• Arch upper body back.
• Keep neck stiff and chin tucked.
• Thrust forward from waist.
• Contact ball on forehead.

Score Your Success

3 penalty points or more = 0 points

1 to 2 penalty points = 2 points

0 penalty points = 4 points

Your score ___

Jump Header Drill 7.   Moving Headers

Stand at one end of a regulation field facing a partner (server) positioned 5 yards away. The server begins to backpedal slowly down the field and you follow, all the while maintaining the 5-yard distance between the two of you. While moving backward, the server tosses a ball up toward you. Move forward, jump up to meet the ball, and head it to the server so that he or she can catch the ball directly out of the air. The server continues to backpedal while repeatedly tossing the ball toward you as you follow, maintaining the 5-yard distance. Jump up and head each toss back to the server. Continue for a total of 50 repetitions, then switch roles with the server and repeat. Award yourself 1 point for each ball headed directly to the server so that he or she can catch the ball out of the air.

To Increase Difficulty

• Increase heading distance to 7 yards.

- Increase jogging speed.
- Increase number of repetitions.

To Decrease Difficulty

- Perform stationary heading.
- Do not require player to jump when heading the ball.

Success Check

- Use a two-foot takeoff to jump up.
- Arch upper body back from vertical.

- Keep eyes open and mouth closed.
- Contact ball on forehead.

Score Your Success

0 to 29 points = 0 points

30 to 37 points = 1 point

38 to 44 points = 3 points

45 to 50 points = 5 points

Your score ___

Jump Header Drill 8. Headers End to End

Use markers to represent two 5-yard-wide goals positioned 15 yards apart. Get in one goal with a ball; your opponent gets in the opposite goal. Toss the ball up so that it drops near the center of the area. Your opponent moves forward and attempts to score by heading the ball past you through the goal. Alternate turns, attempting to score from jump headers. Return to your respective goals after each attempt. Award 2 points for a goal scored and 1 point for a ball headed on goal but saved. Perform 30 headers each. The player scoring more points wins the game.

To Increase Difficulty

- Reduce width of goal to 3 yards.

To Decrease Difficulty

- Increase width of goal to 7 yards.
- Do not require player to jump when heading.

Success Check

- Square shoulders to ball.
- Jump straight up.
- Snap upper trunk forward.
- Contact ball on forehead.
- Head ball on a downward angle toward goal line.

Score Your Success

0 to 19 points = 0 points

20 to 29 points = 2 points

30 to 44 points = 4 points

45 of 60 points = 6 points

Your score ___

Jump Header
Drill 9.   Score by Headers Only (With Neutrals)

Organize two teams of three to five players each. Designate two additional players as neutrals; these players always play with the team in possession of the ball. Play within a 25 by 35-yard area with a small goal (4 yards wide) at the center of each end line. Award one team the ball to begin. Passing is accomplished by throwing and catching rather than kicking. Players score by heading a ball tossed by a teammate through the opponent's

goal. Players may take a maximum of five steps with the ball before passing to a teammate. Neutral players join with the attacking team to create a two-player advantage. Do not use goalkeepers.

Field players can use their hands to intercept opponents' passes and block headers directed at goal. The defending team is awarded the ball when an opponent takes more than five steps with the ball without releasing it, after an opponent's score, when a defending player intercepts a pass, when an opponent drops the ball to the ground, or when the ball that goes out of bounds was last touched by a member of the opposing team. Players are not permitted to wrestle the ball from an opponent. Play for 15 minutes. The team scoring more goals wins the game.

To Increase Difficulty

- Decrease size of goal.
- Play with goalkeepers.

To Decrease Difficulty

- Increase size of goal.

- Play with four neutrals.

Success Check

- Square shoulders to goal.
- Use a two-foot takeoff to jump up.
- Contact the ball on forehead.
- Head the ball down toward the goal line.

Score Your Success

Member of losing team = 0 points

Member of winning team = 1 point

Your score ___

DIVE HEADER

The dive header technique is used to head a ball that is traveling parallel to the ground at waist level or lower. When possible, square your shoulders to the oncoming ball and assume a slightly crouched position (figure 4.2). Move toward the ball, anticipate its trajectory, and dive parallel to the ground to meet it. Tilt your head back with eyes open, mouth closed, and neck firm. Contact the ball on the flat surface of your forehead, just above the eyebrows. Extend arms downward to break your fall to the ground.

Figure 4.2 **Dive Header**

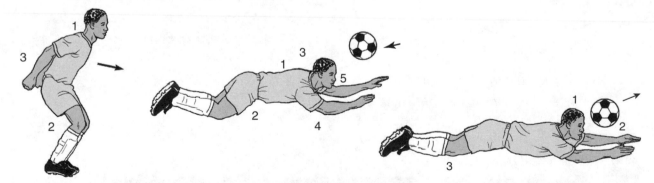

PREPARATION	EXECUTION	FOLLOW-THROUGH
1. Square shoulders to oncoming ball	1. Dive forward to intercept the ball	1. Keep momentum forward through point of contact
2. Bend knees with weight centered over balls of feet	2. Keep body parallel to ground	2. Break fall with arms
3. Draw arms back and to sides	3. Tilt head back with neck firm	3. Jump to feet
4. Focus on the ball	4. Extend arms forward and down	
	5. Keep eyes open and mouth closed	
	6. Contact ball on forehead	

Misstep

The header lacks power or accuracy.

Correction

Lack of power or poor accuracy means you either mistimed the dive or failed to keep your head steady as it contacted the ball. Tilt the head back, keep the neck firm, and contact the ball on the flat surface of your forehead.

Misstep

The ball pops up off your head.

Correction

When the ball pops up, it means you have either contacted the ball too high on your forehead or dipped your head as the ball arrived. Keep your head and neck firmly positioned, and contact the ball on the central area of your forehead, just above the eyebrows.

Dive Header Drill 1. Dive Headers With Partner

Perform this drill on a gymnastics mat or on soft ground. Face a server standing 10 yards away. The server tosses a ball toward you at approximately waist height. Bend the knees slightly, dive forward parallel to the ground, and contact the ball on the flat surface of the forehead. Extend your arms down to break the fall. Score 1 point for heading the ball directly back to the server so that he or she does not have to move more than one step in any direction to collect it. After each header, jump to your feet and prepare to head again. Head 10 tosses in succession, then switch roles with the server.

To Increase Difficulty

- Increase number of repetitions.

To Decrease Difficulty

- Start on all fours rather than diving from standing position.

- Move closer to server.
- Decrease number of repetitions.

Success Check

- Dive parallel to ground.
- Tilt head back with neck rigid.
- Keep eyes open and mouth closed.
- Contact ball on forehead.

Score Your Success

0 to 4 points = 0 points

5 to 7 points = 1 point

8 to 10 points = 3 points

Your score ___

Dive Header Drill 2. Dive Headers in Threes

Play with two teammates within a 10- by 15-yard area. Place two flags to represent a goal 4 yards apart on one end of the area. One player stands in goal as the goalkeeper. One player, the server, stands to the side of the field, about 6 yards out from the end line. You get in position 10 yards front and center of the goal. The drill begins as the server tosses a ball across the goalmouth to simulate a crossed ball, at about waist height.

Judge the flight of the ball and attempt to score using the dive header technique. Award 2 points for a goal scored and 1 point for a ball headed on goal saved by the goalkeeper. Players rotate positions after each attempt on goal. Continue until each player has performed 20 dive headers.

To Increase Difficulty

- Reduce size of goal.

- Increase number of repetitions.

To Decrease Difficulty

- Increase width of goal to 6 yards.
- Do not use a goalkeeper.

Success Check

- Dive parallel to ground.
- Tilt head back with neck rigid.
- Extend arms down to break fall to ground.

- Contact ball on forehead.

Dive Header Drill 3.   Dive Header Competition

Form two equal teams of 4 to 6 players each. Teams stand side by side in single file 15 yards front and center of a regulation-size goal. Station a neutral goalkeeper in the goal and a server 5 yards to each side of the goal. Servers alternate tossing balls into the area front and center of the goal. Players from each team take turns attempting to score off dive headers. The goalkeeper tries to save all shots. Award 2 points for a goal scored and 1 point for a ball headed on goal but saved by the goalkeeper. The first team to score 50 points wins.

To Increase Difficulty

- Decrease width of goal to 6 yards.

To Decrease Difficulty

- Increase width of goal to 10 yards.

Success Check

- Dive parallel to ground.
- Tilt head back with neck stiff.
- Contact ball on forehead.
- Extend arms to cushion fall.

Dive Header Drill 4.   Score Off Diving Headers

Three players participate in this drill. One player (server) stands 10 yards behind a regulation goal with a supply of balls. A second player (attacker) stands on the top edge of the penalty area, facing the goal. The third player gets in position as the goalkeeper. The server chips a ball over the crossbar of the goal so that it drops within the penalty area. The attacker rushes forward and attempts to score off a first-time diving header. A ball headed on goal saved by the keeper counts 1 point; a goal scored counts 2 points. The attacker performs a total of 20 diving headers, after which players switch positions and repeat. Each player keeps track of his or her point total. (Note: This drill is most appropriate for older, experienced players.)

To Increase Difficulty

- Reduce width of goal.

To Decrease Difficulty

- Do not use a goalkeeper.

Success Check

- Dive parallel to ground.
- Tilt head back with neck rigid.
- Contact ball on forehead.
- Keep eyes open and mouth closed.
- Break fall to ground with arms.

FLICKED HEADER

The flicked header can be used in any area of the field, although it is most often used by attacking players attempting to alter the path of flighted balls driven into the goal area. To perform a flicked header (figure 4.3), move toward the oncoming ball and allow it to glance off your forehead as it travels past. The sudden change in trajectory can cause opposing players and the goalkeeper to misjudge the flight of the ball and create confusion within the defense.

Figure 4.3   Flicked Header

PREPARATION

1. Move into position to intercept the oncoming ball

2. Tilt head back with neck firm

3. Keep eyes open and mouth closed

EXECUTION

1. Jump upward to intercept the flight path of the ball

2. Keep arms out to sides for balance

3. Allow lower half of ball to glance off of upper forehead

FOLLOW-THROUGH

1. Flick forehead in direction the ball is traveling

2. Descend to ground

Misstep

You fail to alter the flight path of the ball.

Correction

Be sure to make contact with enough surface area of the ball to alter the trajectory. Move toward the ball, angle your forehead back, and allow the ball to glance off your upper forehead.

Flicked Header Drill 1. Flicked Headers End to End

Two players (servers A and B) face each another at a distance of 20 yards. Server A has the ball to begin. A third player (player C) gets in position midway between the servers. Server A tosses a head-high ball at player C, who moves toward the ball and flicks it past to server B. Server B collects the ball and repeats the sequence in the opposite direction. Player C executes a total of 30 flicked headers, after which the players rotate positions. Continue until each player has executed 30 flicked headers. Award 1 point for each header flicked to the opposite server. (Note: Accurate tosses from servers are essential for this drill to flow smoothly.)

To Increase Difficulty

- Increase distance and velocity of serve.

To Decrease Difficulty

- Decrease distance of serve.
- Do not require players to leave the ground to head the ball.

Success Check

- Tilt head back.
- Keep eyes open and mouth closed.
- Allow ball to glance off top of forehead.

Score Your Success

0 to 9 points = 0 points

10 to 17 points = 1 point

18 to 24 points = 3 points

25 to 30 points = 5 points

Your score ___

Flicked Header Drill 2. Flicked Headers to Goal

A server gets in position 40 yards from goal with a supply of balls. A second player (header) stands at the penalty spot with his or her back to the goal. The server kicks a flighted ball toward the player stationed at the penalty spot. The header moves to intercept the flight of the ball and flick it past into the open goal. After 30 repetitions, players switch roles and repeat the drill. Award 1 point for each flicked header directed into the open goal for a possible maximum of 30 points. (Note: Accurate service is required for this drill to work effectively.)

To Increase Difficulty

- Reduce width of goal to 5 yards.

To Decrease Difficulty

- Header positions closer to goal.
- Server tosses the ball with hands.

Success Check

- Move toward ball.
- Angle head back with neck firm.
- Allow ball to glance off top of forehead.

Score Your Success

0 to 9 points = 0 points

10 to 19 points = 2 points

20 to 30 points = 4 points

Your score ___

SUCCESS SUMMARY OF HEADING SKILLS

To compete successfully at higher levels, you must become competent in executing the various heading techniques. Focus on these key points.

When performing the jump header, contact the ball at the highest point of your jump. Jump early, hold the arched position until the last possible moment, and then snap forward from the waist to contact the ball on your forehead. Keep your head and neck firmly positioned.

When executing a dive header, fully extend your body parallel to the ground as you dive to meet the ball. Tilt the head back, keep the neck firm, and contact the ball on your forehead. Use your arms to break your fall to the ground.

To execute the flicked header, allow the ball to glance off the top of your forehead and go past you rather than heading the ball back in the direction from which it came. Because it's difficult to visualize whether you are heading the ball correctly, have a coach or teammate observe or videotape you performing the different heading techniques. The observer can evaluate your performance and, if necessary, offer helpful feedback.

Each of the drills described in step 4 has been assigned a point value so that you can evaluate your performance and chart your progress. Record your score in the following chart and then total your points to get an estimate of your overall level of competence.

Jump Header Drills

1. Head Juggle With Partner — _____ out of 5
2. Jump and Head a Stationary Ball — _____ out of 5
3. Heading in Pairs — _____ out of 5
4. Repetition Headers — _____ out of 5
5. Toss, Head, and Catch to Score — _____ out of 5
6. Heading Race Front to Back to Front — _____ out of 4
7. Moving Headers — _____ out of 5
8. Headers End to End — _____ out of 6
9. Score by Headers Only (With Neutrals) — _____ out of 1

Dive Header Drills

1. Dive Headers With Partner — _____ out of 3
2. Dive Headers in Threes — _____ out of 5
3. Dive Header Competition — _____ out of 5
4. Score Off Diving Headers — _____ out of 5

Flicked Header Drills

1. Flicked Headers End to End — _____ out of 5
2. Flicked Headers to Goal — _____ out of 4

Total — _____ *out of 68*

A combined score of 60 or more points indicates that you have sufficiently mastered heading skills and are ready to move on to step 5. A score in the range of 45 to 59 is considered adequate. You can move on to step 5 after reviewing and rehearsing each of the heading skills one more time. A score of 44 or fewer points indicates that you have not sufficiently mastered the heading skills described in step 4.

You should review the material and rehearse each of the skills several times before moving on to step 5.

Shooting to Finish the Attack

The most recognized players throughout the soccer world are the goal scorers, players who can determine the outcome of a game with one strike of the ball. The most famous of them all, the incomparable Pele, scored more than 1,200 goals as a professional. Although Pele has been retired as a player for more than 20 years, young soccer players everywhere still revere him and recognize his place in soccer history. During the 2002 World Cup, players such as Ronaldo of Brazil, Michael Owen of England, and Raul of Spain attracted the most fan and media attention, and rightly so. These players and a handful of others make up an elite group of world-class goal scorers, the ultimate marksmen of international soccer.

Scoring goals remains the most difficult task in soccer. The player who can consistently put the ball in the back of the opponent's net is a rare and valuable commodity. Success depends on several factors. The ability to shoot powerfully and accurately with either foot is essential.

Physical assets such as speed, quickness, and strength are definite benefits. Intangibles such as anticipation and composure under pressure are also important. A bit of luck doesn't hurt either, although scoring goals on a regular basis surely isn't the result of blind luck. As the old coaching adage so aptly states, "Good luck generally occurs where preparation meets opportunity." The key word here is *preparation*. You can prepare to take advantage of scoring opportunities by practicing the various shooting skills in exercises that mirror actual game conditions. Develop the ability to shoot the ball (whether it rolls, bounces, or drops from the air) with either foot.

The *instep drive* technique is used for striking a stationary or rolling ball. The *full volley*, *half volley*, and *side volley* techniques are used for striking a bouncing ball or a ball that drops from above. A *swerving shot* bends the ball's trajectory of flight and is particularly effective when taking free kicks and corner kicks.

INSTEP DRIVE SHOT

Use the instep drive technique to strike a rolling or stationary ball. The kicking mechanics are similar to those used when passing with the instep except that there is greater follow-through of the kicking leg.

Approach the ball from behind and at a slight angle (figure 5.1). Plant your supporting foot beside the ball with the knee slightly bent. Keep your head steady and focus on the ball. Draw the kicking leg back with the foot extended and firm. At this point, the knee of the kicking leg should be directly over the ball. Snap the leg straight and contact the center of the ball with the full instep (laces) of your foot. Keep the kicking foot firm and pointed down as it strikes the ball. Square your shoulders and hips to the target, and use a complete follow-through motion to generate maximum power on the shot.

Figure 5.1 | **Instep Drive Shot**

PREPARATION	**EXECUTION**	**FOLLOW-THROUGH**
1. Approach from behind and at a slight angle	1. Point supporting foot toward target	1. Momentum is forward through point of contact
2. Lean forward and plant supporting foot beside ball	2. Square shoulders and hips to target	2. Supporting foot leaves the ground
3. Bend supporting leg and keep arms out to sides for balance	3. Snap kicking leg straight	3. Complete the follow-through kicking motion toward target
4. Draw back kicking leg with foot extended	4. Keep kicking foot pointed downward and diagonally across the ball	
5. Keep the head steady with vision on the ball	5. Contact center of ball with instep	
	6. Keep kicking foot firm throughout	

Misstep

The ball travels up and over the goal.

Correction

This occurs when you lean back as your foot strikes the ball. Plant the supporting foot beside, not behind, the ball. From this position, lean forward slightly, with the knee of the kicking leg positioned directly over the ball. Keep the kicking foot fully extended and pointed down as the instep contacts the center of the ball. Generate forward momentum through the point of contact.

Misstep

The shot lacks power.

Correction

Lack of power is usually due to inadequate follow-through motion of the kicking leg, failure to transfer weight forward as the kicking foot contacts the ball, or failure to keep the kicking foot firm. Generate forward momentum as you drive your foot through the ball. Follow-through motion of the kicking leg should continue forward and upward to waist level or above.

Instep Drive Shot Drill 1.   Hit the Target

Face a teammate (server) standing 10 yards away. The server plays a slowly rolling ball toward you. Shoot the ball first time (without stopping it) directly back at the server using the instep drive technique. Repeat for a total of 40 shots, alternating shots between right and left feet. Award yourself 1 point for each shot aimed directly at the server so that he or she can collect the ball without moving more than one step to either side.

To Increase Difficulty

- Increase distance from server.
- Increase velocity of serve.

To Decrease Difficulty

- Reduce distance to server.
- Take all shots with dominant foot.

- Shoot stationary ball to server.

Success Check

- Square shoulders and hips to target.
- Knee of kicking leg is over ball.
- Kicking foot is extended and firm.
- Head is steady.
- Follow through toward target.

Score Your Success

0 to 25 points = 1 point

26 to 34 points = 3 points

35 to 40 points = 5 points

Your score ____

Instep Drive Shot
Drill 2.   Score Through the Central Goal

Place 2 cones 8 yards apart to represent a regulation-width goal. Partner with a teammate. You get in position with a ball 25 yards from the goal, Your partner (target) stands 5 yards behind the goal, facing you. Dribble forward a few yards and attempt to shoot the ball through the goal (at the target) using the instep drive technique. The target immediately retrieves the ball and returns it to you. Perform a total of 30 shots, alternating shots between left and right feet, and then switch roles with the target player. All shots must be taken from a distance of at least 20 yards. Score 1 point for each shot that travels through the goal below the target's head height.

To Increase Difficulty

- Increase shooting distance to 25 yards.
- Reduce width of goal.

To Decrease Difficulty

- Decrease shooting distance to 15 yards.
- Increase width of goal.
- Shoot a stationary ball.

Success Check

- Square shoulders and hips to goal.

- Position knee of kicking leg over ball.
- Kicking foot is extended and firm.
- Follow through toward target.

Score Your Success

0 to 19 points = 1 points

20 to 24 points = 3 points

25 to 30 points = 5 points

Your score ___

Instep Drive Shot
Drill 3. Combine With the Target and Score

Join with two teammates and get in position on one end of a regulation field. One player is the goalkeeper. A second player (target) gets in position with back to the goal at the top of the penalty area. You stand 30 yards from the goal with a supply of balls, facing the target. To begin the drill, dribble forward a couple of yards and play a firm pass to the target. He or she deflects the ball sideways a couple of feet, just outside the top of the penalty area. Immediately after passing, sprint forward and strike the ball first time on goal (without controlling it) using the instep drive technique. The goalkeeper tries to save all shots. Sprint back to your original position and repeat for a total of 20 shots. Award yourself 1 point for a shot on goal saved by the goalkeeper and 2 points for a goal scored. All shots must be taken from a distance of 18 yards or greater. After 20 shots, players rotate positions and repeat the drill. Continue until each player has taken a turn as the shooter.

To Increase Difficulty

- Increase shooting distance.
- Increase number of repetitions.

To Decrease Difficulty

- Reduce shooting distance to 15 yards.
- Allow two-touch shooting.

Success Check

- Square shoulders and hips to goal.
- Position knee of kicking leg over ball.
- Keep kicking foot extended down and firm.
- Keep the head steady with vision on ball.
- Follow through toward target.

Score Your Success

0 to 15 points = 1 point

16 to 27 points = 3 points

28 to 40 points = 5 points

Your score ___

Instep Drive Shot
Drill 4. Repetition Shooting in the Penalty Area

Play with two teammates within the penalty area of a regulation field. One player is a goalkeeper. A second player (server) stands 25 yards from the goal with a dozen soccer balls. You get in position directly in front of the server with back to the goal, facing the server. The drill begins as the server rolls a ball past you a couple of yards into the penalty area. Turn and sprint to the ball, shoot first time, and sprint immediately back to your original spot. The server rolls a second ball past you to the opposite side. Again turn, sprint to the ball, and shoot to score. You must strike each ball first time, without stopping or controlling it, using the instep drive technique. The server alternates rolling balls to your left and right. Continue until the supply of balls is depleted, then switch positions with the server and repeat. (The goalkeeper remains the goalkeeper.) Award 2 points for each goal scored and 1 point for each shot on goal saved by the goalkeeper. Play two rounds as shooter for a total of 24 shots.

To Increase Difficulty

- Increase shooting distance.
- Increase number of shots to induce physical fatigue.

To Decrease Difficulty

- Reduce shooting distance.

- Decrease speed of repetitions.
- Allow shooter two touches to control and shoot the ball.

Success Check

- Turn and sprint to the ball.
- Square shoulders and hips to goal.
- Position knee of kicking leg over ball.
- Keep kicking foot extended and firm.
- Keep the head steady.
- Follow through toward target.

Score Your Success

0 to 21 points = 1 point

22 to 32 points = 3 points

33 to 48 points = 5 points

Your score ___

Instep Drive Shot Drill 5. Serve and Shoot

Play on one end of a regulation field. Position a server beside the goal with a supply of balls and the goalkeeper in goal. You get in position 25 yards front and center of the goal. To begin the drill, the server kicks a ball toward you, either along the ground or through the air. Move toward the oncoming ball, control and prepare it with your first touch, and shoot on goal with your second touch. All shots must be two-touch shots only and must be taken from a distance of 15 yards or greater from goal. After each shot, return immediately to your starting position and repeat the sequence for a total of 20 shots on goal. The goalkeeper attempts to save all shots. Award 1 point for a shot on goal, 2 points for a goal scored. Keep tally of points scored. After completing 20 shots, switch positions with the server and repeat the drill. The goalkeeper remains the goalkeeper.

To Increase Difficulty

- Have a defending player sprint off the end line to challenge the shooter.
- Reduce width of goal to 6 yards.

To Decrease Difficulty

- Allow three touches to control, prepare, and shoot the ball on goal.

Success Check

- Move forward to receive the ball.
- Push the ball toward the goal with the first touch.
- Strike ball on goal with the second touch.
- Keep shoulders and hips square to the goal.
- Keep knee of kicking leg over ball.
- Keep kicking foot extended and firm.

Score Your Success

0 to 21 points scored = 1 point

22 to 29 points scored = 3 points

30 to 40 points scored = 5 points

Your score ___

Instep Drive Shot Drill 6.　Score Off the Dribble

Form two teams of three to five players each. Teams stand side by side in two single-file lines facing the goal 25 yards away. A neutral goalkeeper positions in goal. The first player in each line alternately dribbles forward at top speed and shoots on goal from a distance of 15 yards or greater. After each shot, the shooter quickly retrieves his or her ball and returns to the end of the line. Continue the drill until each player has attempted 15 shots. Award 1 point for each shot on goal, 2 points for each goal scored. Each player keeps tally of points scored. (Note: Rotate two or three goalkeepers in goal because of the large number of shots taken.)

To Increase Difficulty

- Increase shooting distance.
- Have a defender chase the dribbler.

To Decrease Difficulty

- Reduce dribbling speed.
- Reduce shooting distance.

Success Check

- Dribble at top speed toward goal.
- Square shoulders and hips to target.
- Position knee of kicking leg over ball.
- Keep kicking foot pointed down and firm.
- Completely follow through toward target.

Score Your Success

0 to 14 points = 1 point

15 to 21 points = 3 points

22 to 30 points = 5 points

Your score ___

Instep Drive Shot Drill 7.　Two-on-Two Scoring Derby

Play at one end of a regulation soccer field. Six players are required; one is the goalkeeper and one is the server. The remaining players are divided into two teams of two players each. Both teams take positions in the 18- by 44-yard penalty area. The server stands at the top of the penalty arc with a dozen soccer balls and initiates play by rolling a ball into the penalty area. Both teams vie for possession. The team that wins the ball attempts to score while the other team defends. If a player steals the ball, his or her team immediately goes on the attack and tries to score. The goalkeeper is neutral and attempts to save all shots. The server immediately rolls another ball into the area after the goalkeeper makes a save, when the ball is kicked out of play, or when a goal is scored. Play nonstop until the supply of balls is depleted. The team scoring more goals wins the game. Play a total of five games. Award yourself 1 point for each goal scored.

To Increase Difficulty

- Use markers to designate a smaller goal.
- Add one player who always plays with the defending team, creating a three-on-two-player advantage for the defense.

To Decrease Difficulty

- Use markers to represent an enlarged goal.
- Add one player who always plays with the attacking team, creating a three-on-two-player advantage for the offense.

Success Check

- Combine with your teammate to create scoring opportunities.
- Shoot at every opportunity.
- Favor accuracy over power.

Score Your Success

Average 1 goal scored per game = 1 point

Average 2 goals scored or more per game = 3 points

Your score ___

Instep Drive Shot Drill 8. Score From Distance

Play in a 40- by 60-yard area with a regulation-size goal centered on each end line. Use markers to divide the field lengthwise into three equal zones. Organize two teams of five players each; one player on each team is the goalkeeper. Each team defends a goal. Begin with a kickoff from the center of the field. Regular soccer rules are in effect except that all shots must originate from the middle zone, 20 yards or more from the goal. Award 2 points for a goal scored and 1 point for a shot on goal saved by the goalkeeper. Play for 20 minutes. Players keep individual tallies of points scored.

To Increase Difficulty for Attacking Team

- Decrease width of goal.
- Require first-time shots.
- Add a neutral player who always plays with the defending team.

To Decrease Difficulty for Attacking Team

- Add a neutral player who always plays with the attacking team.
- Allow scores from any distance.

Success Check

- Square shoulders and hips to target.
- Keep kicking foot extended and firm.
- Use a complete follow-through motion.

Score Your Success

0 to 6 points scored = 1 point

7 to 15 points scored = 3 points

16 points or more scored = 5 points

Your score ____

Instep Drive Shot Drill 9. World Cup Scoring Game

Organize four to six teams of two players each. All teams take positions within the penalty area. Each team chooses a country to represent (such as United States, England, Germany, Spain, or any other country). A neutral goalkeeper stands in goal with a supply of balls. The game begins when the goalkeeper tosses a couple of balls toward the outer edge of the penalty area. All teams vie for possession. Teams gaining possession of a ball attempt to score in the full-size goal; all other teams defend. The offside rule is not in effect. A team that loses possession immediately goes on defense; a team gaining possession immediately attacks. The goalkeeper returns the ball into play after each save by tossing it toward the outer edge of the penalty area. Two balls are kept in play at all times.

A team that scores on the goalkeeper advances to the next round of play. After scoring, the players shout their team name and sprint off the field behind the goal to wait for the next round. The round ends when all but one team has scored. That team is eliminated from the World Cup competition. Remaining teams advance to the next round, which is organized in the same manner as the first.

Play a sufficient number of rounds until only one team remains—the World Cup champion.

Eliminated teams practice ball juggling behind the goal until the game is repeated. Play a total of five games.

To Increase Scoring Difficulty

- Increase number of teams to reduce available time and space.
- Position two goalkeepers in goal.

To Decrease Scoring Difficulty

- Increase width of goal.

Success Check

- Turn and shoot at any half chance.
- Square shoulders and hips to goal.
- Keep kicking foot down and firm.
- Shoot low and hard.

Score Your Success

Win 0 or 1 World Cup competitions = 1 point

Win 2 or 3 World Cup competitions = 2 points

Win 4 or 5 World Cup competitions = 3 points

Your score ____

VOLLEY SHOTS

There will be situations in which you won't have time to bring the ball to the ground before shooting on goal. In those instances, your best option is to volley it directly out of the air. Successfully executing a volley shot requires precise timing and proper form. If you perform a volley shot correctly, you can generate tremendous velocity. Some of the most spectacular goals I've witnessed during my long career as a player and coach have been scored off volleys.

Full-Volley Shot

Use the full-volley technique to strike a bouncing ball or a ball that drops from above. Face the ball with shoulders square to the target (figure 5.2). Bend your supporting leg slightly at the knee to maximize balance and body control. Draw the kicking leg back with the foot extended and firm. Keep your head steady with vision focused on the ball. As the ball descends, snap the kicking leg straight and contact the center of the ball with the full instep. Strike the ball when it is as low to the ground as possible. The knee of your kicking leg should be directly above the ball and the kicking foot pointed down at the moment of contact. Use a short, powerful kicking motion as the leg snaps straight.

Figure 5.2 Full-Volley Shot

PREPARATION

1. Move to spot where the ball will drop
2. Face the ball with shoulders square
3. Bend supporting leg at the knee
4. Draw back kicking leg with foot extended
5. Hold arms out to sides for balance
6. Keep head steady and focus on the ball

EXECUTION

1. Square hips to target
2. Have knee of kicking leg over ball
3. Keep kicking foot firm
4. Contact center of ball with instep

FOLLOW-THROUGH

1. Kicking leg snaps straight
2. Momentum is forward

Misstep

The ball travels up and over the goal.

Correction

This will happen if you lean back and reach for the ball as you kick it. Allow the ball to drop as close to the ground as possible before kicking it. The kicking foot is pointed down with the knee over the ball at the moment of contact.

Half-Volley Shot

The half-volley technique is similar in many ways to the full volley. The primary difference is that the ball is kicked at the instant it hits the ground rather than directly out of the air. Anticipate where the ball will drop, then move to that spot (figure 5.3). Draw your kicking leg back with the foot extended and firm. Square shoulders and hips to the target as you snap the kicking leg straight. Strike the center of the ball with the full instep the instant the ball hits the ground. The knee of the kicking leg should be above the ball at the moment of contact. Use a short, powerful snaplike motion of the kicking leg.

Figure 5.3   Half-Volley Shot

PREPARATION	EXECUTION	FOLLOW-THROUGH
1. Anticipate where ball will drop, and move to that spot	1. Square shoulders and hips to target	1. Kicking leg follows through toward target
2. Bend supporting leg at knee	2. Have knee of kicking leg over ball	2. Momentum is forward through point of contact
3. Draw back kicking leg with foot extended and firm	3. Snap kicking leg straight	
4. Hold arms out to sides for balance	4. Keep kicking foot extended and firm	
5. Keep head steady and eyes on ball	5. Strike through center of ball as it hits the ground	

Misstep

The shot slices right or left of the target.

Correction

Precise timing and proper technique are essential. It's too late to contact the ball once it has begun to rebound upward off the ground. Move into position early, judge the descent of the ball, and strike the ball at the exact instant it hits the ground. Square shoulders and hips to the target.

Misstep

The shot travels up and over the goal.

Correction

This will happen if you lean back as your foot contacts the ball. Time your shot release so that your body is moving forward and over the ball as you kick it. Your kicking foot is pointed down with the knee above the ball at the moment of contact.

Side-Volley Shot

Use the side-volley technique to shoot a ball that bounces or drops to your side or to redirect a ball directly out of the air that crosses into the goal area. Face the ball as it approaches (figure 5.4). As the ball arrives, turn your body sideways so that your lead (front) shoulder is pointing in the direction you want the ball to travel. Raise your kicking leg to the side so that it is almost parallel to the ground. Draw back the kicking foot with the leg bent at the knee. Keep your head steady with eyes focused on the ball. Snap the kicking leg straight and contact the top half of the ball with your instep. Follow through by rotating your body toward the target. The kicking-leg motion should travel on a slightly downward plane.

The shot will lack power if you swing your kicking leg at the ball rather than powerfully snap the lower leg through the point of contact. Keep your leg in the cocked position until the last possible moment, then snap it straight and drive the kicking foot through the upper half of the ball with a short, explosive motion.

Figure 5.4 **Side-Volley Shot**

PREPARATION

1. Face the oncoming ball
2. Raise kicking leg to side, parallel to ground
3. Draw back kicking foot with knee bent
4. Balance weight on supporting leg
5. Keep arms out to sides for balance
6. Keep head steady

EXECUTION

1. Rotate a half turn toward ball on balance foot
2. Point front shoulder toward target
3. Snap kicking leg straight
4. Contact top half of ball with instep

FOLLOW-THROUGH

1. Rotate body square to target
2. Angle kicking motion slightly downward
3. Momentum is forward in direction of shot
4. Drop kicking foot to ground

Misstep

The ball travels up and over the goal.

Correction

The knee of the kicking leg must be on an even plane with or above the ball as you kick it. The kicking motion should travel on a downward plane through the top half of the ball.

Misstep

The shot travels wide of the goal.

Correction

Rotate your body toward the target as you kick the ball. At completion of the follow-through kicking motion, you should be square to the goal.

Volley Shot Drill 1. Partner Volley

Face a partner from 8 yards away. Hold the ball in your hands at waist level. Drop the ball and kick a full-volley shot to your partner's chest. He or she catches the ball and volleys it back to you in the same manner. Continue for 30 volleys each, alternating between left and right feet every other shot. Repeat the drill for 30 half-volley shots each, alternating feet with every other shot. Score 1 point for each ball volleyed directly at your part-ner that he or she can catch out of the air. Keep track of points scored.

To Increase Difficulty

- Increase distance to 12 yards.
- Volley a ball tossed to you by your partner.

To Decrease Difficulty

- Decrease distance to 5 yards.

Success Check

- Square shoulders and hips to target.
- Contact ball on full instep.
- Position knee above ball.
- Keep toes down and foot firm.
- Use a short, powerful snap of the kicking leg.

Volley Shot Drill 2.   Toss and Volley to Goal

Get in position 20 yards front and center of a regulation goal with a supply of balls. A goalkeeper plays in goal. Toss a ball into the air so that it drops 3 to 4 yards in front of you. Move forward, allow the ball to bounce once, and execute a full-volley shot on goal. Take 20 full-volley shots followed by 20 half-volley shots for a total of 40 volleys. Alternate left- and right-foot volley shots. Score 1 point for each shot on goal, even if the goalkeeper saves the shot.

To Increase Difficulty

- Increase shooting distance.
- Decrease size of goal.
- Volley a ball tossed by a server.
- Require all volleys to be with your weaker (nondominant) foot.

To Decrease Difficulty

- Reduce shooting distance.
- Increase size of goal.
- Volley the ball directly out of your hands.

Success Check

- Square shoulders and hips to goal.
- Have knee over ball.
- Keep head steady.
- Keep kicking foot down and firm.
- Use a short, powerful follow-through.

Volley Shot Drill 3.   Score From Side Volleys

Get in position 6 to 8 yards front and center of a regulation goal. A server stands on the flank 20 to 25 yards away with a supply of balls. The server crosses or tosses a ball for you to side-volley into the goal. Do not use a goalkeeper. Perform 20 side volleys from the right side, then 20 from the left side. Score 1 point for each side volley kicked into the open goal.

To Increase Difficulty

- Increase shooting distance to 15 yards.

To Decrease Difficulty

- Toss the ball to yourself to side-volley on goal.

Success Check

- Face the server.
- Raise and cock kicking leg with foot extended and firm.
- Rotate on supporting foot as ball arrives.
- Turn lead shoulder to goal.
- Kick on a downward plane through top half of ball.

Volley Shot Drill 4.   Volley Shooting Game

Form two equal teams of four to six players each. Use markers to outline a rectangular playing area 40 by 60 yards. Center a full-size goal on each end line. Do not use goalkeepers. Each team defends a goal and can score in the opponent's goal. Passing among teammates is accomplished by throwing and catching rather than kicking the ball. A player may take no more than four steps with the ball before releasing it to a teammate. Change of possession occurs when a defending player intercepts a pass, when an out-of-bounds ball was last touched by an attacking player, when the ball is dropped to the ground, when a player takes more than four steps with the ball, or after a goal is scored.

Points are scored by volleying a ball tossed by a teammate directly out of the air into the opponent's goal. Players are not permitted to toss the ball to themselves to volley on goal. Although goalkeepers are not designated, all players are permitted to use the hands to catch the ball and to block passes or shots on goal. Play for 15 minutes. The team scoring more goals wins.

Note: Successful execution of full-volley shots requires precise timing and correct technique, so this game may not be appropriate for younger players.

To Increase Difficulty

- Use goalkeepers.

To Decrease Difficulty

- Allow players to volley directly out of their hands.

Success Check

- Square shoulders and hips to target.
- Allow ball to drop as low to the ground as possible.
- Have knee over ball at moment of contact.
- Keep kicking foot extended and firm.
- Keep the shot low.

Score Your Success

Member of losing team = 0 points
Member of winning team = 1 point
Your score ___

SWERVING SHOT

In some situations, the most direct path to goal is not always the best route. This is particularly true on corner kicks and free kicks, during which you may attempt to bend the ball around or over a wall of players. You can cause the ball to swerve and dip in flight by imparting spin to it. Striking the outer half of the ball with the inside of the right instep will cause the ball to bend from right to left. Striking the outer half of the ball with the inside of the left instep will bend the ball from left to right. These types of swerving shots are commonly referred to as *inswingers*.

Begin your approach from behind the ball at a slight angle (figure 5.5). Plant your supporting foot beside or slightly behind the ball. Keep your head steady and eyes focused on the ball. Draw back the kicking leg with the foot extended and firm. Lean slightly back and away from the ball as you strike it. Use an outside-in follow-through motion.

You can swerve the ball in the opposite direction using the outside surface of the instep. Contact the inside half of the ball with the outside of your right instep to make the shot bend from left to right. Contact the inside half of the ball with the outside of your left instep to make the shot bend from right to left. These types of shots are often referred to as *outswingers*. Use an inside-out follow-through motion of the kicking leg. Position the kicking foot down and diagonally inward as it contacts the ball. A complete follow-through motion will generate greater power and swerve.

Figure 5.5 | Swerving Shot

PREPARATION

1. Approach the ball from behind at a slight angle
2. Plant supporting foot beside or slightly behind the ball
3. Draw back kicking leg with foot extended
4. Hold arms out to sides for balance
5. Keep the head steady and eyes on ball

EXECUTION

1. Lean back slightly and away from ball.
2. Contact ball left or right of its vertical midline with inside or outside surface of instep.
3. Keep the kicking foot firm and angled down.

FOLLOW-THROUGH

1. Keep momentum forward through point of contact
2. Use inside-out kicking motion for outside-of-the-instep shot
3. Use outside-in kicking motion for inside-of-the-instep shot
4. Follow-through motion is to waist level or higher

Misstep

The ball fails to curve in flight.

Correction

The shot will not swerve in flight unless you impart sufficient velocity and spin to the ball. Contact the ball left or right of its vertical midline, not directly through its center. Lean away from the ball as you kick it. Use an inside-out kicking motion for an outside-of-the-instep shot, and use an outside-in kicking motion for an inside-of-the-instep shot.

Misstep

The shot lacks power.

Correction

A weak shot usually occurs for one of the following reasons: the kicking foot contacts the ball too close to its outer edge, the kicking foot is not firm as it contacts the ball, or there is insufficient follow-through. Contact the ball just right or left of center, not along its outer edge. Get as much of your instep on the ball as possible while still imparting sufficient spin. Extend and firmly position the kicking foot. A complete follow-through motion coupled with proper kicking mechanics will generate sufficient velocity and spin on the ball to bend the flight path of the shot.

Swerving Shot Drill 1.   Target Practice

Use masking tape to outline a 4- by 4-yard target on a wall or kickboard. Shoot (swerve) stationary balls to hit the target from a distance of 20 yards or greater. Take a total of 30 shots using your favorite (dominant) foot. Award yourself 1 point for each shot that bends in flight and hits inside the square.

To Increase Difficulty

- Reduce size of target to 3 by 3 yards.

To Decrease Difficulty

- Reduce shooting distance.
- Increase size of square to 5 by 5 yards.

Success Check

- Square hips to target.
- Contact ball right or left of vertical midline.
- Impart sufficient spin and velocity on the ball.

Score Your Success

4 points or fewer scored = 0 points

5 to 8 points scored = 2 points

9 to 14 points scored = 3 points

15 to 19 points scored = 4 points

20 to 30 points scored = 5 points

Your score ___

Swerving Shot Drill 2.   Bending Balls From Set Pieces

Place a dozen soccer balls at various spots outside of the penalty area. A goalkeeper positions in the regulation goal. Practice scoring from direct free kicks. Attempt to swerve each shot with the inside or outside surface of the instep. After 12 shots, reposition the balls at different spots and repeat the drill for a total of 24 free-kick attempts. Award yourself 1 point for each shot on goal that bends in flight, and award yourself 2 points for a goal scored. The goalkeeper collects and returns each shot on goal.

To Increase Difficulty

- Shoot from a greater distance.
- Make the goal smaller.

To Decrease Difficulty

- Shoot from 15 yards.

Success Check

- Square shoulders and hips to goal.
- Lean back slightly and away from the ball.
- Keep kicking foot extended and firm.
- Use a complete follow-through motion.

Score Your Success

0 to 24 points = 1 point

25 to 34 points = 3 points

35 to 48 points = 5 points

Your score ___

Swerving Shot
Drill 3.   Swerving Shots From the Run of Play

This drill requires seven players, one a neutral goalkeeper. Play within a 50- by 50-yard field area. Mark off a 25-yard square within the larger field. Position two cones or flags in the center of the 25-yard square to represent an 8-yard-wide goal. The neutral goalkeeper stands in goal and attempts to save all shots. The remaining players divide into two teams of three players each.

Teams compete three-on-three within the larger area. One team begins with possession of the ball; the other team defends. Players score by shooting the ball through either side of the central goal below the height of the goalkeeper. The goalkeeper must readjust position (side of the goal) depending on the location of the ball. Players are not permitted to enter the 25-yard square.

All shots must be taken from outside the 25-yard square and must be swerved with the inside or outside surface of the instep. A ball that goes out of play is returned by a throw-in. If the defending team gains possession of the ball, it immediately switches to the attack and tries to score. After making a save, the goalkeeper tosses the ball to a corner of the playing area where both teams compete for possession. Play for 15 minutes. Each player keeps tally of the number of swerving shots he or she kicks on goal. (Note: This drill is most appropriate for older, experienced players.)

To Increase Difficulty for the Attacking Team

- Reduce size of goal.
- Limit players to three or fewer touches to pass or shoot the ball.
- Add a neutral player who always plays with the defending team to create a one-player advantage.

To Decrease Difficulty for the Attacking Team

- Enlarge the goal.
- Add a neutral player who always plays with the attacking team to create a one-player advantage.

Success Check

- Square shoulders and hips to goal.
- Impart spin and velocity on the shot.
- Shoot at every opportunity.

Score Your Success

4 shots on goal or fewer = 1 point

5 to 9 shots on goal = 2 points

10 shots on goal or more = 3 points

Your score ___

SUMMARY OF SHOOTING SUCCESS

Developing your ability to shoot with power and accuracy is the first step toward becoming a proficient goal scorer. Focus on these key points. Square shoulders and hips to the target. Shift momentum forward with the knee of the kicking leg above the ball as you prepare to strike it. Drive your kicking foot through the point of contact. Keep your head steady and the kicking foot extended and firm throughout the kicking motion. Use a complete follow-through when executing the instep drive and swerving shots. Use a short, powerful leg snap when executing the full-volley, half-volley, and side-volley techniques.

Once you're able to shoot consistently with power and accuracy in a low-pressure, practice-type environment, move on to more gamelike situations that involve the pressures of limited time and space and physical fatigue as well as the challenge of determined opponents. If necessary, you can modify the drills described in step 5 to match your level of expertise.

Each of the drills described in step 5 has been assigned a point value so that you can evaluate your performance and chart your progress. Record your scores in the following chart and then total the points to get a rough estimate of your overall level of success.

Instep Drive Shot Drills

1. Hit the Target _____ out of 5

2. Score Through the Central Goal _____ out of 5

3. Combine With the Target and Score _____ out of 5

4. Repetition Shooting in the Penalty Area _____ out of 5

5. Serve and Shoot _____ out of 5

6. Score Off the Dribble _____ out of 5

7. Two-on-Two Scoring Derby _____ out of 3

8. Score From Distance _____ out of 5

9. World Cup Scoring Game _____ out of 3

Volley Shot Drills

1. Partner Volley _____ out of 5

2. Toss and Volley to Goal _____ out of 5

3. Score From Side Volleys _____ out of 5

4. Volley Shooting Game _____ out of 1

Swerving Shot Drills

1. Target Practice _____ out of 5

2. Bending Balls From Set Pieces _____ out of 5

3. Swerving Shots From the Run of Play _____ out of 3

Total _____ *out of 70*

A combined score of 60 or more points indicates that you have sufficiently mastered the shooting skills and are prepared to move on to step 6. A total score in the range of 45 to 59 is considered adequate. Move on to step 6 after you have reviewed and rehearsed each of the shooting techniques one more time. If you had fewer than 45 points, you need to polish up your shooting skills. Review all of the material in step 5, rehearse each of the shooting techniques, and then progress through each of the drills at least one more time to improve your overall score before moving on to step 6.

Goalkeeping

The goalkeeper can be considered the one true specialist on the soccer team. Assigned the task of protecting a goal 8 feet high and 24 feet wide, the keeper stands as the final obstacle opponents must bypass in order to score. The goalkeeper is the only player allowed to use the hands to control the ball within the team's penalty area.

Goalkeeper is a difficult and demanding position to play, one that requires a special type of athlete. Top-flight netminders combine a high degree of mental toughness with outstanding physical ability. Most are tall and rangy and have excellent jumping ability. They are able to catch and hold powerful shots that arrive from different angles and distances. They are willing and able to propel their bodies through the air to make a save or dive at the feet of a rushing opponent to smother the ball on a breakaway. Superior levels of agility, balance, and body control enable goalkeepers to react instantly to rapidly changing situations that occur in the goalmouth. Powerful legs and upper bodies enable them to leap up to

catch balls served into the goalmouth and, when necessary, fend off the determined challenge of opponents attempting to win the ball.

In short, the goalkeeper must be willing to do whatever it takes to make the big save—and preventing goals is only half the job! Once the goalkeeper makes the save, he or she is responsible for initiating the team's attack by distributing the ball accurately to teammates.

Important goalkeeping skills include the basic goalkeeper stance, commonly referred to as the *ready position;* receiving skills for low (ground-level), medium-high, chest-high, and high balls; diving skills; and the distributing skills of rolling, throwing, dropkicking, and punting. The modern goalkeeper must also be proficient in the basic footwork used by field players. Recent changes in rules prohibit the goalkeeper from handing a ball passed back to him or her from a teammate, so it is important that the goalkeeper be comfortable and competent using the feet to play the ball.

READY POSITION

The goalkeeper must maintain good balance and body control at all times. All movements begin with the goalkeeper positioned in the standard goalkeeper posture, commonly referred to as the ready position (figure 6.1). Assume the ready position whenever an opponent has the ball within shooting distance of your goal. Face the ball with shoulders square and feet approximately shoulder-width apart. Keep your head and upper body erect with knees bent. Center your body weight forward over the balls of the feet so that your heels elevate slightly off the ground. Position your hips and buttocks as if you were sitting on a medium-high stool. Carry your hands at approximately waist level with palms forward and fingers pointing up. Keep your head steady with your focus on the ball.

From the ready position you will be able to move quickly in any direction. You need to set your feet in the ready position before the shot, because it will be difficult to react quickly if your feet are still moving at the moment the shot is released.

Figure 6.1   Ready Position

1. Stand forward of the goal line
2. Align body with ball
3. Keep head steady and eyes on ball
4. Square shoulders and hips to ball
5. Keep upper body erect
6. Weight is forward over balls of feet
7. Keep hands at waist level with palms forward and fingers pointing up
8. Bend knees for maximum balance
9. Set feet before shot
10. Be prepared to reposition in response to the location of the ball

Misstep

You are unable to quickly move laterally to make the save.

Correction

Set your feet just before the shot to ensure maximum balance and body control.

RECEIVING GROUND BALLS

Consistency is a trait of top-flight netminders. Therefore, making the routine play on a regular basis is equally as important, if not more so, than the occasional spectacular save. Most of your saves should be of the routine variety unless your teammates fail to provide much of a defense in front of you. Three different techniques are used to receive ground balls, depending on the nature of the shot. You must become competent in performing each skill.

Standing Save

A ball rolling directly at the goalkeeper is received using the scoop technique. This is commonly referred to as the *standing save* (figure 6.2). Shuffle sideways to a position between the ball and the goal. (Note: Do not cross your legs when moving sideways.) Come to the set position with legs straight and feet planted a few inches apart.

As the ball arrives, bend forward at the waist and extend your arms down, palms facing forward, hands slightly cupped. Forearms are parallel to each another, and fingertips should almost touch the ground. Do not attempt to catch a rolling ball directly in your hands. Instead, allow the ball to roll up onto your wrists and forearms and then return to an upright position with the ball clutched securely against your chest.

Figure 6.2   Standing Save

PREPARATION	EXECUTION	FOLLOW-THROUGH
1. Get in ready position between ball and goal	1. Allow ball to roll onto wrists and forearms	1. Clutch ball against chest with forearms
2. Focus on the ball	2. Keep legs straight	2. Return to standing position
3. Bend forward at the waist	3. Keep feet only a few inches apart	3. Distribute the ball to a teammate
4. Extend arms down	4. Withdraw body slightly on impact	
5. Turn palms forward and cup palms		

Misstep

The ball rolls between your legs and into the goal.

Correction

If possible, always position your body behind the ball with feet only a few inches apart. If the ball should inadvertently slip between your hands, it will rebound off your legs rather than roll past you into the goal.

Misstep

The ball rebounds off your hands into the path of a rushing opponent.

Correction

Do not attempt to catch a rolling ball directly in your hands. Instead, allow the ball to roll up onto your wrists and forearms, and clutch it to your chest as you return to a standing position.

Tweener Save

A rolling ball arriving to the goalkeeper's side is commonly referred to as a *tweener* and is received using the tweener save technique. This shot is far enough away to make the standing save impossible but not so far as to require a diving save. The tweener technique also can be used to block a close-in shot that is bouncing, skipping, or arriving with some velocity.

To make the tweener save (figure 6.3), shuffle sideways (laterally) across the goal. Extend your lead foot in the direction you are moving with the leg bent at the knee. Kneel on the trailing leg and position it parallel to the goal line. To prevent the ball from squeezing through your legs, allow only a few inches of open space between the heel of your lead foot and the knee of the trailing leg. From the kneeling position, bend your upper body forward with shoulders square to the oncoming ball. Allow the ball to roll up onto your wrists and forearms before clutching it to your chest.

Figure 6.3   Tweener Save

PREPARATION

1. Shoulders and hips are square
2. Feet are shoulder-width apart
3. Hands are at waist level with palms forward
4. Focus on the ball

EXECUTION

1. Shuffle sideways to intercept the ball
2. Kneel on trailing leg and position it parallel to goal line
3. Lean forward at waist
4. Keep shoulders square to ball
5. Palms are forward and fingers are extended
6. Allow ball to roll onto wrists and forearms

FOLLOW-THROUGH

1. Clutch ball to chest with forearms
2. Return to upright position
3. Distribute the ball

Misstep

The ball rebounds off your hands into the area in front of the goal.

Correction

This can occur if you try to catch the ball directly in your hands rather than allowing it to roll up onto your wrists and forearms. Use a scooping motion of the arms to receive the ball, and clutch the ball to your chest before you return to a standing position.

Forward Vault

The conventional standing save is not appropriate when fielding a low, powerfully driven shot coming directly at you or a ball that skips immediately in front of you. This is especially true when playing on a slippery field on which the ball accelerates when it hits standing water or wet grass. To compensate for the added velocity of such shots, use the *forward vault* technique (figure 6.4) to receive the ball.

Face the ball with shoulders square. Bend forward at the waist, bend your knees, and vault toward the ball and down to the ground. Extend your arms and hands beneath the ball with palms facing up. Allow the ball to contact your wrists and forearms rather than your hands. Fall forward and trap the ball between your forearms and chest. Extend and slightly spread your legs behind you for balance and support.

Figure 6.4 | **Forward Vault**

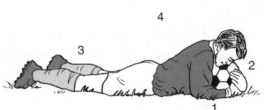

PREPARATION

1. Begin in the ready position
2. Square shoulders and hips to ball
3. Bend forward at the waist with knees bent
4. Focus on the ball

EXECUTION

1. Vault forward to ground
2. Extend arms beneath the ball with palms facing up
3. Allow ball to contact wrists and forearms

FOLLOW-THROUGH

1. Fall forward onto forearms
2. Trap ball between forearms and chest
3. Extend legs behind and spread slightly
4. Scramble to feet and distribute the ball

Misstep

The ball slips through your arms, between your legs, and into the goal.

Correction

This error recently occurred with my starting goalkeeper, who I might add is a fine player. To avoid this misstep, position your forearms close together beneath the ball as you vault forward. Keep your arms extended and parallel to one another with forearms a few inches apart as you receive the ball. Scoop the ball and clutch it between your chest and forearms.

Receiving Ground Balls Drill 1. Standing Save Drill

Two servers (A and B), each with a ball, face each other 12 yards apart. You get in position midway between the servers. Server A begins the drill by rolling a ball toward you. Receive the ball using the standing save (scoop) technique and toss it back to server A. Immediately turn to receive a rolling ball from server B. Continue until you have received 30 balls using the standing save technique. Score 1 point for each ball received and held without rebound.

To Increase Difficulty

- Increase velocity of serves.
- Increase number of repetitions.

To Decrease Difficulty

- Scoop a slowly rolling ball.

Success Check

- Bend forward at waist.
- Keep legs together and straight.
- Allow ball to roll onto wrists and forearms.
- Scoop ball to chest.
- Return to upright position.

Score Your Success

0 to 24 points = 1 point

25 to 27 points = 3 points

28 to 30 points = 5 points

Your score ___

Receiving Ground Balls Drill 2. Scoop Save and Change Lines

Four goalkeepers participate in this drill. Goalkeepers A and B stand in single file and face goalkeepers C and D at a distance of 15 yards. Goalkeeper A rolls a ball toward goalkeeper C and sprints to the end of that line. Goalkeeper C moves forward to meet the ball, receives the ball using the scoop technique, rolls the ball to goalkeeper B in the opposite line, and sprints to the end of that line. Goalkeeper B executes a standing save, rolls the ball to goalkeeper D, and sprints to the end of that line. Continue the drill until each goalkeeper has received 30 rolling balls. Award 1 point for each ball properly received using the standing (scoop) save.

To Increase Difficulty

- Increase velocity of the serves.

To Decrease Difficulty

- Reduce velocity of serves.

Success Check

- Square shoulders and hips to the ball.
- Bend forward at the waist
- Keep legs together and straight.
- Allow ball to roll onto wrists and forearms.
- Scoop ball to chest.
- Return to upright position.

Score Your Success

0 to 24 points = 1 point

25 to 27 points = 3 points

28 to 30 points = 5 points

Your score ___

Receiving Ground Balls
Drill 3.   Saving the Tweener Ball

Take a position in goal next to the right goalpost. Two servers take positions in line with each goalpost, 10 yards out from the goal line. Server A (directly in front of you) rolls a ball to your left toward the center of the goal. Move laterally to receive the ball using the kneeling (tweener) save technique. Return the ball to server B and continue to shuffle sideways across the goal until you reach the left goalpost. At that point, server B rolls the ball to your right toward the center of the goal. Move laterally toward the ball, receive it using the kneeling save, and return the ball to server A. Continue shuffling sideways from post to post for a total of 20 tweener saves. Score 1 point for each properly executed save.

To Increase Difficulty

- Increase velocity of serves.
- Increase speed of repetitions.
- Increase number of repetitions.

To Decrease Difficulty

- Decrease speed of repetitions.
- Decrease number of repetitions.

Success Check

- Extend lead foot toward ball.
- Kneel on trailing leg.
- Align trailing leg parallel to goal line.
- Allow ball to roll up onto wrists and fore-arms.
- Clutch ball to chest.

Score Your Success

0 to 14 points = 1 point

15 to 17 points = 3 points

18 to 20 points = 5 points

Your score ___

Receiving Ground Balls
Drill 4.   Forward Vault to Save

Kneel facing a partner who is also kneeling 5 yards away. Toss a ball so that it skips immediately in front of your partner, who falls forward to receive the ball using the forward vault technique. He or she returns the ball in a similar manner for you to receive using the forward vault technique. Continue the drill until each player has executed 20 saves using the forward vault. Award 1 point for each ball held without a rebound.

To Increase Difficulty

- Vary trajectory and velocity of serves.
- Execute the forward vault from a squat position.
- Execute the forward vault from a standing position.

To Decrease Difficulty

- Roll the ball slowly to your partner.

Success Check

- Fall forward.
- Scoop the ball with palms up and forearms underneath the ball.
- Keep forearms parallel to each other.
- Clutch ball to chest.

Score Your Success

0 to 14 points = 1 point

15 to 17 points = 3 points

18 to 20 points = 5 points

Your score ___

Receiving Ground Balls
Drill 5. Collecting Through Balls

Goalkeepers A and C get in position 10 yards apart. Goalkeeper B stands midway between A and C with legs apart. Goalkeeper A rolls the ball through B's legs toward C. Goalkeeper C quickly moves forward and uses the forward vault technique to collect the ball as it rolls through B's legs. Goalkeeper C must vault to B's side after receiving the ball. After players return to their original positions, C rolls the ball through B's legs, and A saves using the forward vault. Goalkeepers rotate positions after 20 saves and repeat the drill so that each keeper attempts 20 forward vault saves. Award 1 point for each ball received without rebound.

To Increase Difficulty

- Increase velocity of serves.
- Increase number of repetitions.

To Decrease Difficulty

- Decrease velocity of serves.

Check Your Success

- Dive forward and down to ground.
- Keep palms up and forearms parallel.
- Slip forearms beneath the ball.
- Clutch ball to chest.

Score Your Success

0 to 13 points = 1 point

14 to 16 points = 3 points

17 to 20 points = 5 points

Your score ___

Receiving Ground Balls
Drill 6. Ground Ball Keeper Wars

Place two 6-yard-wide goals with nets 20 yards apart. Station a goalkeeper (A and B) in each goal. Goalkeeper A begins with the ball and attempts to score on B by rolling or dropkicking the ball past B and into the goal. B attempts to save the shot and then tries to score on A in a similar manner. Keepers are permitted only one step before shooting on goal. All shots must be driven along the ground. Goalkeepers should use either the standing save, tweener save, or forward vault, depending on the nature of the shot. Award 1 point for each goal scored. Play for 15 minutes and keep track of the score.

To Increase Difficulty for Defending Goalkeeper

- Increase width of goal.
- Reduce distance of shot.

To Decrease Difficulty for Defending Goalkeeper

- Decrease width of goal.
- Increase distance of shot.

Check Your Success

- Square up with oncoming ball.
- Choose appropriate receiving technique.
- Clutch ball to chest.
- Do not give up rebounds.

Score Your Success

Lose the competition = 0 points

Win the competition = 2 points

Your score ___

RECEIVING AIR BALLS

The space front and center of the goal is considered the goalkeeper's personal domain, an area that he or she must control in order to be successful. To dominate the goal box, you must be able to receive and control driven balls that arrive through the air. Powerful shots from outside the penalty area and balls crossed or lofted into the goalmouth pose a definite challenge. The technique used for receiving the ball depends on the height, velocity, and trajectory of the ball.

Medium-High Shots

A medium-high shot is defined as one that arrives between your ankles and waist. Use a scoop technique similar to the standing save to receive a ball that is arriving at approximately ankle height. Position your body between the ball and the goal with legs straight and feet a few inches apart. Bend forward at the waist with arms extended down, fingers pointing forward, and palms turned up. Receive the ball on your wrists and forearms and then secure it against your chest. Do not attempt to catch a medium-high shot directly in the palms of your hands.

Receive a ball arriving at waist height by bending forward at the waist with forearms parallel and extended down (figure 6.5). Receive the ball on the insides of the forearms, just below the elbows. As the ball arrives, jump back a few inches to absorb its impact. The greater the velocity of the shot, the more cushion you must provide to prevent the ball from bouncing away from you.

Figure 6.5	Receiving a Medium-High Shot

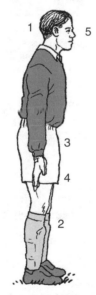  

PREPARATION

1. Get in line with the oncoming ball
2. Keep legs straight with feet planted a few inches apart
3. Extend arms down and keep forearms parallel
4. Point fingers forward and turn palms up
5. Focus on the ball

EXECUTION

1. Bend forward at the waist
2. Bend knees
3. Allow the ball to contact your wrists and forearms

FOLLOW-THROUGH

1. Jump back a few inches to cushion shot
2. Allow the ball to roll up onto forearms
3. Clutch the ball against chest with your forearms
4. Distribute the ball

Misstep

You fail to hold the ball.

Correction

Do not attempt to catch the ball in your hands. Instead, allow the ball to contact your wrists and forearms first before clutching it to your chest.

Receiving Medium-High Shots
Drill 1.   Pingers With Partner

Goalkeepers A and B face one another at a distance of 8 yards. Goalkeeper A volleys (pings) the ball at B at approximately waist level, who receives the ball using the scoop technique. Goalkeeper B returns the ball to A in a similar manner. Goalkeepers must receive the ball using the scoop technique. Get your body behind the ball. Lean forward with forearms extended beneath the ball and palms up. Trap the ball against your body. Perform 30 repetitions each. Score 1 point for each ball received and held without rebound.

To Increase Difficulty

- Vary the serve.
- Play for time—perform as many reps as possible in a specified time limit.

To Decrease Difficulty

- Decease velocity of serve.

Check Your Success

- Align your body with the oncoming ball.
- Keep legs straight with feet planted a few inches apart.
- Extend arms down and keep forearms parallel.
- Bend forward at the waist.
- Allow ball to contact wrists and forearms.

Score Your Success

0 to 19 points = 1 point

20 to 25 points = 3 points

26 to 30 points = 5 points

Your score ___

Receiving Medium-High Shots
Drill 2.   Save, Turn, and Save Again

Goalkeepers A and B, each with a ball, get in position 20 yards apart. Goalkeeper C stands midway between them. Goalkeeper A tosses or kicks a medium-high shot to goalkeeper B, who scoops the ball and returns it to A. B immediately turns to receive a medium-high shot from goalkeeper C. Repeat for 20 repetitions, after which players rotate positions and repeat. Award 1 point for each ball received and held without rebound. Serves should be aimed directly at the goalkeeper.

To Increase Difficulty

- Increase velocity of serve.

To Decrease Difficulty

- Decease velocity of serve.

Check Your Success

- Align with the oncoming ball.
- Keep legs straight with feet planted a few inches apart.
- Extend arms down and keep forearms parallel.
- Bend forward at the waist.
- Contact ball on wrists and forearms.

Score Your Success

0 to 13 points = 1 point

14 to 17 points = 3 points

18 to 20 points = 5 points

Your score ___

Receiving Medium-High Shots
Drill 3. Collecting Medium-High Balls

Play with one goalkeeper and six field players within an area approximately 40 yards square. Position flags to represent a regulation-width goal at one end of the area. The goalkeeper takes position in goal. The field players pass two balls among themselves while moving throughout the area. On the goalkeeper's command, the player with the ball hits a medium-high shot directly to the keeper, who receives the ball and immediately distributes it to the nearest open player. The keeper then demands a ball from a different field player. All shots must be from a distance of 10 yards or greater from the goal. The goalkeeper continuously receives and distributes the ball for 15 minutes. Assess 1 penalty point for each ball not secured and held.

To Increase Difficulty

• Increase velocity of serves.

• Include three balls in the drill.

To Decrease Difficulty

• Have servers toss the ball softly to the keeper.

Check Your Success

• Keep legs straight with feet planted a few inches apart.

• Extend arms down and keep forearms parallel.

• Bend forward at the waist.

• Contact ball on wrists and forearms and secure to chest.

Score Your Success

6 penalty points or more = 1 point

4 or 5 penalty points = 3 points

0 to 3 penalty points = 5 points

Your score ____

Chest-High and Head-High Shots

A shot arriving at chest or head height is received with shoulders square to the oncoming ball. Position your hands in what is generally referred to as the *W (window) position* (figure 6.6). Fingers are spread and extended toward the oncoming ball with thumbs almost touching behind. Position forearms behind the ball and parallel with one another. Extend your arms toward the ball with slight flexion at the elbow. Instead of using the scoop technique used for receiving a medium-high shot, you should attempt to catch the chest-high and head-high shot on the fingertips. As the ball arrives, withdraw your arms to cushion the impact and then secure the ball to your chest.

Follow the *hands-eyes-head (HEH) principle* when receiving a chest-high or head-high ball (figure 6.7). Position your hands, eyes, and head in direct line with the ball as you receive it. Watch the ball into your hands by looking through the

Figure 6.6 W position of the hands.

window formed by your thumbs and index fingers. There should be little or no sound as the ball contacts your fingertips. Keepers often refer to this as having soft hands.

Figure 6.7 Receiving the Chest-High or Head-High Shot

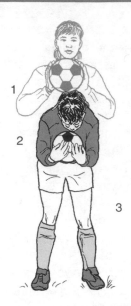

PREPARATION

1. Square shoulders and hips to oncoming ball
2. Position feet approximately shoulder-width apart
3. Carry hands at chest level with palms forward
4. Extend fingers
5. Keep head steady with vision on ball

EXECUTION

1. Put hands in W position
2. Slightly bend elbows
3. Look through window as the ball arrives
4. Receive ball on fingertips

FOLLOW-THROUGH

1. Withdraw hands and arms
2. Secure ball to chest
3. Distribute the ball

Misstep

The ball slips through your hands.

Correction

Position your hands close together to form the window. Thumbs and forefingers should almost touch behind the ball as you receive it.

Misstep

The ball bounces off your hands.

Correction

Receive the ball on the fingertips, not the palms. To soften the impact, withdraw your arms and hands as the ball arrives.

Receiving Chest- and Head-High Shots
Drill 1.   The W Catch

Hold a ball with both hands at approximately chest level. Bounce the ball hard off the ground and receive it with hands positioned in the W position before the ball rises above your waist. Repeat 50 times. Score 1 point for each ball received and held.

To Increase Difficulty

- Bounce and catch the ball while walking at a fast pace.

To Decrease Difficulty

- Bounce ball more softly off the ground.

Success Check

- Catch ball on fingertips.
- Keep thumbs behind the ball.
- Withdraw hands to cushion impact.

Score Your Success

0 to 39 points = 1 point

40 to 44 points = 3 points

45 to 50 points = 5 points

Your score ___

Receiving Chest- and Head-High Shots
Drill 2.   Toss and Catch Using HEH

Goalkeepers A and B face each other at a distance of 8 yards. Goalkeeper A tosses a ball to the right or left of B's head. Goalkeeper B receives the ball while adhering to the HEH principle. Goalkeeper B then tosses the ball to A, who receives it in the same manner. Repeat for 40 tosses each. Award 1 point for each ball caught with hands-eyes-head in line.

To Increase Difficulty

- Increase velocity of tosses.
- Perform drill while shuffling sideways.

To Decrease Difficulty

- Reduce distance between keepers.

- Toss ball very softly.

Success Check

- Keep head steady and focus on the ball.
- Align hands, eyes, and head with ball.
- Hold hands in W position.
- Receive ball on fingertips.

Score Your Success

0 to 35 points = 0 points

36 to 39 points = 1 point

40 points = 3 points

Your score ___

Receiving Chest- and Head-High Shots
Drill 3.   Catching Chest- and Head-High Balls

Goalkeepers A and C, each with a ball, face each other at a distance of 15 yards. Goalkeeper B gets in position midway between A and C. Goalkeeper A tosses a chest-high or head-high ball to B, who receives it with hands in the W position, forearms parallel, and elbows tucked in slightly. Goalkeeper B returns the ball to A and immediately turns to receive a chest- or head-high ball tossed by C. Continue for 60 repetitions, then rotate positions and repeat. Score 1 point for each ball caught and held with proper form.

To Increase Difficulty

- Increase velocity of serves.

- Increase speed of repetitions.

To Decrease Difficulty

- Reduce number of repetitions.

Check Your Success

- Square the shoulders and hips.
- Carry hands at chest level with palms turned forward.
- Extend fingers toward ball.

- Hold hands in W position with elbows bent.
- Look through window as ball arrives.
- Receive ball on fingertips.

Score Your Success

0 to 49 points = 1 point

50 to 54 points = 3 points

55 to 60 points = 5 points

Your score ___

High Balls and Crosses

A high ball is defined as any ball arriving into the goal area above head height. Crosses are driven balls sent into the goalmouth from a flank area of the field. Both high balls and crosses present a difficult challenge for the goalkeeper. In most instances, you will have to get airborne to receive and control the ball and at the same time fend off the challenge of an opponent trying to head the ball into the goal.

As a general rule, you should try to catch the high ball or cross rather than box or parry (push or deflect the ball wide of or over the goal) it away. If the high ball is uncatchable, use an alternative technique, discussed later in this step. (See pages 105, 110-111.) While preparing to catch the high ball or cross, face the ball with shoulders square. Take a moment to judge the ball's trajectory before moving toward the ball. If

you have to get airborne to receive the ball, use a *one-leg takeoff* to generate maximum upward momentum. The jumping technique looks similar to that used when shooting a layup in basketball. Try to catch the ball at the highest point possible by extending your arms overhead.

It's important to leap up off the correct foot. To receive a high ball arriving from the flank (figure 6.8), move toward the ball and thrust your arms and outside leg (the leg toward the field) up in one fluid movement with the knee pointed toward the oncoming ball. Shoulders and hips are square to the oncoming ball. The inside leg (the leg closest to the goal) remains straight and serves as the balance leg. Hold your hands in the W position and employ the HEH principle. Watch the ball into your hands and then secure it to your chest. Drop to the ground on your balance leg.

| Figure 6.8 | Receiving High Balls and Crosses |

PREPARATION

1. Face the ball with shoulders square
2. Move toward the ball
3. Keep head steady and vision on ball

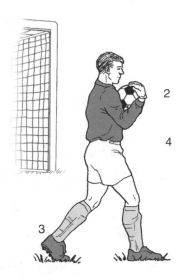

EXECUTION

1. Use one-leg takeoff to jump up
2. Thrust arms and outside leg up in one fluid motion
3. Keep inside leg straight
4. Extend arms up, hands in W position
5. Use the hands-eyes-head (HEH) principle
6. Receive ball at highest point of jump on fingers and palms

FOLLOW-THROUGH

1. Withdraw arms and hands
2. Secure ball to chest
3. Descend to ground
4. Distribute the ball

Misstep

An opponent beats you to the ball and heads it into the goal.

Correction

Move toward the ball, jump early, and catch the ball at the highest point of your jump. Thrust your arms and takeoff leg up in one fluid motion.

Receiving High Balls and Crosses
Drill 1. Collecting the High Ball

Toss a ball high in the air as you jog slowly across the field. Use a one-leg takeoff to jump up and catch the ball at the highest point of your jump. Toss and receive 40 high balls. Alternate using right- and left-leg takeoffs to jump up. Score 1 point for each high ball received with proper form at the highest possible point.

To Increase Difficulty

• Compete against a teammate who is also jumping to catch the same ball.

To Decrease Difficulty

• Rehearse the one-leg takeoff movement without catching a high ball.

• Don't leave the ground when receiving the ball.

Success Check

- Square shoulders and hips to the ball.
- Thrust arms and leg up in one smooth motion.
- Hold hands in the W position.
- Catch ball at highest point of jump.

Receiving High Balls and Crosses
Drill 2.   High Balls Side to Side

Set up three cones in the shape of a triangle, with approximately 8 yards between cones. The goalkeeper gets in position at the apex of the triangle. The server stands 10 yards in front of the base of the triangle, facing the goalkeeper. The server tosses or volleys a ball up into the air so that it drops near one of the cones at the base of the triangle. The goalkeeper moves forward, catches the ball at the highest possible point, and returns it to the server. The goalkeeper quickly backpedals to his or her starting point and repeats the drill. The goalkeeper receives 30 high balls, 15 to each base cone. Score 1 point for each high ball received using the proper technique.

To Increase Difficulty

- Add an opponent who contests the goalkeeper for the ball.

To Decrease Difficulty

- Rehearse the jumping movement without actually leaving the ground.

Check Your Success

- Use one-leg takeoff to jump.
- Thrust arms and outside leg up in one fluid motion.
- Keep inside leg straight.
- Extend arms with hands in W position.
- Receive ball on fingers and palms at highest point of jump.

Receiving High Balls and Crosses
Drill 3.   High-Ball Pressure Training

Four servers position an equal distance apart around the center circle of a regulation field; the goalkeeper positions in the center of the circle. Each server in turn tosses a high ball that drops near the center of the circle. The goalkeeper squares shoulders and hips to the ball, jumps up using the correct takeoff leg, and catches the ball at the highest possible point. Continue for 40 tosses. Goalkeeper alternates between left and right legs for takeoff. Score 1 point for each ball received with proper technique.

To Increase Difficulty

- Increase number of repetitions.
- Station two goalkeepers within the circle who compete for the high ball.

To Decrease Difficulty

- Reduce number of repetitions.
- Do not require the goalkeeper to leave the ground.

Success Check

- Use one-leg takeoff to jump.
- Point knee of takeoff leg toward ball.
- Extend arms and hands above head.
- Hold hands in W position.

21 points or fewer = 1 point

22 to 29 points = 2 points

30 to 35 points = 3 points

36 to 40 points = 5 points

Your score ___

Receiving High Balls and Crosses
Drill 4.   Catching Crosses

Set up two regulation-size goals opposite each other, one on the end line of the field and the other at the top edge of the penalty area. Two players (servers) get in position on each flank in the space between the edge of the penalty area and the touchline. Goalkeepers A and B take position in each goal. Goalkeeper A starts the drill by rolling a ball to one of the flank players. The flank player controls the ball and serves a cross to goalkeeper B. Goalkeeper B receives the ball at the highest possible point and distributes it to a flank player on the opposite side of the field. That player controls the ball and crosses it into the goal for goalkeeper A to collect and distribute. Continue until each goalkeeper has the opportunity to receive 30 crossed balls. Award 1 point for each cross successfully received and held using the proper technique.

To Increase Difficulty

- Station an attacking player in the goal area to contest the goalkeeper for the crossed ball.

To Decrease Difficulty

- Flank players toss soft crosses to the goalkeeper.

Check Your Success

- Square up with oncoming ball.
- Thrust arms and outside leg up in one fluid motion.
- Extend arms up with hands in W position.
- Use HEH principle; keep hands, eyes, head in line.
- Receive ball on fingers and palms at highest point of jump.
- Withdraw arms and hands.
- Secure ball to chest.

Score Your Success

0 to 19 points = 1 point.

20 to 24 points = 3 points.

25 to 30 points = 5 points.

Your score ___

Uncatchable High Balls

In most cases, you should attempt to catch a high ball or crossed ball. However, there are exceptions to every rule. For example, you may have difficulty gauging the flight of a ball that is dipping or swerving as it enters the goal area, adverse weather conditions may create doubt as to whether you will be able to hold the ball, or opposing players may aggressively challenge for the ball as you attempt to catch it. If you have any doubts about your ability to catch and hold the ball, it's best to choose safety first. Rather than trying to catch the ball, you can box, or punch, it away from the goalmouth. The decision whether to catch or box is a critical one that you must make swiftly and decisively. Choosing the wrong course of action can result in goals scored against you.

As a general rule, you should box the ball rather than catch it if one or more of the following conditions are present:

- The goalmouth is crowded with players and you do not have a clear path to the ball.

- There is a strong likelihood that you will collide with an opponent who is also challenging for the ball.

- You are knocked off balance as you jump up to receive the ball.

- The ball is hard to handle because of rain, snow, or sleet.

- Footing is poor and you are unsure whether you can get to the ball.

You can box the high ball with one or two hands. Your choice of technique depends on the angle of the ball's approach, your position in relation to the ball and opponents, and your degree of confidence in boxing.

Use the *two-fist boxing technique* when you can move directly toward the oncoming ball with shoulders square. The objective when boxing is to direct the ball away from the goalmouth toward a less dangerous scoring area. You accomplish this by sending the ball high, far, and wide toward a flank area of the field. Boxing the ball high into the air will give teammates precious moments to regroup and reorganize. Boxing the ball as far as possible reduces the likelihood of an opponent's volleying the ball back at the goal as it drops to the ground. Boxing the ball toward the flank area removes the ball from the dangerous scoring zone immediately front and center of the goal.

To execute the two-fist boxing technique (figure 6.9), form two solid fists with knuckles facing forward and thumbs on top. Position your hands side by side with wrists firm and arms held tightly against your sides. Elbows are bent at approximately 90 degrees. As the ball arrives, thrust your arms forward in unison using a short, compact, powerful movement. Keep your wrists firm and fists together, and contact the ball just below its horizontal midline. Box the ball at the highest possible point.

Figure 6.9　Two-Fist Boxing

PREPARATION

1. Square shoulders and hips to the ball
2. Position fists side by side with wrists firm
3. Bend elbows and hold them tightly to sides

EXECUTION

1. Extend arms toward the ball in a short, powerful movement
2. Keep fists together with wrists firm
3. Contact ball below its horizontal midline
4. Contact ball at highest possible point

FOLLOW-THROUGH

1. Follow through motion in the direction you want the ball to go
2. Box the ball high, far, and wide of the goal area

Misstep

The clearance lacks height and distance.

Correction

Generate maximum power by keeping your arms tight to your sides with elbows bent at 90 degrees. Thrust your arms and fists forward to meet the ball as it arrives. Use a short, compact extension of the arms rather than a looping movement.

A ball driven from the flank that travels across the goalmouth poses a different challenge. Because the ball is moving at a high velocity and is not coming directly at goal, it is easier to continue the ball's flight toward the opposite flank rather than trying to box it back in the direction it is coming from. In this situation, box the ball across your body using a *one-fist technique* (figure 6.10). A ball crossed from the opponent's right flank (your left) is boxed with the left hand to continue its flight toward the opponent's left flank (your right). A ball served from the opponent's left flank is boxed with the right hand toward the opponent's right flank. The boxing motion is short and compact. A powerful extension of the arm angled across your body will provide the greatest degree of control. Avoid a wide, looping-type arm motion. Keep the fist tight and wrist firm.

You also can use a slight variation of the one-fist boxing technique in those rare instances when you are caught off the goal line with a high ball dropping behind you. If you cannot backpedal and catch the ball cleanly, use the one-fist boxing technique to punch the ball over the crossbar and out of play. Take a deep drop step with the foot farthest from the ball, angle your body sideways to the ball, and box the ball over the bar with a short, powerful extension of the arm. When boxing a ball that is dropping over your left shoulder near the crossbar, take a drop step left and box across the body with the right hand. To box a ball dropping over your right shoulder, take a drop step right and box across the body with the left hand.

Figure 6.10 One-Fist Boxing

PREPARATION

1. Judge the flight of the ball
2. Form a solid fist with arm held against chest
3. Keep the head steady and vision focused on ball

EXECUTION

1. Step toward ball
2. Punch ball toward opposite flank with short, compact extension of arm across chest
3. Keep wrist firm

FOLLOW-THROUGH

1. Direct ball toward opposite flank with follow-through motion of arm

Misstep

You box the ball straight up into the air.

Correction

Box the ball across your body to keep it traveling toward the opposite flank. The boxing motion should be compact and powerful.

There is an alternative method that you can use to handle a high ball dropping behind you. In many cases, the *open-palm technique* (figure 6.11) is actually preferable to one-fist boxing because it provides a greater degree of control. Rather than boxing with your fist, simply guide the ball over the crossbar with your open hand. This is commonly referred to as turning or palming the ball over the bar.

Begin by executing a drop step with the foot farthest from the ball. For example, do a drop step with the left foot when preparing to palm a ball crossed from your right side (the opponent's left) that is dropping over your left shoulder. As the ball arrives, extend your right arm and hand up and across your body to guide the ball over the crossbar. After turning the ball over the bar, rotate your body to face the ground as you fall. Arms and hands contact the ground first. Tuck your shoulder and roll to further cushion the impact.

Figure 6.11 — Palming With One Hand

PREPARATION

1. Judge flight of ball
2. Do a drop step with foot farthest from ball
3. Turn body sideways to ball

EXECUTION

1. Extend arm up and across body
2. Guide ball over bar with palm of hand
3. Watch the ball travel over crossbar

FOLLOW-THROUGH

1. Rotate body to face ground
2. Tuck shoulder to roll as you contact ground

Misstep

You slap at the ball and it drops behind you into the goal.

Correction

You should virtually carry the ball over the bar with your palm and fingers. Don't slap it.

Handling Uncatchable High Balls
Drill 1. Two-Fist Boxing

Goalkeepers A, B, and C get in position in line, about 6 yards apart. Goalkeeper A kneels and faces B and C, who are standing. Goalkeeper B, stationed between A and C, has the ball to begin. Goalkeeper B tosses a high ball toward A. Goalkeeper A, while kneeling, uses a two-fist technique to box the ball over B's head to C. Goalkeeper A performs 15 repetitions, then players rotate positions and repeat. Keep track of the number of balls boxed directly to the target.

To Increase Difficulty

• Increase distance between goalkeepers.

To Decrease Difficulty

• Decrease distance between goalkeepers.

Success Check

• Position fists side by side.
• Hold elbows tight to sides.
• Extend arms in a short, powerful motion.
• Contact ball below its horizontal midline.
• Follow through in the direction you want the ball to go.

Score Your Success

0 to 9 balls boxed directly to target = 1 point

10 to 13 balls boxed directly to target = 3 points

14 to 15 balls boxed directly to target = 5 points

Your score ___

Handling Uncatchable High Balls
Drill 2. One-Fist Boxing

Goalkeepers A, B, and C get in position in line, 8 yards from each other. Goalkeeper B, stationed between A and C, kneels sideways to A and C. Goalkeeper A begins the drill by tossing a ball about 2 feet above B's head. Goalkeeper B continues the flight of the ball to goalkeeper C by boxing the ball across his or her body. Goalkeeper C catches the ball and tosses it back at B, who continues the ball's flight to A by boxing it across the body with the opposite arm. Goalkeeper B boxes 20 tosses (10 with each fist), after which players rotate positions and repeat. Keep track of the number of balls boxed directly to the target. (Note: It's important that the serves be accurate.)

To Increase Difficulty

• Increase distance between goalkeepers.
• Box from a standing position.
• Increase speed or number of repetitions.

To Decrease Difficulty

• Reduce distance between players to 5 yards.

Success Check

• Use short, compact extension of the arm across chest.
• Keep wrist firm.
• Contact underside of ball.
• Follow through to continue the ball's flight.

Score Your Success

0 to 10 balls boxed directly to target = 1 point

11 to 15 balls boxed directly to target = 3 points

16 to 20 balls boxed directly to target = 5 points

Your score ___

Handling Uncatchable High Balls
Drill 3. Two-Fist Boxing Over an Opponent

Two pairs of goalkeepers (A and B, C and D) participate in this drill. Goalkeepers A and B stand between C and D, who get in position 15 yards apart and act as servers. Each server has a ball. Goalkeeper A stands about 1 yard directly behind B. Both players face C to begin. Goalkeeper C tosses a high ball toward A who steps forward, jumps vertically upward above B (stationary obstacle), and boxes the ball back to C. Goalkeepers A and B then turn and face D, who serves a high ball to B. Goalkeeper B jumps upward and boxes the ball over A and back to D. Each goalkeeper performs 15 repetitions, after which A and B switch positions with the servers and repeat the drill. Keep track of the number of serves boxed directly to the target. Serves should be of sufficient height to allow the goalkeeper an opportunity to time his or her approach, jump up, and box the ball.

To Increase Difficulty

- Box as many balls as possible in 60 seconds.

To Decrease Difficulty

- Do not require keeper to box over an opponent.

Success Check

- Put fists together to form solid block.
- Extend arms in short, powerful motion.
- Contact lower half of ball.
- Follow through toward target.

Score Your Success

0 to 9 balls boxed directly to target = 1 point

10 to 12 balls boxed directly to target = 3 points

13 to 15 balls boxed directly to target = 5 points

Your score ____

DIVING TO SAVE

Diving (figure 6.12) is probably the most acrobatic of all goalkeeping skills. It's used in situations where you must leave your feet and propel your body sideways through the air to make the save. The initial movement begins from the ready position. Step in the direction of the dive with the foot nearest the ball, and then push off that foot to initiate the dive. For example, step sideways and push off your right foot when diving to your right. The opposite leg and arm follow to generate additional momentum in the direction of the dive. Extend both arms toward the ball with hands in a sideways version of the W position. Receive the ball on your fingertips and palms with the lower hand behind the ball and elbow tucked to your side. Contact the ground on your side, not your belly.

You must avoid giving up rebounds in the goal area. If you are unsure about being able to hold the ball at the completion of your dive, follow this basic rule of goalkeeping: *When in doubt, parry it out.* Rather than try to catch the ball in your hands, simply parry past the goalpost. To parry the ball wide of the goal, deflect it with the open palm of your lower hand. Angle your hand slightly back with the wrist firm. Contact the inside half of the ball.

Figure 6.12 Diving to Save

PREPARATION

1. Begin in the ready position
2. Step sideways with the foot nearest the ball

EXECUTION

1. Vault toward ball
2. Thrust opposite arm and leg in direction of dive
3. Extend arms and hands toward ball
4. Position hands in sideways W
5. Receive ball on fingertips and palms

FOLLOW-THROUGH

1. Ball contacts ground first, then forearm, shoulder, hip, and finally legs
2. Regain footing and distribute the ball

Misstep

You dive flat on your belly.

Correction

Contacting the ground on your side will protect your lower back from a rushing opponent and will enable you to receive the ball using the HEH (hand-eyes-head) principle.

Diving Drill 1. Diving From Knees

Kneel on both knees with a ball placed within reach to each side. Fall sideways and pin the stationary ball to the ground. Emphasize the correct diving form. Contact the ground on your side while placing one hand behind the ball and one on top to pin it to the ground. Repeat 10 times to each side.

To Increase Difficulty

• Move balls farther away.

• Increase number of repetitions.
• Increase speed of repetitions.
• Dive from a squat position.

To Decrease Difficulty

• Decrease number of repetitions.

Success Check

• Tuck elbow of lower arm to side.

- Contact ground on side and hip.
- Pin ball with one hand on top of the ball and one behind.

Score Your Success

14 or fewer dives using correct form = 1 point

15 to 18 dives using correct form = 2 points

19 or 20 dives using correct form = 3 points

Your score ___

Diving Drill 2. Dive to Save a Rolling Ball

Stand in the ready position facing a server who is 8 yards away. The server rolls a ball 3 to 4 yards to your side. Dive sideways to pin the ball, jump to your feet, and return the ball to the server. Repeat the drill to the opposite side. Attempt 10 saves to each side. As a variation, have the server toss the ball at waist height. (Note: Perform this drill on a soft field surface.)

To Increase Difficulty

- Increase velocity of serves.
- Increase speed of repetitions.
- Increase number of repetitions.

To Decrease Difficulty

- Reduce distance of dive.

Success Check

- Step sideways with foot nearest ball.
- Vault toward the ball.
- Extend arms and hands.
- Contact ground on side.
- Pin ball to ground.

Score Your Success

0 to 14 successful dives = 1 point

15 to 17 successful dives = 3 points

18 to 20 successful dives = 5 points

Your score ___

Diving Drill 3. Flying Side to Side

Begin in a squat position facing a server 8 yards away. The server tosses a chest-high ball 3 to 4 yards to your side. Step toward the ball, vault through the air, and make the save. The ball should contact the ground first, followed by your forearms, shoulders, hips, and legs. Quickly jump to your feet and return the ball to the server. Repeat dive to the other side. Repeat the exercise at maximum speed for 30 seconds, then rest for 30 seconds, then repeat again.

To Increase Difficulty

- To the goalkeeper's side, place an obstacle (ball, cone, small hurdle) that the goalkeeper must dive over to save the ball.

To Decrease Difficulty

- Reduce the diving distance.

Success Check

- Step sideways toward the ball.
- Thrust opposite arm and leg in direction of dive.
- Extend arms and hands.
- Position hands in sideways W.
- Receive ball on fingertips and palms.

Score Your Success

Fail to hold all tosses = 3 points

Hold all tosses = 5 points

Your score ___

Diving Drill 4. Keeper Wars

Set up two full-size goals 20 yards apart. Station a goalkeeper in each goal. One goalkeeper has the ball to begin. Goalkeepers alternate turns trying to score on one another. The shooting goalkeeper may take three steps forward from his or her goal before releasing the shot. The defending goalkeeper may advance off the line to narrow the shooting angle. Award 2 points for a ball saved and held without rebound, 1 point for a shot saved but not held. Play to a predetermined number of points or a time limit.

To Increase Difficulty

- Reduce the shooting distance.

To Decrease Difficulty

- Increase the shooting distance.
- Decrease width of goal.

Success Check

- Begin in ready position.
- Move forward of goal line to narrow the shooting angle.
- Initiate dive toward ball.
- Extend arms and hands toward ball.
- Receive ball on fingertips and palms.
- Ball contacts ground first followed by forearm, shoulder, hip, and legs.
- Parry wide of the goal if you can't hold the ball.

Score Your Success

Losing goalkeeper = 1 point

Winning goalkeeper = 3 points

Your score ___

DISTRIBUTING THE BALL

Once the ball is secured, you must initiate your team's attack by quickly distributing the ball to a teammate. You can do this by rolling, throwing, or kicking the ball. The rolling technique is generally used to release the ball to a nearby teammate who is not under immediate pressure from an opponent. Throwing is an effective means of distributing the ball over greater distances, typically to teammates positioned in the middle third of the field or in flank areas along the touchlines. Kicking is the optimal choice when the objective is to quickly send the ball down the field into the opponent's half. In most cases, a goalkeeper who distributes the ball by kicking will sacrifice accuracy for greater distance.

Rolling

Rolling, or bowling, the ball is an effective way to distribute the ball accurately over a short distance. After making the save, you initiate an immediate counterattack by rolling the ball to a nearby teammate. Cup the ball in the palm of your hand, step toward the target, and release the ball with a bowling-type motion (figure 6.13). Release the ball at ground level to prevent bouncing.

Figure 6.13 | Rolling the Ball

PREPARATION

1. Square shoulders to target
2. Hold ball securely in hands
3. Choose your target

EXECUTION

1. Cup ball in palm of hand
2. Draw back arm and ball
3. Step toward target with leg opposite throwing arm

FOLLOW-THROUGH

1. Release ball at ground level with bowling-type motion
2. Follow through with arm toward target
3. Resume erect posture

Misstep

Ball bounces toward the target.

Correction

Release the ball at ground level with a smooth motion.

Throwing

You can distribute the ball over longer distances by throwing or kicking it. Throwing has the advantage of greater accuracy and quicker delivery. Use the *baseball throw* (figure 6.14) to distribute the ball over distances of 20 to 35 yards. Hold the ball in the palm of the hand next to your ear. Step toward the target and use a three-quarter or overhand throwing motion to release the ball. Snap your wrist toward the target to add velocity to the throw.

Figure 6.14 | Baseball Throw

1. Face the target
2. Hold ball in palm of hand
3. Cock arm behind ear
4. Step toward target with foot opposite throwing arm
5. Using three-quarter throwing motion, snap wrist toward target
6. Follow through toward target, momentum moving forward

Use the *javelin throw* (figure 6.15) to deliver the ball over distances of 40 yards or greater. Curl your hand around the ball, encasing it with the fingers, palm, and wrist. Bring the throwing arm back with the ball at approximately waist level. Arch back, step toward the target, and snap your upper body forward from the waist.

The throwing motion moves along an upward arc and ends with a whiplike action above your head. You can release the ball at any point along the throwing arc. The sooner you release the ball along the throwing arc, the higher the trajectory.

Figure 6.15 | Javelin Throw

1. Encase ball in fingers, palm, and wrist
2. Bring back throwing arm
3. Point opposite arm toward target
4. Arch upper body back
5. Hold ball at waist level
6. Step toward target with foot opposite throwing arm
7. Whip throwing arm along upward arc, releasing ball
8. Follow through with the throwing arm, momentum moving forward

Misstep

Throw is inaccurate.

Correction

Step toward the target. When using the baseball throw, snap your wrist toward the target as you release the ball. When using the javelin throw, point your nonthrowing arm toward the target as you prepare to deliver the ball. The follow-through motion should be directed at the target.

Misstep

Throw lacks distance.

Correction

When executing the baseball throw, use a complete follow-through motion of the throwing arm. When using the javelin throw, fully extend the throwing arm behind and employ a whiplike motion of the arm along an upward arc to propel the ball toward the target. Generate momentum forward toward target.

Kicking

Kicking is a less accurate means of distribution than throwing, but it is a viable option if your objective is to deliver the ball quickly into the opponent's end of the field. Kicking is also a good choice in adverse weather conditions. By immediately sending the ball far down the field, you eliminate the risk of possession loss in your end of the field. The most common kicking techniques used for distributing the ball are the full-volley punt and dropkick.

For the *full-volley punt* (figure 6.16), hold the ball in the palm of the hand opposite the kicking foot. Extend the arm forward with the ball held at approximately waist level. Step forward with the nonkicking foot, release the ball, and volley it directly out of the air. Square shoulders and hips to the target and contact the center of the ball with the instep. Keep the kicking foot fully extended and firmly positioned. Use a complete follow-through motion of the kicking leg to generate distance and height on the punt.

Figure 6.16 Full-Volley Punt

1. Keep head steady and vision on ball
2. Step toward the target with nonkicking foot and release the ball
3. Swing kicking leg forward and drive instep through lower half of ball
4. Keep foot extended and firm
5. Square shoulders and hips to the target
6. Follow through to waist level or higher

The *dropkick* (figure 6.17), or half volley, is a good choice on windy days because the ball's trajectory is generally lower than that of a full-volley punt. A lower trajectory means the ball's flight path will not be affected as much by swirling and gusty winds. The lower trajectory also will make it easier for teammates to receive and control the ball. The kicking mechanics for a dropkick are similar to a full volley except that the ball is kicked just as it hits the ground rather than directly out of the air. Hold the ball in the palm of the hand opposite the kicking foot with the arm fully extended. Step forward and release the ball. Drive the instep of the kicking foot through the ball the moment the ball contacts the ground. Square your shoulders and hips to the target as your foot contacts the ball.

Figure 6.17 Dropkick

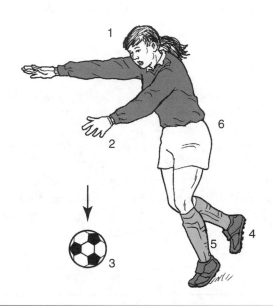

1. Face the target
2. Extend arm opposite the kicking foot with ball in palm of hand
3. Lean forward, step toward the target, and release the ball
4. Drive instep through center of ball the moment the ball hits the ground
5. Keep kicking foot extended and firm
6. Square hips and shoulders to target
7. Bring momentum forward through point of contact
8. Follow through to waist level or higher

Misstep

The punt or dropkick angles to the right or left of the target.

Correction

Square shoulders and hips to the target as you kick the ball. Contact the center of the ball with the full instep.

Misstep

The punt or dropkick lacks distance.

Correction

Keep the kicking foot firm as it contacts the ball. Use a complete follow-through motion of kicking leg to waist level or higher.

Keeper Distribution Drill 1. Toss to the Target

Play on one-half of a regulation-size field. Four servers, each with a ball, stand at various distances from the goal. Three additional players, designated as targets, take positions at various distances from the goal. A goalkeeper stands in goal. Servers alternate turns kicking a ball into the goal area for the goalkeeper to receive and control. After collecting the ball, the goalkeeper immediately distributes the ball by throwing it to one of the designated targets who change location (distance from goal) and position with every repetition. The goalkeeper chooses the method of distribution appropriate for the distance the ball must travel:

- Roll the ball when the target is 15 to 20 yards from goal.
- Use a baseball throw when the target is 25 to 40 yards from goal.
- Use a javelin throw when the target is 45 yards or more from goal.

A throw is considered accurate if the target does not have to move more than three steps in any direction to receive the ball. Perform 15 repetitions of each type of throw. Award 1 point for each accurate toss for a maximum total of 45 points.

To Increase Difficulty

- Define an accurate throw as one that drops within two steps of the target player.

To Decrease Difficulty

- Define an accurate throw as one that drops within five steps of the target player.

Success Check

- Step toward target.
- Use appropriate throwing technique.
- Use complete follow-through motion.

Score Your Success

0 to 24 points = 0 points

25 to 29 points = 1 point

30 to 34 points = 3 points

35 to 45 points = 5 points

Your score ___

Keeper Distribution Drill 2. Kick to the Target

Get in position within the penalty area with a supply of balls. Attempt to punt (volley) or half-volley the ball so that it lands within the center circle of the field. Score 2 points for each ball that drops within the circle on the fly and 1 point for a ball that bounces into the circle. Execute 20 volley punts and 20 half-volley punts. Keep track of points scored.

To Increase Difficulty

- Decrease size of target area.
- Increase distance to target area.

To Decrease Difficulty

- Increase size of target area.

Success Check

- Square shoulders to target.
- Extend arms with ball held at approximately waist height.
- Keep head steady and vision on ball.
- Contact ball through its center.
- Follow through toward the target.

Score Your Success

0 to 39 points = 0 points

40 to 49 points = 1 point

50 to 59 points = 3 points

60 to 80 points = 5 points

Your score ___

Keeper Distribution Drill 3. Distribution Circuit

Goalkeepers A, B, C, and D get in position at various locations on the playing field. Goalkeeper A stands in one penalty area. Goalkeeper B assumes a position on the flank outside the penalty area near the touchline. Goalkeeper C gets in position within the center circle, and goalkeeper D stands in the opposite penalty area. The drill begins as goalkeeper A distributes the ball to B by rolling it. Goalkeeper B receives the ball and delivers it to C using the baseball throw. Goalkeeper C receives the ball and delivers it to D using the javelin throw. Goalkeeper D completes the circuit by returning the ball to A via a dropkick or punt. Repeat the circuit 5 times, after which goalkeepers rotate positions and repeat the drill. Continue the drill until each keeper has performed five repetitions of each distribution technique for a total of 20 attempts. Award 1 point for each repetition performed with correct technique.

To Increase Difficulty

- Require keeper to distribute the ball to moving targets.

To Decrease Difficulty

- Reduce distance to targets.

Check Your Success

- Step toward target.
- Use appropriate throwing or kicking technique.
- Use complete follow-through motion.

Score Your Success

14 points or fewer scored = 1 point

15 to 17 points scored = 2 points

18 to 20 points scored = 3 points

Your score ___

SUCCESS SUMMARY OF GOALKEEPING

If you are new to the goalkeeper position, you should begin by slowly rehearsing each technique until you feel comfortable with the movements. As you gain confidence, increase the speed and intensity of your training. Eventually you will be able to progress to more challenging game-simulation situations. If you are really serious about becoming a top goalkeeper, I recommend that you read *The Soccer Goalkeeper, Third Edition* (Luxbacher 2002). This book provides an in-depth analysis of the skills and tactics used by the number one player on the soccer field.

Each of the drills described in step 6 has been assigned a point value to help you evaluate your performance and chart your progress. Record your score in the following chart. Total your points to get an estimate of your overall mastery of goalkeeping skills.

Receiving Ground Balls

1. Standing Save Drill _____ out of 5

2. Scoop Save and Change Lines _____ out of 5

3. Saving the Tweener Ball _____ out of 5

4. Forward Vault to Save _____ out of 5

5. Collecting Through Balls _____ out of 5

6. Ground Ball Keeper Wars _____ out of 2

Receiving Medium-High Shots

1. Pingers With Partner _____ out of 5

2. Save, Turn, and Save Again _____ out of 5

3. Collecting Medium-High Balls _____ out of 5

Receiving Chest- and Head-High Shots

1. The W Catch _____ out of 5

2. Toss and Catch Using HEH _____ out of 3

3. Catching Chest- and Head-High Balls _____ out of 5

Receiving High Balls and Crosses

1. Collecting the High Ball _____ out of 5

2. High Balls Side to Side _____ out of 5

3. High-Ball Pressure Training _____ out of 5

4. Catching Crosses _____ out of 5

Handling Uncatchable High Balls

1. Two-Fist Boxing _____ out of 5

2. One-Fist Boxing _____ out of 5

3. Two-Fist Boxing Over an Opponent _____ out of 5

Diving

1. Diving From Knees _____ out of 3

2. Dive to Save a Rolling Ball _____ out of 5

3. Flying Side to Side _____ out of 5

4. Keeper Wars _____ out of 3

(continued)

(continued)

Keeper Distribution

1. Toss to the Target   _____ out of 5

2. Kick to the Target   _____ out of 5

3. Distribution Circuit   _____ out of 3

Total   _____ **out of 119**

A combined score of 100 points or greater indicates that you have achieved competency in performing fundamental goalkeeping skills and are prepared to move on to step 7. A score in the range of 80 to 99 is considered adequate, but you still need to polish up some of the techniques. Before moving on, review the skills that are giving you the most difficulty. A score of 79 points or fewer suggests that you have not sufficiently mastered the goalkeeping skills described in step 6. Rehearse and practice each of the skills several more times before moving on to step 7. (Note: If you are primarily a field player, feel free to move on to step 7 at your discretion. You need not master all of the goalkeeping skills.)

Winning One-on-One Matchups

A soccer game is 90 minutes of flowing action, an interconnected series of constantly changing situations, each lasting only a few moments before evolving into something new and different. Your ability to do the right thing, to choose the most appropriate action in a given situation, will in large part determine your performance on the soccer pitch. In short, you must be able to read each situation and react accordingly. The ability to make good decisions swiftly and consistently is referred to as *tactical speed*. All elite players and elite teams demonstrate a high level of tactical speed.

You can improve your ability to read the game by developing a thorough understanding of the tactical principles on which players' actions are based. Soccer tactics provide a frame of reference for decision making, problem solving, and playing cooperatively with teammates. Tactics are applied on three levels: individual, group, and team. Individual tactics deal with the principles of attack and defense applicable in one-on-one (1v1) situations. Group tactics involve two or more players (2v1, 2v2, 3v2, and so on) working in combination. Team tactics are applied to the group as a whole with the ultimate goal of maximizing team performance above and beyond the ability of the individual players.

To improve tactical speed, it is best to start with the most fundamental tactical unit, the individual player. Although soccer is in the purest sense a team game, virtually every situation in some manner or another involves a one-on-one matchup—the player with the ball versus the opponent who is responsible for defending against him or her. It is not uncommon to hear coaches say, "We lost the game because we lost the majority of the one-on-ones," and that observation is very true. These minicompetitions waged between opposing players are links in the chain of events that collectively determine the outcome of the game. Step 7 provides information that will improve your ability to win the one-on-one matchup.

INDIVIDUAL ATTACK TACTICS

There are no offensive or defensive specialists in soccer. All players, including the goalkeeper, must be prepared to defend when the opponents have the ball and contribute to the attack when their team has the ball. More important, players must be willing and able to make an immediate transition from one role to the other.

In our discussion of soccer tactics we will speak of the first, second, and third attacker and the first, second, and third defender. Individual tactics deal primarily with the first attacker and the first defender. The player with the ball, the first attacker, is the focal point of individual attack tactics. When in the role of first attacker, you should base your decisions and subsequent actions on the following guidelines.

Maintain Possession of the Ball

It's pretty simple. Your team cannot score without the ball. Likewise, the opposing team cannot score when your team has the ball. So the first order of business is to maintain possession of the ball once you have it. Use the dribbling and shielding skills discussed in step 1 to protect the ball from opponents trying to steal it from you (figure 7.1).

Figure 7.1 Protect the ball by positioning your body between the ball and the opponent.

Turn to Face the Opponent's Goal

Simply retaining possession of the ball won't necessarily result in goals scored. The advantage still lies with the defending team as long as you are facing your own goal and not in a position to penetrate with the ball. Shift the advantage to your favor by turning with the ball to face the opponent's goal, a position from which you can penetrate the opposing defense by dribbling, passing, or shooting. Before attempting to turn with the ball, you must first separate from the defender who is marking you.

In soccer an important equation always holds true: *Space equals time*. That is, the more space you can create between yourself and the opponent marking you, the more time you will have to maneuver with the ball and make plays. In essence, you automatically become a better player simply by creating more space and time for yourself.

You can lose a marking defender through the use of *body feints*. Body feints are deceptive body and foot movements designed to mislead, or unbalance, an opponent. A slight dip of the shoulder or a quick step over the ball may be all you need to get your opponent leaning the wrong way (figure 7.2). Sudden changes of speed and direction can also create distance between you and the defender.

Penetrate With the Ball

The next step is to penetrate the opposing defense via the pass or dribble. When doing so, consider your location on the field, the risk of losing possession versus the potential reward of penetrating that area, and your technical strengths and weaknesses.

Practice safety first when in your defending half of the field, an area where possession loss can be very costly. Passing the ball forward to a teammate stationed in a more advanced position is the optimal choice of penetration when you're positioned in your own half. Even if the pass is cut off, your team will still have a sufficient number of players behind the ball to thwart

Figure 7.2 Body feints are one way to create space for yourself: *(a)* step over the ball; *(b)* dribble away with the outside of the other foot.

an immediate counterattack by the opponents. Conversely, loss of possession on the dribble in your own half of the field may prove more costly because many of your teammates will already be ahead of the ball, a situation that provides the opposing team an opportunity to mount an immediate attack on your goal.

Penetration by dribbling is used to best advantage in the attacking third of the field nearest the opponent's goal. The risk of possession loss in this area is overshadowed by the potential reward of bypassing a defender to create a scoring opportunity. When on the dribble, take the most direct route toward the goal, an action that

will draw the first defender (nearest defender) to you. This tactic is commonly referred to as *taking on* or *committing* the defender; it forces that player to either step forward to tackle the ball from you or withdraw to delay your forward movement. If the defender commits to the tackle, it may open up passing lanes to teammates in more forward positions, or it may provide an opportunity for you to dribble past the defender to create a numbers-up situation (numerical advantage) on the attack. Once you have beaten a defender on the dribble, continue at speed directly at the goal. You should never have to pass the same defender twice.

Misstep

The defender kicks the ball away as you attempt to turn.

Correction

Separate yourself from the marking defender before attempting to turn with the ball. Use body feints coupled with sudden changes of speed and direction to create space in which to execute a spin turn.

Misstep

You are indecisive in your actions and fail to attack the defense.

Correction

Once you have turned with the ball, dribble immediately toward goal to commit the nearest defender. Depending on the situation, you can then penetrate by passing to a teammate in a more forward position or by dribbling past the defender.

Individual Attack Drill 1. One-on-One Possession

Play one-on-one within a 10- by 20-yard area. You begin with the ball. Try to keep the ball from your opponent through close control of the ball coupled with sudden changes of speed and direction. Play for 30 seconds, rest for 30 seconds, and repeat. Score 1 point each time you can maintain possession of the ball for a 30-second round. Play 10 rounds as the attacker, then switch roles and play 10 rounds as the defender.

To Increase Difficulty

- Add a second defender to the drill.
- Decrease size of playing area.

To Decrease Difficulty

- Score 1 point for a 15-second possession time.

- Increase size of playing area.

Success Check

- Position body to shield the ball.
- Maintain space between ball and defender.
- Use sudden changes of speed and direction.
- Use deceptive body feints.

Score Your Success

0 to 3 points = 1 point

4 to 6 points = 3 points

7 to 10 points = 5 points

Your score ____

Individual Attack Drill 2. Turn on the Defender

Form two teams (A and B) of two players each. Play within a 10- by 20-yard field area. One player from each team acts as a target. Targets, each with a ball, get in position on opposite end lines while their partners take positions in the middle of the field area. Target A begins by passing the ball to his or her teammate, who attempts to turn and play the ball forward to target B. The middle player on team B attempts to prevent the turn and deny penetration via the pass or dribble. The middle player for team A scores 1 point for turning with the ball to face the defender and 1 additional point for playing the ball accurately to target B. The middle player has 15 seconds once he or she receives the ball to turn and play the ball to the opposite target. After a score or 15 seconds, whichever comes first, the round ends, and target B serves a ball to his or her teammate. Each middle player plays 10 rounds as the attacker for a maximum possible total of 20 points.

To Increase Difficulty

- Reduce size of playing area to limit attacking space.

- Allow only 10 seconds to turn and penetrate opposite end line.

To Decrease Difficulty

- Reduce the number of rounds.

Success Check

- Check to the ball.
- Receive and shield the ball from the defender.
- Create separation from the marking defender.
- Turn and take on the defender.

Score Your Success

0 to 7 points as attacker = 1 point

8 to 11 points as attacker = 3 points

12 to 20 points as attacker = 5 points

Your score ____

Individual Attack
Drill 3.   Penetrate a Layered Defense

Four players participate in this drill. Use markers to divide a 10- by 40-yard area into four consecutive 10- by 10-yard zones. One player (the attacker) gets in position with the ball in zone 1; the remaining players (the defenders) get in position on the end lines of zones 2, 3, and 4, respectively. On command, the attacker attempts to dribble the length of the field from zone 1 through zone 4. To score 1 point, the attacker must dribble past the defender in a zone while staying within the side boundaries of the area. Defenders are restricted to movement within their assigned zone. If the attacker dribbles past the defender in a zone, the attacker continues forward to take on the defender in the next zone. If a defender tackles the ball, he or she immediately returns it to the attacker, who then continues forward to take on the defender in the next zone. Award 1 point for each defender beaten, for a possible total of 3 points per round. After taking on the defender in zone 4, the attacker remains there to play as a defender for the next round. Each of the original defenders moves forward one zone. The player who moves into zone 1 becomes the attacker for round 2. Continue until each person has played

5 rounds as the attacker, for a maximum possible total of 15 points per player. The player with the most points wins the game.

To Increase Difficulty

- Reduce width of field to 5 yards.

To Decrease Difficulty

- Widen field to 15 yards.

Success Check

- Attack (dribble at) the defender at speed.
- Use deceptive body feints to unbalance defender.
- Employ sudden changes of speed to accelerate past the defender.

Score Your Success

4 points or fewer = 1 point

5 to 9 points = 3 points

10 to 15 points = 5 points

Your score ____

Individual Attack
Drill 4.   One-on-One to a Central Goal

Play one-on-one within a 20- by 20-yard area. Place flags 3 yards apart near the center of the area to represent a common goal. You begin with possession of the ball; your opponent plays as the defender. The objective is to beat your opponent and pass or dribble the ball through either side of the central goal. Award yourself 1 point for each goal scored. Change of possession occurs when the defender steals the ball, when the ball travels outside of the area, and when a goal is scored. Players alternate from attack to defense with each change of possession. Play two 5-minute halves with a short rest between. The player scoring the most points wins the game.

To Increase Difficulty for Attacker

- Decrease width of goal to 2 yards.

To Decrease Difficulty for Attacker

- Increase width of goal to 4 yards.

Success Check

- Protect the ball from the defender.
- Turn with ball when possible.
- Take on defender via pass or dribble.

Score Your Success

Lose the game = 0 points

Win the game = 3 points

Your score ____

Individual Attack Drill 5. Four-Goal Game

Use markers to outline a 25- by 25-yard field area. Position flags to represent a 3-yard-wide goal at the midpoint of each sideline. Form two teams of four players each; number players on each team 1 through 4. Teams take positions on opposite sidelines. To begin, the coach calls a number (for example, 2) and kicks a ball into the field. The number 2 players from each team sprint into the area to compete one-on-one. The player who wins the ball can score by dribbling through any of the four goals; the other player defends. Player roles reverse on change of possession. After each score, or when the ball goes out of the area, the coach immediately kicks another ball into the field area. Play continuously for 60 seconds, after which the coach signals a different pair into the square. Play a total of 15 minutes (3 rounds for each pair) and keep track of goals scored by each player.

To Increase Difficulty

- Lengthen the round to 90 seconds.

- Station a neutral defender within the area who joins with the original defender to create a 1v2 situation.

To Decrease Difficulty

- Shorten round to 30 seconds.

Success Check

- Be first to the ball.
- Protect the ball and maintain possession.
- Use body feints to unbalance the defender.
- Be direct—attack the nearest goal.

Score Your Success

0 to 2 goals scored in 3 rounds = 1 point

3 goals or more scored in 3 rounds = 3 points

Your score ___

INDIVIDUAL DEFENSE TACTICS

Individual defense tactics apply to the defending player positioned nearest the opponent with the ball. This player, hereafter referred to as the *first defender,* is responsible for applying immediate pressure at the point of attack. Ultimately the first defender would hope to win the ball, but that is not his or her sole objective. The most important responsibility of the first defender is to delay the attack and deny penetration to provide teammates time to reorganize behind the ball. The temptation to immediately jump in on the tackle must be tempered by the fact that a miscalculation will leave the defender beaten and out of the play.

Top defenders always appear in complete control of their actions. They never look rushed or hurried, and they don't sell themselves by recklessly diving in at every opportunity to challenge for the ball. When the time is right, they commit to the tackle with power and determination. Your decisions on the soccer field will dictate your actions and obviously play a critical

role in your ability to defend in 1v1 situations. Making good decisions is an integral part of solid individual defensive play. When in the role of first defender, base your decisions and subsequent actions on the following general guidelines.

Assume Proper Marking Position

The first step in the process of regaining possession of the ball is to assume the correct starting position in relation to the opponent, the ball, and your goal. Always get in position *goal side* (that is, between the ball and the goal you are defending; see figure 7.3). From a goal-side position, you can keep both the ball and the opponent you are responsible for marking in view at all times. It's generally to your advantage to position slightly to the inside of the opponent, shading him or her toward the center of the field. From there you can shut off the attacker's most direct route to goal.

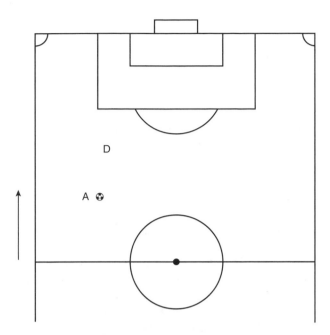

Figure 7.3 Goal-side position.

Determine Appropriate Marking Distance

How tight should you mark when defending one-on-one? There are several variables to consider. You must be close enough to prevent the attacker from turning with the ball to face you, but not so tight that he or she can spin off and dribble past.

As a general rule, take a position a step or two off the attacker with clear vision of the ball. If the attacker tries to turn, you can step in to tackle the ball. If you can prevent the turn and force the opponent to play the ball back or square, then you have done your job.

If the opponent you are marking does not have the ball, you must adjust your position

accordingly. In this situation, your starting position must enable you to be first to any pass slotted into the space in front of the opponent, but it must also allow you to challenge for the ball or intercept the pass should the ball be played directly to that player. As your opponent moves farther from the ball, you can afford to extend the marking distance (figure 7.4). If the ball is subsequently passed to that player, you can close the distance while the ball is in flight to challenge for the ball.

Also take into account the area of the field and the ability of the opponent. As a general rule, the closer the opponent is to your goal, the tighter the marking distance. An opponent within scoring range must be denied the space and time needed to release a shot or pass the ball forward.

Finally, an opponent who has great speed and quickness should be afforded a bit more space to prevent him or her from merely pushing the ball past and outracing you. Mark more tightly if the opponent is highly skilled but relatively slow. In that situation, you must deny the time and space required to use those skills to beat you.

Close Down the Space

Quickly reduce the distance between you and the opponent when you see that he or she is about to receive the ball. Ideally you should arrive at about the same moment as the ball or just before. If possible, angle your approach so as to limit the attacker's options. For example, you can funnel the opponent into space along a touchline or force him or her into the space occupied by a covering defender. In all cases you must maintain good balance and body control.

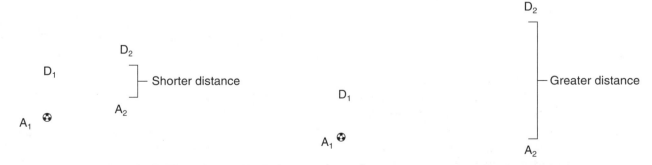

Figure 7.4 Marking distance: *(a)* support attacker close to the ball; *(b)* support attacker farther from the ball.

Slow your approach as you near the attacker, shorten your strides, and shift into a slightly crouched posture with knees bent (figure 7.5). Maintain a low center of gravity with weight centered over the balls of the feet. Assume a staggered stance, with feet a comfortable distance apart and one foot slightly forward of the other. Having your feet in the staggered position will eliminate the possibility of having the ball pushed between your legs, a dribbling maneuver commonly referred to as the *nutmeg.* You also will be able to respond quickly to the opponent's sudden changes of speed and direction.

Figure 7.5 Assume a defensive posture: bent knees, staggered stance, vision on the ball.

Prevent the Turn

Once an attacker turns with the ball to face your goal, his or her options dramatically increase. The greatest danger is that he or she will now be able to serve a penetrating pass into the space behind you or attempt to beat you on the dribble. That being the case, it's in your best interest to prevent an opponent who has his or her back to your goal from turning with the ball. The marking position should be relatively tight but not so close that the attacker can spin with the ball and roll off you. Get in position so that you have a clear view of the ball and are ready to step forward to tackle the ball if the opponent attempts to turn.

Jockey and Delay

If by chance the opponent successfully turns with the ball to face you, your immediate priority is to deny penetration. Try to jockey, or channel, the attacker into areas in which space is limited, such as toward the touchline or into a covering defender, or force him or her to pass the ball square or backward. If you can successfully deny or at least delay penetration, even for a few moments, then your teammates will have time to organize behind (on the goal side of) the ball.

Commit to the Tackle

Always be alert for an opportune moment to win the ball. Step forward quickly, and fully commit to the tackle if you sense that the attacker has allowed the ball to get too far from his or her feet. Use the tackling techniques described in step 1 to regain possession of the ball and go on the attack.

Misstep

The opponent turns with the ball to face your goal.

Correction

You must get in position at the appropriate distance to deny your opponent the space required for turning with the ball.

Misstep

You commit recklessly to the tackle and are beaten on the dribble.

Correction

Your first priority in a 1v1 situation is to prevent penetration, not necessarily win the ball. Get in position at an appropriate marking distance with feet in a staggered stance and weight evenly distributed. Challenge for the ball only when a teammate is covering the space immediately behind you or when you are extremely confident that you can successfully execute the tackle.

Individual Defense Drill 1.   Defend the End Line

Play on a 10- by 30-yard field area. Get in position on one end line as the defender; your opponent (attacker) stands on the opposite end line. The coach (server) begins play by kicking a ball to the attacker, who controls the ball and attempts to dribble the ball past you over your end line. Move forward quickly off the end line to close the distance to the ball. You score 1 point if you successfully tackle the ball or kick the ball out of the field area. After each round, return to your respective starting positions and repeat. Play 20 rounds as the defender, then switch roles and repeat.

To Increase Difficulty for Defender

- Increase width of field.

To Decrease Difficulty for Defender

- Decrease width of field to 5 yards.

Success Check

- Quickly close distance to attacker.
- Maintain balance and body control.
- Use a staggered defensive stance.
- Deny penetration.
- Tackle the ball.

Score Your Success

0 to 9 points = 1 point

10 to 14 points = 3 points

15 to 20 points = 5 points

Your score ____

Individual Defense Drill 2.   Deny the Turn

Six players participate in this drill. Four players stand an equal distance apart around the perimeter of the center circle, two in each half of the field. One player in each half (server) has a ball to begin; the other (target) does not. A single defender and an attacker are stationed within the circle.

The drill begins as one of the servers plays a ball to the attacker, who attempts to turn with the ball and play it to the target player positioned on the opposite half of the circle. The defender quickly closes the distance to the ball to prevent the turn and deny penetration. Play continues until the defender wins the ball or the attacker plays the ball to the target player. At this point, the second server plays a ball to the attacker, and the round is repeated in the opposite direction. Award the defender 1 point for each round in which he or she prevents the attacker from turning and playing the ball to the target player on the opposite side of the circle. Play a total of 10 rounds and keep track of points scored by the defender. Repeat until each player has taken a turn as the defender.

To Increase Difficulty for Defender

- Increase size of area.
- Position two attackers within the center circle.

To Decrease Difficulty (for Defender)

- Reduce size of area.

Success Check

- Assume goal-side position.
- Quickly close distance to ball to deny the turn.
- Maintain balance and body control.
- Deny penetration via the dribble or pass.
- Tackle the ball.

Score Your Success

0 to 3 points = 1 point

4 to 6 points = 2 points

7 to 10 points = 3 points

Your score ____

Individual Defense Drill 3.   The Gauntlet

Play with four to six teammates. Use markers to outline a rectangular field area of 15 by 30 yards with a 5-yard-deep safety zone at each end. Get in position in the center of the area as the lone defender. Your teammates (attackers), each with a ball, stand in a safety zone at one end of the field. On command, all attackers leave the safety zone and attempt to dribble past you into the safety zone at the opposite end of the field. You can prevent the dribblers from reaching the opposite safety zone by tackling the ball and kicking it outside of the field area. Award yourself 1 point for each time you tackle a ball or kick it out of the area. A dribbler whose ball is kicked out of the area quickly retrieves it and rejoins the game for the next round. Dribblers who reach the safety zone remain there until you give the command to return to the original safety zone. Repeat for 15 rounds and a maximum possible total of 15 points.

To Increase Difficulty for Defender

- Increase width of field.

To Decrease Difficulty for Defender

- Narrow the field.

Success Check

- Maintain balance and body control.
- Delay or deny penetration.
- Funnel the dribbler into tight spaces.
- Tackle with power and determination.

Score Your Success

0 to 7 points = 1 point

8 to 11 points = 2 points

12 to 15 points = 4 points

Your score ___

Individual Defense Drill 4.   One-on-One Marking Game

Form two teams of three players each. Use markers to outline a playing area of 25 by 40 yards with a goal 4 yards wide at the center of each end line. Each team defends a goal. Do not use goalkeepers. Begin with a kickoff from the center of the field. Require strict one-on-one marking of opponents. Regular soccer rules apply except that the offside law is waived. Because goalkeepers are not used and shots may be taken from anywhere on the field, marking must be very tight to prevent long-range goals. Change of possession occurs when a defending player steals the ball, when the ball goes out of play, or when a goal is scored. The team scoring the most goals wins the game.

To Increase Difficulty for Defending Players

- Increase width of field.
- Place three small goals on each end line to provide attackers with additional scoring options.

To Decrease Difficulty for Defending Players

- Reduce width of field.
- Reduce size of goal.

Success Check

- Maintain goal-side position.
- Keep knees bent and center of gravity low.
- Place feet in staggered position.
- Apply immediate pressure on attacker with the ball.
- Deny penetration via the pass or dribble.

Score Your Success

Member of losing team = 1 point

Member of winning team = 2 points

Your score ___

SUCCESS SUMMARY OF INDIVIDUAL TACTICS

Practicing one-on-one tactics is challenging and fun. The exercises are highly competitive and physically demanding, and they test your ability to execute skills and make decisions under gamelike conditions. Once you've sufficiently mastered the basics of individual attack and defense, get together with a group of teammates and organize a one-on-one tournament where each player plays a game against every other player. Keep tally of wins and losses to determine a tournament winner. Your coach can observe the tournament and analyze your performance.

Each of the drills provided in step 7 has been assigned a point value to help you evaluate your performance and measure progress. Record your scores in the following chart. Total your points to obtain an estimate of your overall level of success.

Individual Attack

    1. One-on-One Possession   _____ out of 5

    2. Turn on the Defender   _____ out of 5

    3. Penetrate a Layered Defense   _____ out of 5

    4. One-on-One to a Central Goal   _____ out of 3

    5. Four-Goal Game   _____ out of 3

Individual Defense

    1. Defend the End Line   _____ out of 5

    2. Deny the Turn   _____ out of 3

    3. The Gauntlet   _____ out of 4

    4. One-on-One Marking Game   _____ out of 2

Total   _____ *out of 35*

A combined score of 30 points or more suggests that you have mastered the fundamentals of individual attack and defense tactics. You are ready to move on to group tactics. A score in the range of 24 to 29 is considered adequate. You should review and rehearse the individual attack and defense tactics once again before moving on to step 8. If you scored 23 points or fewer, you have more work to do. Review the material once again and perform all the drills at least one more time. When you are confident and competent in your ability to execute individual tactics, you can move on to the next step.

Attacking As a Group

While the skills and individual tactics discussed thus far are essential for winning the one-on-one battles, the team as a whole will not experience success unless players can also combine their efforts toward a common goal. Much like the pieces of a puzzle, individual players must fit together in the correct combinations to complete the picture. When players are willing and able to work together, team performance can far exceed the collective efforts of individual performances. Ultimately that is the goal of all team sports, that the so-called whole (team) be greater than its individual parts (players). Conversely, when teammates cannot or will not work in combination, team performance will suffer regardless of how talented the players are.

Group attack tactics typically involve two or more players working together to maintain possession of the ball, penetrate the opposing defense, and create scoring opportunities. Step 7 discussed in depth the role of the first attacker, that being to penetrate the opposing defense via the pass or dribble. In most cases, the first attacker will need the help of teammates to accomplish that aim. That is where group tactics come into play.

Group attack involves the coordinated involvement of the first, second, and third attackers. The overriding goal of group attack tactics is to position more attacking players than defending players in the vicinity of the ball to create what is commonly referred to as a *numbers-up situation,* and then exploit that advantage through tactics that include support (depth), give-and-go (wall) passes, double passes, takeovers, and overlaps.

The second attacker's primary role is to provide immediate passing options, or *support,* for the player on the ball. He or she also plays an important role in executing the give-and-go pass, the double pass, and the takeover maneuvers. The third attacker's job is to provide passing options away from the ball, usually by making penetrating diagonal runs through the defense or overlapping runs behind the defense.

Successfully executing group attack tactics requires an understanding of each attacker's role in the specific tactic coupled with the ability to perform the requisite skills involved. An adequate level of technical ability (skill) is a prerequisite for tactical execution. At the end of the day it doesn't really matter that you know where to be, when to run, or how to perform a specific tactic if you are unable to pass, receive, dribble, and shoot the ball effectively. For that reason players must master the skills discussed in steps 1 through 5 before focusing their efforts on the tactical aspects of the game.

GROUP SUPPORT

Players in position off the ball are responsible for providing passing options for the player on the ball. This tactic, referred to as support, puts more attackers than defenders in the vicinity of the ball and thus increases the likelihood that the team will be able to maintain possession. Conversely, failure to provide adequate support will leave the first attacker isolated with few options, a situation that shifts the advantage to the defense. When determining when, where, and how to get in position for optimal support, consider the number of support players needed, the angle of support, and the distance of support.

Too few attacking players in the vicinity of the ball (a lack of support) will limit the first attacker's options, while too many can be a disadvantage because they draw additional defenders to the area. As the area around the ball becomes crowded with players, it becomes increasingly difficult to find the space and time required to develop passing combinations. As a general rule, three attacking players should provide close support to the first attacker, one player to each side and slightly ahead of the ball to provide width and the third support player behind the ball to provide depth (figure 8.1).

Imagine three lines drawn from the ball, one to each of the support players. The angle formed between any two support players and the ball should be 90 degrees or greater (figure 8.2). A single defending player cannot possibly cover two or more support players when they are positioned at wide angles, but the defending player may be able to do so if the support players are positioned at a narrow angle (less than 90 degrees) of support.

How close to the ball should support players be? Base your decision on the position of the defenders and the area of the field. As a general rule, position yourself within 3 to 4 yards of the ball when the first attacker is being challenged by an opponent, a situation in which he or she may have to release the ball quickly. Extend the distance of support, possibly to 8 to 10 yards, if a defender is not in position to challenge for the ball or if the space around the ball is not crowded with players. In all cases, you should maintain a clear passing lane to the ball.

Reduce the distance of support as the ball moves closer to the opponent's goal. The defending team usually will consolidate players in the dangerous scoring zone front and center of their goal. Tighter support in that area opens up the possibility of executing the give-and-go pass or takeover maneuver to penetrate a packed defense. The distance of support can be extended as the ball moves farther from the defending team's goal.

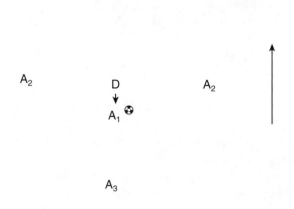

Figure 8.1 Support in attack. Attackers near the ball provide passing options for the player on the ball. A1 = player on the ball; A2 = support attackers; A3 = support behind the ball; D = defender.

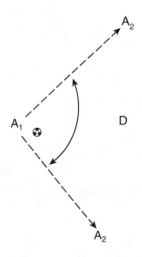

Figure 8.2 Wide angle of support.

Misstep

A single defender is able to shut off the passing lanes to two or more attackers.

Correction

Support players should form a wide angle (90 degrees or greater) from the ball so as to maintain open passing lanes to the ball. They should not get in position behind the defender or at a narrow angle in which the defender can intercept the pass.

Misstep

Support players fail to readjust position in response to the movement of the ball.

Correction

Soccer is a fluid game, and as such your position of support is in a state of constant flux. As the ball is passed from one attacker to another, the players providing support must adjust their positions accordingly.

Attacking Support
Drill 1. Triangular Possession (Three-on-One)

A single defender plays against three attackers within a 12- by 12-yard grid. The attackers try to keep the ball away from the defender within the boundaries of the grid. Attackers are unrestricted in their movement within the grid and are allowed unlimited touches to pass and receive the ball. The emphasis is on proper support movement and positioning of the second attackers. Award 1 point for eight or more consecutive passes without a loss of possession. Play continuously for 5 minutes.

To Increase Difficulty for Attackers

- Decrease size of grid.
- Limit attackers to two touches to receive and pass the ball.
- Add a defender to create a 3v2 situation.

To Decrease Difficulty for Attackers

- Increase size of grid.
- Add an attacker to create a 4v1 situation.

Success Check

- Get in position at wide angles of support.
- Prepare the ball with the first touch.
- Use the correct pace and accuracy of passes.

Score Your Success

0 to 3 points in 5 minutes = 1 point

4 to 6 points in 5 minutes = 2 points

7 points or more in 5 minutes = 4 points

Your score ___

Attacking Support Drill 2. Four-Sided Support Game

Eight players participate in this exercise. Use markers to outline a 25- by 25-yard playing area. A support player stands at the midpoint of each of the four sides. Organize the remaining players into two teams of two players each. Award one team possession of the ball to begin. The objective is to maintain possession of the ball within the grid. The four support players join the team with the ball to create a 6v2 player advantage for the

attack. Support players, however, are restricted in their movements. They are permitted to move laterally along the sidelines but may not enter the field area. Support players may receive the ball from and pass the ball to central players only—they may not pass among themselves—and are limited to two touches to receive and pass the ball. Change of possession occurs when a defending player steals the ball or when the ball goes out of play. Award 1 team point for 6 consecutive passes without a loss of possession. Play for 5 minutes, after which central players switch positions with support players and repeat the game.

To Increase Difficulty for Attackers

- Limit the support players to one-touch (first-time) passes.
- Award 1 team point for 10 consecutive passes without a loss of possession.

To Decrease Difficulty for Attackers

- Permit support players to pass among themselves.

Success Check

- Move the ball quickly to unbalance defenders.
- Support players move laterally to provide passing options.

Score Your Success

0 to 3 points in 5-minute game = 1 point

4 to 7 points in 5-minute game = 3 points

8 points or more in 5-minute game = 5 points

Your score ___

Attacking Support Drill 3.   Possess to Penetrate

Use markers to outline a 15- by 20-yard playing area. Designate two players as defenders and four players as attackers. Attackers attempt to keep the ball from the defenders within the area by passing among themselves, and they try to *split* defenders (pass the ball between defenders) when possible. (This type of pass is commonly referred to as the *killer pass*, a pass that penetrates the defense.) If a defender steals the ball or the ball leaves the playing area, the ball is quickly returned to an attacker and play resumes. Attackers are limited to three touches to receive and pass the ball. Award the attacking team 1 point for 6 consecutive passes without a loss of possession, and 2 points for a completed pass that splits the defenders. Play for 5 minutes, then designate two different players as defenders and repeat. Play three rounds with all players taking a turn as attackers.

To Increase Difficulty for Attackers

- Award 1 point for 10 consecutive passes.
- Restrict attackers to two-touch passing.
- Reduce size of playing area.

- Add a defender and play 4v3.

To Decrease Difficulty for Attackers

- Increase size of playing area.
- Add an attacker and play 5v2.

Success Check

- Commit a defender before passing.
- Support players get in position at wide angles to the ball.
- Readjust position in response to movement of the ball.
- Recognize opportunities for the killer pass.

Score Your Success

7 points or fewer in a 5-minute round = 1 point

8 to 14 points in a 5-minute round = 3 points

15 points or more in a 5-minute round = 5 points

Your score ___

Attacking Support Drill 4.   Double-Grid Four-on-Two (Plus Two)

Set up two adjacent 15- by 15-yard grids with a 5-yard space between grids. Four attackers and two defenders are in grid A, and two additional players are in grid B. The four attackers in grid A attempt to keep the ball from the two defenders (4v2) by passing among themselves. Attackers are limited to three touches or fewer to receive and pass the ball. Once the attackers have completed a minimum of four consecutive passes, they can play the ball to the two players stationed in grid B. Two attackers from grid A immediately sprint to grid B to join the two players already there to create a four-player team in grid B. The two defenders in grid A also sprint to grid B to create a 4v2 situation in that grid.

If a defender wins the ball, he or she immediately passes the ball to one of the players in the opposite grid. The two defenders follow the pass to form a new four-player attacking team in the other grid. Two of the original attackers sprint into the opposite grid to serve as defenders. Play continuously for 10 minutes. Award 1 point each time the attacking team completes four or more consecutive passes and plays the ball into the opposite grid.

To Increase Difficulty for Attackers

- Reduce size of grid to 10 by 10 yards.
- Add a third defender to create a 4v3 situation in each grid.

- Limit attackers to two touches or fewer.

To Decrease Difficulty for Attackers

- Increase size of grid.
- Add an extra attacker to create a 5v2 situation in each grid.

Success Check

- Get a good first touch of the ball, away from defensive pressure.
- Provide support at wide angles to the ball.
- Make hard support runs to opposite grid when ball changes location.

Score Your Success

4 points or fewer when playing as an attacker = 1 point

5 to 9 points when playing as an attacker = 3 points

10 points or more when playing as an attacker = 5 points

Your score ___

GIVE-AND-GO (WALL) PASS

The most fundamental numbers-up situation is two attackers versus one defender. The give-and-go pass, or wall pass (figure 8.3), is an effective way to penetrate past the defender in a 2v1 situation.

The concept of give-and-go is simple. The player with the ball (first attacker) dribbles at the defender, causing the defender to commit to the first attacker. As the defender closes to tackle, the first attacker passes the ball to a nearby teammate (second attacker) and sprints forward into the space behind the defender to collect a return pass.

The first and second attackers must each fulfill specific responsibilities in order for the give-and-go pass to work effectively. An accurate and properly paced pass coupled with correct timing of the pass and run are essential for success. If performed correctly, the give-and-go pass is almost impossible to defend.

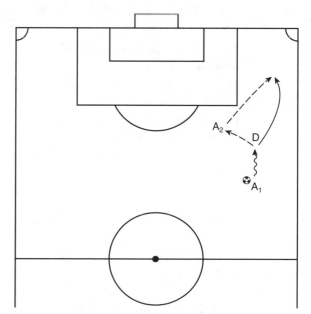

Figure 8.3 Give-and-go pass. The first attacker passes to the second attacker and then runs forward into open space to receive a return pass.

The player on the ball (first attacker) must initiate the action. Perform the following steps in the order listed:

1. *Take on the defender*. Dribble directly at (take on) the defender when you recognize that a potential give-and-go situation exists. This action is designed to freeze the defender.

2. *Commit the defender*. Dribbling directly at the defender will draw him or her to you.

3. *Pass the ball*. As the defender closes to tackle, pass the ball to the wall player using the outside surface of your instep. Pass the ball to the wall player's lead foot.

4. *Sprint forward into space*. After releasing the ball, sprint into the space behind the defender.

5. *Collect the return pass*. Receive a return pass from the wall player.

The wall player (support attacker) must perform the following steps in the order listed:

1. *Move quickly to a position ahead and to the side of the first attacker*. Get in position 3 to 4 yards to the side of the defending player at an angle approximately 45 degrees from the ball.

2. *Get in position sideways in relation to the ball*. Use an open stance with your body angled sideways toward the first attacker. Use your lead foot to redirect the pass.

3. *Redirect the ball*. Position your lead foot to redirect the pass from the first attacker into the space behind the defender.

4. *Support the ball*. Sprint forward to support your teammate. Another give-and-go situation could develop immediately.

Misstep

You (the first attacker) fail to commit the defender before releasing the ball.

Correction

Dribble directly at the defender. Release the pass as the defender steps forward to tackle the ball.

Misstep

You commit the defender and pass to the wall, but the wall is unable to redirect the ball into the space behind the defender.

Correction

This misstep can occur for two reasons. First, the wall may be positioned too far away from you. The proper support distance of the wall player is 3 to 4 yards to the side of the defender. Positioning at a greater distance will allow the defender sufficient time to readjust his or her position to block the passing lane. Execution of the give-and-go may also break down if you (the first attacker) fail to sprint forward after passing to the wall.

DOUBLE PASS

The double pass (figure 8.4) is simply a wall pass followed by a second entry pass to the original wall player. After redirecting the ball into the space behind the defender, the wall player makes a diagonal penetrating run ahead of the ball to receive a return pass from the first attacker. Each player has specific obligations.

The first (player on the ball) attacker's primary responsibility is to dribble at and commit the defender to him or her. As the defender closes, release the pass to the lead foot of the wall using outside-of-the-foot technique and then sprint forward into space behind the defender to collect a return (wall) pass. After receiving the ball, you complete the double pass by passing the ball forward to the original wall player, who has sprinted into position ahead of the ball.

The support (wall) player's initial responsibility is to get in position as the wall 3 to 4 yards to the side of the defending player while at the same time maintaining a clear passing lane to the ball. Position your body sideways to the first attacker. As the ball arrives, redirect the pass into the space behind the defender, and then sprint forward ahead of the ball to receive a second pass from the first attacker to complete the double pass.

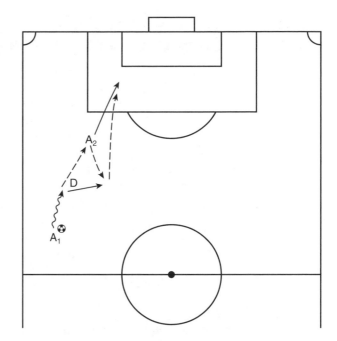

Figure 8.4 Double pass. The first attacker passes to the second attacker (wall) and runs into open space past the defender. The second attacker returns the ball to the first attacker, runs ahead of the ball, and receives a return pass.

Misstep

The double-pass combination fails to materialize.

Correction

You must first execute a successful wall pass to set up the double pass. Once the wall player has redirected the initial pass behind the defender, he or she must sprint ahead of the ball to receive a return pass.

Wall Pass and Double Pass Drill 1.   Playing the Wall

Partner with a teammate. Execute the give-and-go against an imaginary defender as you jog the length of the field. Score 1 point for each properly executed wall pass. Perform the drill at half speed to begin, then gradually progress to full speed. Execute 40 wall passes, 20 playing as the first attacker and 20 as the second (wall) attacker, for a maximum possible total of 40 points.

To Increase Difficulty for Attackers

• Add a defender to the drill.

To Decrease Difficulty for Attackers

• Practice wall passes off a kick (rebound) wall.

Success Check for First Attacker

• Dribble at imaginary defender.

• Pass with outside surface of foot.

• Sprint forward into space.

Success Check for Support Player (Wall)

• Get in position sideways to first attacker.

• Redirect pass into space behind imaginary defender.

• Move forward to support the ball.

Score Your Success

0 to 24 points = 1 point

25 to 34 points = 3 points

35 to 40 points = 5 points

Your score ___

Wall Pass and Double Pass
Drill 2. Two-on-One in the Box

Partner with a teammate to play against a third player (defender) within a 12- by 12-yard grid. Use dribbling, shielding, and passing skills to maintain possession from the defender within the area. Your team is allowed an unlimited number of touches to pass and receive the ball. Score 2 points each time you and your partner execute a give-and-go pass to beat the defender. Score 1 point each time you and your teammate combine for five or more consecutive passes. Play for 5 minutes, then switch defenders and repeat.

To Increase Difficulty for Attackers

- Reduce size of grid.
- Award 1 point for seven consecutive passes.
- Limit attackers to three touches to pass and receive the ball.

To Decrease Difficulty for Attackers

- Increase size of grid.
- Award 1 point for three consecutive passes.

Success Check

- Commit the defender.
- Maintain clear passing lane to the ball.
- Execute one–two passing combination.

Score Your Success

0 to 9 points in 5-minute game = 1 point

10 to 14 points in 5-minute game = 3 points

15 points or more in 5-minute game = 5 points

Your score ___

Wall Pass and Double Pass
Drill 3. Two-on-One to the End Line

Use markers to outline a 15- by 25-yard field area. You and a teammate get in position on one end line of the field. A third player (the defender) stands on the opposite end line with a ball. The defender initiates play by serving the ball to you and immediately sprinting forward to defend. You and your partner attempt to take on and beat the defender to the end line either by dribbling past the defender or by executing a wall pass or double pass. Score 1 team point if you and your partner beat the defender and penetrate the end line with the ball. If the defender wins the ball, the play is dead and players return to their original positions. Repeat 20 times for a maximum possible total of 20 points.

To Increase Difficulty for Attackers

- Restrict the attacking team to a 10-yard-wide zone when attempting to beat the defender.

To Decrease Difficulty for Attackers

- Add a third attacker to the drill.

Success Check

- Commit the defender.
- Support player gets in position to side of defender.
- Execute wall pass or dribble past defender.
- Penetrate at speed to end line.

Score Your Success

0 to 9 points = 1 point

10 to 14 points = 3 points

15 to 20 points = 5 points

Your score ___

Wall Pass and Double Pass
Drill 4.   Two-on-One (Plus One) Transition Game

Organize into two teams of two players each. Use markers to outline a playing area 20 by 25 yards with a 4-yard-wide goal at the midpoint of each end line. Each team defends a goal and can score in the opponent's goal. Begin the game with a kickoff from the center of the field. The rules of play follow: The team with possession scores points by kicking the ball through the opponent's goal or by executing a successful wall pass. The defending team has one player as a goalkeeper and one as a defender. Change of possession occurs when the defender steals the ball, the goalkeeper makes a save, the ball last touched by a member of the attacking team goes out of bounds, or a goal is scored.

When the defender gains possession of the ball, he or she must pass back to the goalkeeper, who can then sprint forward out of the goal to join in an attack on the opponent's goal. The team losing possession must now defend. One player sprints back to play as the goalkeeper while the other is the defender. The action is continuous as teams attack with two players and defend with one player and a goalkeeper. Teammates alternate playing goalkeeper. Award 1 team point for each wall pass that beats a defender and 1 additional point for each goal scored. Play for 15 minutes and keep track of points. The team that scores more points wins the game.

To Increase Difficulty for Attackers

- Decrease size of goal.
- Decrease width of field.
- Limit players to three touches or fewer.

To Decrease Difficulty for Attackers

- Increase size of goal.

Success Check

- Immediately transition from defense to attack.
- Take on and commit defender.
- Execute wall pass.
- Penetrate to goal.

Score Your Success

Losing team = 0 points

Winning team = 2 points

Your score ___

Wall Pass and Double Pass
Drill 5.   Small-Sided Game With Multiple Scoring Options

Form two teams of five players each. Use markers to outline a 40- by 50-yard playing area with a 4-yard-wide goal on the center of each end line. Each team defends a goal and can score in the opponent's goal. Do not use goalkeepers. Begin with a kickoff from the center of the field. Regular soccer rules apply except for the method of scoring. Teams are awarded points as follows:

- 1 point for a successful give-and-go pass
- 1 point for a successful double pass
- 2 points for a goal scored

Play for 20 minutes. The team scoring more points wins the game.

To Increase Difficulty for Attacking Team

- Reduce size of field to limit space and time.
- Restrict players to three touches or fewer to pass and receive the ball.
- Reduce width of goal.

To Decrease Difficulty for Attacking Team

- Enlarge the goals.

Success Check

- Recognize and exploit opportunities for the give-and-go pass.
- Provide support for the player on the ball.

- Recognize opportunities for the double pass.
- Maintain open passing lanes.
- Penetrate to goal.

TAKEOVERS

The takeover maneuver, typically used to free an attacker in 2v2 situations, can be likened to the pick in basketball. If executed properly, it is an excellent way to create gaps of open space in areas where there originally were none.

To perform the takeover (figure 8.5), the player on the ball, who is marked tightly by the first defender, dribbles the ball laterally across the field toward a nearby teammate (receiver) who is moving toward the dribbler. As the dribbler passes the receiver, he or she leaves the ball. The receiver accepts the ball and continues forward in the opposite direction into the space vacated by the original dribbler. In the process of exchanging the ball, the defender who was trailing the original dribbler is momentarily screened from the ball, which creates an opportunity for the receiving player to penetrate by dribbling, passing, or shooting. The original dribbler also has the option of decoying the takeover and keeping the ball.

It's important for the dribbler to shield the ball from the trailing defender at the moment the ball is exchanged. To do so, he or she controls the ball with the outside foot farthest from the defender. The receiver angles his or her approach to collect the ball with the inside foot

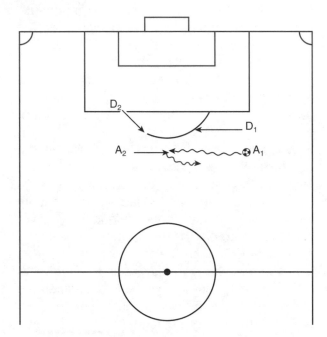

Figure 8.5 A takeover is used to lose a defender in a tight space.

(foot closest to the dribbler). This maneuver is sometimes referred to as the *same-foot exchange*. The right-foot-to-right-foot and left-foot-to-left-foot rule always applies with respect to executing a takeover.

Misstep

The defender kicks the ball away as you attempt to exchange possession.

Correction

Control the ball with the foot opposite the trailing defender. In that position, you can maintain distance between the ball and the opponent, and you may also cause the defender to lose sight of the ball momentarily during the exchange of possession.

OVERLAP

The overlap maneuver is a two- or three-player combination designed to get a defender or midfielder forward from a wide position into a more penetrating attacking position. Overlaps are generally used as a means of getting in on the flank to create a numbers-up situation.

To execute an overlap (figure 8.6), the player on the ball dribbles at the nearest defender to commit him or her. At the same time, a teammate sprints around and past (overlaps) the ball into a more forward position. This action creates space for the first attacker to play the ball diagonally forward for the overlapping player to run on to.

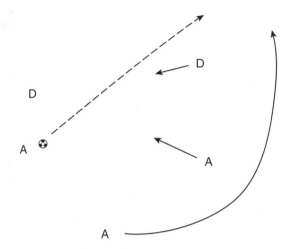

Figure 8.6 Overlap. Player bends his or her run around a teammate to overlap the ball and get in a more advanced attacking position.

Misstep

The first attacker is stripped of the ball, and as a result the overlapping player is caught on the wrong side of the ball in a poor defensive position.

Correction

Do not execute an overlap run unless the player on the ball is in position to serve the ball forward. Once he or she is facing forward and is in no danger of losing the ball, sprint ahead of the ball to receive the pass.

Takeovers and Overlaps Drill 1. Multiple Takeovers

Play within the penalty area. Divide the team into two groups (A and B) of equal numbers. The players in group A each have possession of a ball; group B players do not. On command, all players begin moving throughout the area. Those with a ball dribble, and those without a ball jog. Dribblers look to exchange their balls via a takeover move with a player who does not have a ball, and then immediately look to get a ball back by executing a takeover with a different player. All takeovers should adhere to the same-foot guideline—right foot to right foot or left foot to left foot. Perform a minimum of 50 takeovers for each player.

To Increase Difficulty

- Execute takeover maneuver at game speed.
- Add three neutral defenders who try to prevent takeovers.

To Decrease Difficulty

- Perform drill at half speed.

Success Check

- Dribble at nearby teammate.
- Exchange ball using same-foot technique.
- Shield the ball with your body as you exchange with a teammate.

Score Your Success

34 takeover maneuvers or fewer without error = 1 point

35 to 46 correct takeover maneuvers without error = 3 points

47 to 50 correct takeover maneuvers without error = 5 points

Your score ____

Takeovers and Overlaps Drill 2.   Overlap Your Pass

Play on a 25- by 35-yard field with a small goal at the midpoint of each end line. Form two teams of two players each. Each team defends a goal and can score in the opponent's goal. Designate one additional player as a neutral player who plays with the team in possession to create a 3v2-player advantage for the attack. Do not use goalkeepers.

Regular soccer rules apply except for the following restriction: Players must overlap the teammate to whom they pass the ball. This restriction creates a continuous series of overlapping runs throughout the game. Play for 15 minutes and keep track of goals scored. Individual players keep track of the number of overlap runs executed.

To Increase Difficulty

- Play even numbers (3v3).

To Decrease Difficulty

- Play 3v1.

Success Check

- Play the ball accurately to a teammate's feet.
- Overlap the ball.
- Look for a return pass.

Score Your Success

Execute 19 or fewer overlapping runs = 1 point

Execute 20 to 24 overlapping runs = 2 points

Execute 25 or more overlapping runs = 3 points

Your score ___

Takeovers and Overlaps Drill 3.   Take Over and Score

Play on one end of a field with a full-size goal centered on the end line. Form two equal teams (A and B) of four to six players each. Teams get in single-file lines facing each other on opposite sides of the penalty arc at the outer edge of the penalty area. Players on team A each have a ball; team B players do not. Put a goalkeeper in goal.

The first player for team A dribbles directly at the first player from team B and executes a takeover at the top of the penalty area. The team B player pushes the ball into the penalty area and shoots to score. The team A player who exchanged the ball bends his or her run toward goal to finish any rebounds off the goalkeeper. Players switch lines after each attempt at goal. Continue the drill until each player has executed a total of 20 takeovers. Score 1 point for each successful takeover performed at game speed.

To Increase Difficulty

- Add a trailing defender to the drill who attempts to disrupt the takeover.

To Decrease Difficulty

- Perform drill at half speed.

Success Check

- Control ball with foot farthest from imaginary defender.
- Adhere to same-foot rule when executing a takeover.
- Curl your run into the penalty area after exchanging the ball.

Score Your Success

0 to 13 points = 1 point

14 to 17 points = 3 points

18 to 20 points = 5 points

Your score ___

Takeovers and Overlaps
Drill 4.   Three-Player Flank Overlap

Divide the team into three groups. Group A players, each with a ball, stand in single file on the midline next to the touchline. Group B players stand within the center circle. Group C players get in position 35 yards front and center of the goal, facing the center circle.

The drill begins as the first player in group A passes the ball to a player in group C and then sprints (overlaps) down the sideline. The receiving (target) player first-times the ball back to a group B player who controls the ball and releases a diagonal penetrating pass to the overlapping player from group A. The overlapping player controls the ball, dribbles to the end line, and crosses it into the goalmouth. The group B and group C players involved in the three-player passing sequence sprint forward into the goal area to finish the cross. Players switch groups after each overlap attempt. The neutral goalkeeper attempts to save all shots. Continue until each player has executed 15 overlap runs.

To Increase Difficulty

- Place two defenders within the penalty area to defend the cross.

To Decrease Difficulty

- Perform drill at half speed.

Success Check

- Play a firm pass into target (group C player).
- Sprint forward to a position ahead of ball.
- Receive the ball and cross it into goal area.

Score Your Success

Execute 9 or fewer overlap runs at game speed = 1 point

Execute 10 to 14 overlap runs at game speed = 2 points

Execute 15 overlap runs at game speed = 3 points

Your score ___

SUCCESS SUMMARY OF GROUP ATTACK

Successful execution of group attack tactics depends in large part on your ability to read the situation correctly, choose the most appropriate action, and then implement that action through precise skill execution. In essence, you must determine what to do and when to do it and then be physically able to do it.

Improved tactical awareness should be a continuing pursuit for all players, particularly those at higher levels of competition. You can improve your understanding of group attack tactics through exercises that simulate situations you will face in the match. Even veteran professionals can sharpen their decision-making skills through repetitive practice in game-simulated situations.

Each of the drills described in step 8 has been assigned a point value to help you evaluate individual and group performance. Record your scores in the following chart and then total the points to get an estimate of your overall level of competence.

Attacking Support

1. Triangular Possession (Three-on-One)   _____ out of 4

2. Four-Sided Support Game   _____ out of 5

3. Possess to Penetrate   _____ out of 5

4. Double-Grid Four-on-Two (Plus Two)   _____ out of 5

Wall Pass and Double Pass

1. Playing the Wall   _____ out of 5

2. Two-on-One in the Box   _____ out of 5

3. Two-on-One to the End Line   _____ out of 5

4. Two-on-One (Plus One) Transition Game   _____ out of 2

5. Small-Sided Game With Multiple Scoring Options   _____ out of 3

Takeovers and Overlaps

1. Multiple Takeovers   _____ out of 5

2. Overlap Your Pass   _____ out of 3

3. Take Over and Score   _____ out of 5

4. Three-Player Flank Overlap   _____ out of 3

Total   _____ *out of 55*

A combined score of 45 or more points suggests that you have sufficient mastery of the tactical concepts in step 8 and are ready to move on to step 9. A score in the range of 36 to 44 is considered adequate. Rehearse each tactic a few more times to become more comfortable with the maneuvers. If you scored fewer than 36 points, you need to review the material again, progress through the drills, and improve your point total before moving on to the step 9.

Defending As a Group

Attacking and defending tactics can be likened to the opposite sides of the same coin. Although their objectives are mirror opposites, the two are forever linked in the sense that players must make quick and effective transitions from one to the other at each change of possession.

Attacking tactics are designed to stretch the opposing team side to side and end to end, to provide multiple options for the player on the ball, to get behind the opposing defense through cooperative play sprinkled with individual brilliance, and to finish with a score. Conversely, defending tactics are designed to compact the field vertically and horizontally, to reduce the space and time available for attacking players, to position a significant number of players behind the ball, to limit options for the player on the ball, and to deny penetration. Once a defender wins the ball, he or she becomes the first attacker, and the team as a whole makes an immediate switch from defense to offense. The opposing team must immediately take on a defensive posture.

Pressure, cover, and *balance* are essential group defensive tactics that apply to all systems and styles of play. Every player, including the goalkeeper, should understand the important role that each of these tactics plays in the team's overall defensive scheme. Just as attacking players must work together to create scoring opportunities, defending players must effectively combine to ensure defensive pressure, cover, and balance if the team is to deny opponents the space and time necessary for scoring goals.

PRESSURE, COVER, AND BALANCE

The defender closest to the ball, referred to as the *first defender,* is responsible for applying immediate pressure at the point of attack (see step 7). The objective of this action is to deny the opposition penetration via the pass or dribble, a delaying tactic designed to buy defending play-ers sufficient time to recover to positions on the goal side of the ball.

As the first defender applies pressure on the ball, the *second (cover) defender* gets in position to protect the space behind and to the side of the first defender. If the first defender is beaten

149

on the dribble, the covering defender can step forward to close down the dribbler and deny penetration. The second defender is also in position to cut off passes slotted through the space behind the first defender, and as such must be aware of support (second) attackers positioned near the ball. The covering defender functions somewhat like the free safety in American football, a player who is available to cover space and help teammates when needed.

Third defenders are responsible for providing balance in defense. Defensive balance is designed to protect the vulnerable space ahead of the ball, particularly the open space behind the defense on the side of the field opposite the ball.

First Defender

The defender nearest the ball is responsible for applying direct pressure on the opponent with the ball. To do so, he or she quickly closes the distance to the ball while maintaining balance and body control. The first defender's priorities are to prevent the opponent on the

ball from penetrating the defense via the pass or dribble, to limit the opponent's options by reducing available space and time, to force the opponent to pass the ball square or backward, or to dribble or pass the ball into space occupied by the second (covering) defender (figure 9.1). The first defender's primary objective is not necessarily to win the ball, although he or she should attempt to do so if the opportunity presents itself.

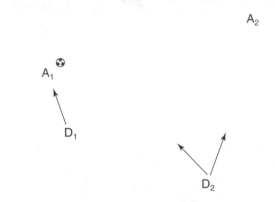

Figure 9.1 First defender applies pressure on the ball while second defender covers space behind first defender.

Misstep

The first defender is beaten on the dribble before a second defender is in cover position.

Correction

Your primary responsibilities as first defender are to delay the attack and deny penetration. Do not dive in on the tackle until a teammate (second defender) is in position to protect the space behind you. Attempt to jockey and delay the attacker until help arrives.

Second (Cover) Defender

The covering defender has two primary responsibilities. First, he or she must protect the space behind and to the side of the first defender. To accomplish that aim, the second defender gets in position to prevent an opponent's pass through that space, and he or she must be ready and able to step forward should the first defender be beaten on the dribble. Second, the covering defender must be aware of opponents (support attackers) in the vicinity of the ball. To fulfill both obligations, the covering defender must be in position at the proper angle and distance from the first defender.

To achieve the proper angle of cover, the second defender gets in position behind and to the side, not directly behind, the first defender. From this starting position, the second defender can cut off passes through that space and also close down on a nearby support attacker if the ball is passed to that player. The covering defender maintains a clear view of the ball and should be able to adjust position quickly in response to the first defender's movements. Ideally there should be a covering defender in position diagonally behind and to each side of the first defender. When properly positioned, the three defending teammates form a triangular shape (figure 9.2).

150

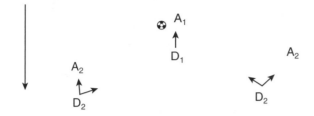

Figure 9.2 Proper angle of cover for the second defender. The second defender protects space behind the first defender and can also apply pressure to the support attacker.

The distance of cover varies depending on the area of the field and position of nearby opponents. Defensive coverage must be very compact (tight) in the dangerous scoring zone front and center of your goal, an area where opponents must be denied the time and space required to release a shot on goal. The distance of cover can be extended as the ball moves farther away from your goal. For example, when the ball is within 30 yards of goal, the appropriate cover distance may be as little as 2 yards, whereas 5 to 6 yards may be more appropriate when the ball is near midfield. It all depends on the immediate situation. Keep in mind that the covering defender is also responsible for marking an opponent (second attacker) in the vicinity of the ball. As a general rule, the closer that opponent is to the ball, the tighter the coverage. The distance of cover can be extended as the opponent moves farther from the ball (figure 9.3).

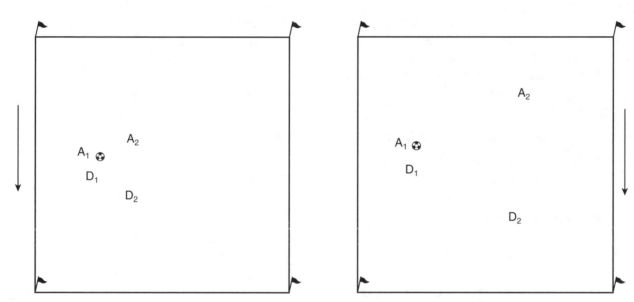

Figure 9.3 Distance of cover changes depending on whether the opponents are *(a)* closer to the ball or *(b)* farther from the ball.

Misstep

The cover defender gets in position behind and in direct line with the first defender.

Correction

A covering defender should position behind and to each side of the first defender. The three players form a triangular shape with the first defender at the apex of the triangle.

Misstep

The cover defender gets in position too far from the first defender.

Correction

Get in position at a distance from which you can provide tight cover for the first defender and also apply pressure on the ball should it be played to a second attacker in the vicinity of the ball.

Defensive Pressure and Cover
Drill 1. Two-on-Two Game

Organize into two teams of two players each. Use markers to outline a 15- by 25-yard field area with a 4-yard-wide goal centered on each end line. Begin with a kickoff from the center of the field. Each team defends a goal and can score goals by kicking the ball through the opponent's goal below knee height. Do not use goalkeepers. Teams switch from attack to defense and vice versa on each change of possession. Teammates must play in combination defensively to ensure adequate pressure and cover. The first defender applies pressure on the ball while the second defender gets in position to prevent a penetrating pass through the space beside and behind the first defender. The second defender must also be in a position to immediately challenge for the ball should it be passed to a nearby support attacker. Play for 15 minutes continuously and keep tally of goals scored.

To Increase Difficulty for Defending Team

- Require teams to defend two small goals, one at each corner of each end line.
- Increase the size of field to create more attacking space and time.

- Add a neutral player who always joins the team with possession to create a 3v2 advantage for the attack.

To Decrease Difficulty for Defending Team

- Make the goals smaller.
- Reduce width of field.

Success Check

- First defender applies immediate pressure at point of attack.
- Second defender gets in position at proper distance and angle of cover.
- Teammates readjust positions in response to movement of ball.

Score Your Success

Concede 11 goals or more in 15 minutes = 1 point

Concede 6 to 10 goals in 15 minutes = 3 points

Concede 0 to 5 goals in 15 minutes = 5 points

Your score ___

Defensive Pressure and Cover
Drill 2. Prevent Penetration Two-on-Four

Designate a team of two defenders and a team of four attackers. Use markers to outline a 15- by 15-yard playing grid. The attacking team attempts to keep the ball from the defending team within the grid. Award the attacking team 1 point each time attacking players complete six consecutive passes and 1 additional point for each pass completed that splits (goes between) the defenders. Award the defending team 1 point each time defenders win possession of the ball or force the attackers to play the ball outside the field area. If the defenders win the ball, they immediately return it to the attacking team and the game continues. Play for 10 minutes and keep track of points scored.

To Increase Difficulty for Defenders

- Enlarge the playing area.
- Add an attacker to the game to create a 2v5 situation.

To Decrease Difficulty

- Reduce field area to 10 by 10 yards.
- Limit attackers to three touches or fewer to pass and receive the ball.

Success Check

- First defender applies immediate pressure on opponent with the ball.

- Limit the attacker's passing options.
- Make the play predictable.
- Cover defender positions to prevent the pass that splits the defenders.

Score Your Success

Defenders score fewer points than attackers = 0 points for each defender

Defenders and attackers score equal number of points = 2 points for each defender

Defenders score more points than attackers = 4 points for each defender

Your score ____

Defensive Pressure and Cover
Drill 3.   Three-on-Two (Plus One) Game

Form two teams of three players each. Play on a 20- by 30-yard field with a 4-yard-wide goal centered on each end line. Award one team possession of the ball to begin. The team with the ball attacks with three players; the opponents defend with two field players and a goalkeeper. The attacking team scores 1 point by kicking the ball directly to the opposing goalkeeper. The defending team attempts to win the ball and prevent the opponent from scoring. If a defending player steals the ball, he or she must pass it back to his or her goalkeeper before the team can initiate an attack on the opponent's goal. The goalkeeper can then move forward to join his or her teammates in the attack. One player on the team that lost possession retreats into the goal to be the goalkeeper. The remaining teammates assume roles of first and second defenders. Teams switch between attack and defense with each change of possession. Change of possession occurs when a defender steals the ball, when a point is scored, or when the ball leaves the playing field. Teammates alternate playing goalkeeper. Play nonstop for 15 minutes and keep track of points scored.

To Increase Difficulty for Defenders

- Increase width of field.
- Increase size of goal.
- Add a neutral player who always joins with the team in possession to create a 4v2 (plus 1) situation.

To Decrease Difficulty for Defenders

- Make the field narrower.
- Reduce width of goal.
- Limit attackers to three or fewer touches to receive and pass the ball.

Success Check

- Apply immediate pressure at point of attack.
- Deny penetration via the dribble.
- Position to prevent passes that split (go between) the defenders.

Score Your Success

Member of losing team = 1 point

Member of winning team = 3 points

Your score ____

Defensive Pressure and Cover
Drill 4.   Pressure and Cover to Deny Penetration

Play within a 20- by 20-yard field area. Two defenders stand in the center of the area; one attacker get in position at the midpoint of each sideline for a total of four attackers. The server (coach) stands outside the field area with an ample supply of balls.

To begin, the server passes a ball to one of the attackers. The player receiving the ball (first attacker) attempts to dribble directly across the square to the opposite sideline. The two defenders work in combination to deny penetration. The first defender steps to confront the dribbler while the second positions to provide cover (support) for his or her teammate. If the dribbler cannot immediately penetrate past the defenders, he or she passes the ball diagonally to an attacker on a different sideline. After receiving the ball, that player becomes the first attacker and immediately tries to dribble across the grid to the opposite sideline. Defenders immediately adjust position to deny penetration by the new attacker.

If a defender wins the ball or the ball is kicked out of the area, the server immediately plays another ball to a different attacker, and the exercise continues. An attacker who successfully dribbles across to the opposite sideline scores 1 point. The attacker returns to his or her original sideline by running along the outside of the grid. In the meantime, the server plays a ball to a different attacker, and the game continues. Play for 5 minutes, then designate two different defenders and repeat the drill. Play several rounds so that each player takes a turn as a defender.

To Increase Difficulty for Defenders

- Increase size of grid.
- Place two attackers at the midpoint of each sideline to create two-on-two (2v2).

To Decrease Difficulty

- Reduce size of grid to 10 by 10 yards.

Success Check

- First defender applies immediate pressure at point of attack.
- Maintain balance and body control.
- Second defender covers space behind first defender.

Score Your Success

Concede 9 points or more in 5 minutes = each defender earns 1 point

Concede 4 to 8 points in 5 minutes = each defender earns 3 points

Concede 0 to 3 points in 5 minutes = each defender earns 5 points

Your score ___

Defensive Pressure and Cover
Drill 5. Three-on-Two in Each Zone

Use markers to outline a field area 35 by 50 yards, bisected lengthwise by a midline. Place a regulation-size goal at each end of the field with a goalkeeper in each goal. Organize two teams of five players each. For each team, designate three players as attackers and two as defenders. The three attackers take positions in the opponent's half of the field, and the two defenders team up in their own half. This creates a three-on-two (3v2) situation in each half. Each team defends its goal and can score in the opponent's goal.

Players are restricted to movement within their assigned half of the field. A defender who steals the ball passes it to a teammate in the opposite half to initiate the counterattack. Otherwise, regular soccer rules are in effect. The team conceding fewer goals wins.

To Increase Difficulty for Defenders

- Increase size of field.

- Add an attacker to each team to make it four-on-two (4v2) in the defending zone.

To Decrease Difficulty for Defenders

- Add a defender to each team to make it three-on-three (3v3) in each half.
- Limit attackers to three or fewer touches to pass and receive the ball.

Success Check

- Apply immediate pressure at the point of attack.
- Deny penetration via the dribble.
- Protect the space behind the first defender.
- Force the attackers to take poor angle shots.

Score Your Success

Team concedes fewer goals than opponents
= each team member earns 2 points

Your score ___

Third Defender

While the first defender applies pressure at the point of attack and the second defender positions to provide cover, the third defender's responsibility is to ensure defensive balance (figure 9.4). The third defender(s) locates diagonally behind the second defender along the line of balance, an imaginary diagonal line that begins at the ball and extends toward the goalpost farthest from the ball. From a position along the line of balance the third defender can accomplish three important objectives: protect the space behind the second defender, keep the ball in view, and keep the opponent he or she is marking in view.

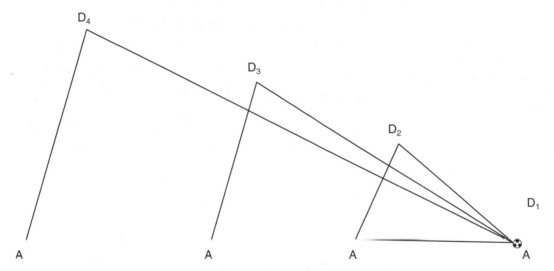

Figure 9.4 Defenders are in proper balance to deny penetrating pass and at correct distance to close in on the opponents they are marking.

Misstep

The third defender gets in position square to the covering defender.

Correction

The third defender should be positioned diagonally behind, not beside, the second defender along an imaginary line extending toward the far goalpost. From that position, the third defender will be able to intercept a ball played into the space behind the second defender. The line of balance changes with the movement of the ball.

Misstep

The third defender takes a position too close to the second defender and is vulnerable to a long diagonal pass directed into the space behind him or her.

Correction

Don't be overly concerned about providing tight cover for the second defender. If the ball is played into the space between you and the second defender, you should be able to close the distance while the ball is in flight.

Defensive Cover and Balance
Drill 1.   Three-on-Three (Plus One) Possession

Use markers to outline a 30- by 30-yard playing area. Organize two teams of three players each. Designate one additional neutral player who will join the team in possession to create a four-on-three situation for the attack. Station both teams and the neutral player within the playing area. Use colored scrimmage vests to differentiate teams from each other and the neutral player. Award one team possession of the ball to begin.

The team with the ball (plus the neutral player) tries to complete as many consecutive passes as possible without loss of possession. The three defenders work in combination to apply pressure, cover, and balance. Change of possession occurs when a defending player steals the ball or when the ball last touched by a member of the attacking team goes out of play. Teams are awarded 1 point for five consecutive passes without loss of possession and 2 points for eight or more consecutive passes. Play for 15 minutes. The team conceding fewer points wins the game.

To Increase Difficulty for Defending Team

- Increase size of playing area.

- Add a second neutral player to create a two-player advantage for the attackers.

To Decrease Difficulty for Defending Team

- Decrease size of playing area.
- Restrict attackers to three touches or fewer to pass and receive the ball.

Success Check

- First defender applies immediate pressure on the ball.
- Second defender provides coverage.
- Third defender provides balance.
- Teammates must move in unison to maintain proper defensive positions.

Score Your Success

Member of team conceding fewer points = 2 points

Your score ___

Defensive Cover and Balance
Drill 2.   Five-on-Three (Plus Two) Game

Play on a field 40 by 30 yards. Position two 5-yard-wide goals on each end line, approximately 10 yards apart. Organize two teams of five players each. Each team must defend the two goals on its end line and can score in either of the opponent's goals. Award one team possession of the ball to begin. The team with the ball attacks with five players. The opponents defend with three field players and one goalkeeper in each goal. A defending player who steals the ball must pass the ball back to one of his or her goalkeepers before the team can initiate a counterattack. Both goalkeepers join the attack to create a five-on-three situation in the opposite direction. Teams switch from defense to attack and vice versa with each change of possession. Regular soccer rules apply except for the method of scoring. A team scores

1 point for eight consecutive passes without loss of possession and 2 points for each goal scored. Play for 15 minutes and keep track of points.

To Increase Difficulty for Defending Team

- Increase length and width of field.
- Enlarge goals.

To Decrease Difficulty for Defending Team

- Reduce size of goal.
- Reduce size of field.
- Limit attackers to two touches to pass and receive the ball.

Success Check

- Apply pressure at point of attack.

- Deny penetration via the dribble.
- Cover space behind and to sides of first defender.
- Force attackers to take shots from poor (narrow) angles to goal.

Defensive Cover and Balance
Drill 3. Four-on-Four-on-Four in Penalty Area

Play within the penalty area (44 by 18 yards). Organize three teams of four players each. Designate one team of four as the defending team; the remaining two teams combine to form an eight-player attacking team. The attacking team attempts to keep the ball from the defending team. Attackers are limited to two touches or fewer to receive and pass the ball. Change of possession occurs when a defender steals the ball, when an attacker plays the ball out of the area, or when an attacker takes more than two touches to receive and pass the ball. The team whose player error caused the loss of possession becomes defenders; the original defending team becomes attackers. Defending teams are assessed 1 penalty point each time the attacking team completes eight or more passes in succession without a loss of possession. Play for 20 minutes. The team conceding the fewest penalty points wins the game.

To Increase Difficulty for Defending Team

- Allow the attackers four touches or fewer to receive and pass the ball.
- Increase size of field.
- Assess 1 penalty point for six consecutive passes.

To Decrease Difficulty for Defending Team

- Reduce size of field.
- Require attackers to play one-touch soccer.

Success Check

- Defenders work in combination to compact space and limit attacking options.
- Defender nearest the ball applies immediate pressure.
- Nearby teammates provide coverage behind and to side of first defender.
- Defender farthest from ball provides balance in defense.

Defensive Cover and Balance
Drill 4. Ten-on-Five (Plus Five) Over and Back

Divide the group into two teams (A and B) of 10 players each. Play on an 80- by 50-yard field area, divided lengthwise by a midline. Teams A and B take positions in opposite halves of the field and are differentiated with colored scrimmage vests. The coach functions as the server and stands outside of the field near the midline with a supply of balls.

The game begins as the server kicks a ball into the half of the field occupied by team A. Team B immediately sends five players across the midline into team A's half to win the ball. Team A players attempt to maintain possession of the ball by passing among themselves. Players are limited to two touches or fewer to receive and pass the ball. If a team B player wins the ball, he or she kicks the ball across the midline to a teammate in the opposite half. The five team B players who won the ball immediately sprint into their half to join their teammates. Team A, which lost possession, sends five players into team B's half of the field to win the ball back.

Teams continue switching from one half to the other with every change of possession, playing 10 attackers versus 5 defenders in each half. The five defending players should work in combination to employ the group defense tactics of pressure, cover, and balance. The first defender to the ball applies pressure, covering defenders provide support behind and to the sides of the first defender, and remaining defenders get in position to provide coverage and balance. A team scores 1 point for 10 or more consecutive passes. The team conceding fewer points wins the game. Play for 15 minutes continuously.

To Increase Difficulty for Defending Team

- Permit the attackers four or fewer touches to receive and pass the ball.
- Increase size of field.

To Decrease Difficulty for Defending Team

- Restrict attackers to one-touch soccer (for high-level players only).
- Allow seven players to cross the midline to attempt to win the ball back.

Success Check

- Close the distance to the ball quickly.
- Deny penetration at point of attack.
- Compact the space behind the ball.
- Limit options for player on the ball.
- Keep the play in front of the defense (prevent passes that split the defense).

Score Your Success

Member of team conceding greater number of points = 2 points

Member of team conceding fewer points = 4 points

Your score ____

Defensive Cover and Balance
Drill 5.   Defending Numbers Down

Organize one team of six players and one team of four players. Use markers to outline a field area of 40 by 50 yards. Position a regulation goal at the center of one end line. Position two small goals, each 3 yards wide, at each corner of the opposite end line. Station a goalkeeper in the regulation goal; do not use goalkeepers in the small goals. The team with four players (numbers-down team) defends the large goal and can score in either of the small goals. The six-player team defends the two small goals and can score in the large goal, and its players are limited to three touches or fewer to receive, pass, and shoot the ball. The six-player team is awarded 2 points for each goal scored in the large goal. The four-player team scores 1 point for each goal it scores in the small goals. Play for 15 minutes and keep track of points scored.

To Increase Difficulty for Numbers-Down Team

- Allow the six-player team unlimited touches to receive, pass, and shoot the ball.

To Decrease Difficulty for Numbers-Down Team

- Make the field narrower.
- Restrict the six-player team to two touches or fewer.

Success Check

- Apply immediate pressure at the point of attack.
- Prevent penetration via pass or dribble.
- Compact space behind the ball.
- Balance on the side of the field opposite the ball.
- Prevent shots front and center of the goal.

Score Your Success

Member of team scoring fewer points = 1 point

Member of team scoring the more points = 3 points

Your score ____

Defensive Cover and Balance
Drill 6.   Five-on-Five (Plus One) Game

Organize into two teams of five field players and one goalkeeper each. Designate one additional neutral player who plays with the team in possession. Use markers to outline a 60- by 50-yard field. Position a regulation-size goal at each end of the field and a goalkeeper in each goal. Award one team possession of the ball to begin. Each team defends a goal and can score in the opponent's goal. Regular soccer rules apply. The overriding emphasis is on execution of group defense tactics. The defender nearest the ball applies pressure at the point of attack, nearby teammates (second defenders) provide cover, and defenders farthest from the ball (third defenders) provide balance. Defending players adjust their positions and responsibilities depending on the movement of the ball. Play for 25 minutes. The team conceding fewer goals wins the game.

To Increase Difficulty for Defending Team

- Designate two neutral players who play with the attacking team to create a two-player advantage for attackers.

To Decrease Difficulty for Defending Team

- Limit players to three touches or fewer to receive, pass, and shoot the ball.

Success Check

- First, second, and third defenders coordinate their play.
- Deny penetration at point of attack.
- Protect space behind and to sides of first defender.
- Third defender takes a position along a line of balance.
- Compact the space and limit attacker's options.

Score Your Success

Member of team conceding more goals = 3 points

Member of team conceding fewer goals = 5 points

Your score ____

SUCCESS SUMMARY OF GROUP DEFENSE

Successful execution of group defense tactics requires the properly coordinated efforts of two or more teammates. You must be prepared to fulfill the role of a first, second, or third defender, depending on the game situation, and understand the importance of each role as it relates to the other two. As clichéd as it may sound, teamwork is absolutely essential to your success. Communication among defending players can help toward that aim. For example, when playing as the covering (second) defender, you can verbally inform the pressuring (first) defender to channel the attacker in a specific direction or cue him or her when to challenge for the ball.

Each of the drills described in step 9 has been assigned a point value to help you evaluate performance and chart progress. Some of the drills, by necessity, are evaluated on the play of the group rather than on the performance of each player. As a consequence, the point value as applied to a specific player may be not be entirely accurate. For example, a player in a five-on-five game may correctly apply the principles of the first, second, and third defenders but still receive a low score if the team as a whole does not perform well. However, an important responsibility when playing group defense is getting the group to perform as one, so each player should act as a coach on the field in that respect. Record your scores in the following chart and then total the points to get an estimate of your overall level of competence.

Defensive Pressure and Cover

1. Two-on-Two Game — ___ out of 5

2. Prevent Penetration Two-on-Four — ___ out of 4

3. Three-on-Two (Plus One) Game — ___ out of 3

4. Pressure and Cover to Deny Penetration — ___ out of 5

5. Three-on-Two in Each Zone — ___ out of 2

Defensive Cover and Balance

1. Three-on-Three (Plus One) Possession — ___ out of 2

2. Five-on-Three (Plus Two) Game — ___ out of 2

3. Four-on-Four-on-Four in Penalty Area — ___ out of 5

4. Ten-on-Five (Plus Five) Over and Back — ___ out of 4

5. Defending Numbers Down — ___ out of 3

6. Five-on-Five (Plus One) Game — ___ out of 5

Total — ___ out of 40

A score of 32 points or more suggests that you have sufficiently mastered the defensive concepts covered in step 9 and are ready to move on to team tactics. A combined score in the range of 26 to 31 points is considered adequate. Review and rehearse each tactic a few more times before moving on to step 10. If you scored 25 points or fewer, you need to review the material again, progress through the drills, and improve your point total before moving forward.

Attacking As a Team

While outstanding individual effort can sometimes break down a defense and create a scoring opportunity out of nothing, in most instances a goal scored is the result of the coordinated efforts of teammates. To casual observers it may appear that a group of individuals are thinking as one. Players seemingly know in advance where their teammates will move and when they will pass the ball. In a sense they actually are thinking as one!

Team tactics are designed to focus the efforts of 11 individuals toward a common goal, to ensure that everyone is on the same page, so to speak. The primary objectives of team attack are to outnumber opponents in the area around the ball, to create and exploit gaps of open space within the opposing defense, and to ultimately finish the attack with a goal scored. The teamwork required to achieve those objectives will occur only when players have a clear idea of what the team is trying to accomplish when it has possession of the ball. That is where team attack tactics come into play.

Top-flight attacking teams are not simply a product of good fortune. For the team to score goals on a regular basis, its players must incorporate into their play specific principles of team attack that are universal to all game situations and systems of play. A summary of these principles follows.

PLAYER MOBILITY

Time-motion studies demonstrate that on average a soccer player has the ball for only 3 to 4 minutes of a 90-minute match, which means that for the remaining 86 minutes or so you will be playing without the ball. It is of the utmost importance that your movement without the ball be efficient and purposeful. The team cannot afford any spectators on the field—players who are willing to work when they have the ball at their feet but basically stand and watch the action when they don't. When your team has the ball, you should be moving constantly to make yourself available for passes and to create space for your teammates. Off-the-ball (without the ball) movement is designed to create passing options for the player on the ball, to draw opponents into poor defensive positions, and to clear space for teammates to fill. It is an essential component of team attack.

Diagonal runs are penetrating runs directed diagonally through the opponent's defense.

Diagonal runs can begin from a flank area and travel diagonally through the center of the defense, or they can begin from a central area and travel toward the flank (figure 10.1).

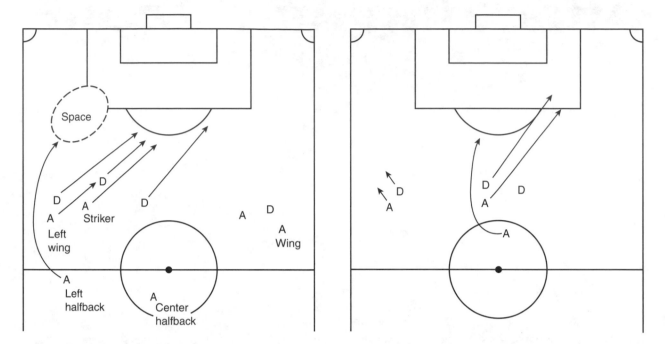

Figure 10.1 Diagonal runs: *(a)* from the flank through the center; *(b)* from center toward the flank.

Diagonal runs have several advantages over square runs, which travel flat across the field. Because diagonal runs slice through the defense, they force opponents to mark you. This action can draw defenders into poor defensive positions and at the same time create open space for teammates to fill. Diagonal runs also position the runner to receive the ball with his or her body between the trailing defender and the ball, because the defender will usually be goal side and inside of an attacker. Finally, a diagonal run that originates from the flank and travels inward puts the runner in excellent position to split the defense and score should he or she receive the ball while cutting through the center of the defense.

Checking runs are used to create distance between yourself and the defender marking you (figure 10.2). Initiate the movement with a short, sudden burst of speed forward, as if you are going to run past the defender to receive the

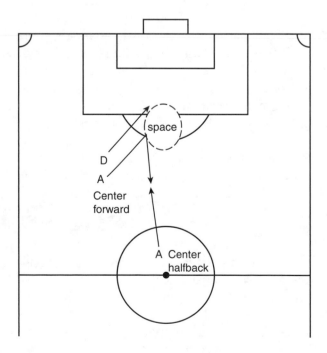

Figure 10.2 An example of a checking run.

ball. Defending players are trained to maintain a goal-side position between their opponent and the goal so the defender will retreat in response to your movement. As the defender retreats, suddenly check back toward the ball. This sudden change of direction will increase the distance between the marker and you. You can take advantage of the extra space to receive the ball and turn to face the defender.

COMBINATION PLAY FOR DEPTH AND WIDTH

In step 8, we discussed how the player on the ball should have teammates positioned behind, to each side, and ahead of him or her. The function of the player behind the ball is to provide depth in attack and to do what the player with the ball is not always able to do—pass the ball forward. For example, if the player on the ball has his or her back to the opponent's goal, he or she can pass the ball back to the trailing teammate, who can then pass the ball forward to a different player. Teammates positioned slightly ahead and to each side of the first attacker provide short, safe passing options; teammates positioned ahead of the ball provide an option for the penetrating pass. This concept of group support can be extrapolated to the team as a whole.

When on attack, the team should attempt to stretch the field vertically and horizontally so as to maximize use of the available space. A team that couples effective passing combinations with proper player positioning can force the opponent to cover a larger field area, increasing the likelihood of gaps of space within the defense, space that can be exploited by the attacking team. Passes must vary in type, distance, and direction in order to keep opponents from closing down around the ball. The positioning of attacking players to ensure width and depth is commonly referred to as the *proper attacking shape* (see figure 10.3).

Depth in attack is also achieved by positioning one or more players ahead of the ball at all

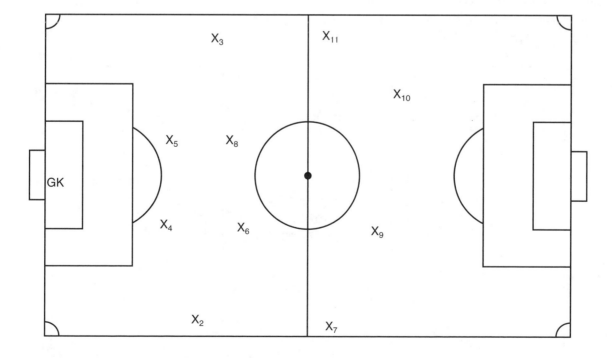

Figure 10.3 Positioning for width and depth in attack.

times. These front-running players stretch the field vertically and spearhead the attack. At the same time, the team has one or more players on each flank near the touchlines to stretch the field horizontally. Flank players (wingers) on the side of the field nearest the ball, and to some extent weak-side players on the side of the field opposite the ball, provide width in attack. Weak-side players are in particularly good position to make diagonal penetrating runs through the center of the opponent's defense (figure 10.4).

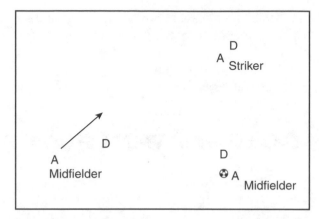

Figure 10.4 Penetrating runs from the weak side.

IMPROVISATION

Defending tactics are designed to make the opponents play as predictably as possible. It follows that when your team is on the attack it is to your advantage to improvise and do the unexpected. Dribbling at opportune times is an excellent means of incorporating improvisation in attack and can effectively serve to break down an opposing defense. On the flip side, indiscriminate dribbling at inappropriate times can just as quickly destroy the continuity required to produce an effective attack. To clarify when and where to use dribbling skills to best advantage, we can divide the playing field lengthwise into three zones—the rear (defending) third, the

middle (midfield) third, and the front (attacking) third (figure 10.5).

A smart player weighs the risk versus safety of dribbling in different areas of the field. The rear, or defending third, of the field nearest your goal is referred to as a no-risk zone, an area where the team can ill afford to lose possession. Rather than attempt to advance the ball by dribbling past opponents in this area, it is safer to advance the ball by passing it to a teammate located in a more forward position. Even if the pass is cut off, you are still in position to defend the counterattack.

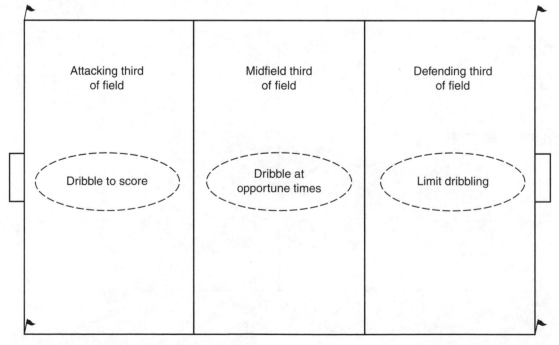

Figure 10.5 Risk and safety in the three zones of the field.

In the middle third of the field, players are willing to accept a moderate risk of loss of possession. Most teams try to strike a balance between safety (passing) and risk (dribbling) in the middle third, so you will generally see dribbling skills used with somewhat greater frequency in that area of the field. Beat an opponent on the dribble and you immediately put that player on the wrong side of the ball and create a numbers-up situation for your team as you move forward into the front third of the field. Even if you are stripped of the ball, you still have time to recover on goal side and defend, because the ball is 50 yards or more from your goal. Excessive dribbling in the middle third is never prudent because it tends to slow the attack and makes play predictable.

The front third of the field is the area in which players are most willing to accept the risk of possession loss in an effort to create a goal-scoring opportunity. Dribbling skills are used to best advantage in the attacking third of the field near the opponent's goal, an area where the positive benefits of beating an opponent on the dribble outweigh the potential negative consequences of loss of possession. If you can penetrate past an opponent by dribbling in the front third, you've probably created an excellent scoring opportunity for yourself or a teammate. Loss of possession in this area will not pose an immediate threat to your own goal. Learn to recognize situations that warrant appropriate use of dribbling skills, and take advantage of them.

TOTAL TEAM SUPPORT

Soccer is sometimes referred to as a game of triangles. This analogy refers to the general positioning of players in relation to their teammates as they move throughout the field area. If the 10 field players position themselves at the proper depth and angle of support with respect to nearby teammates, then the organization of players does resemble a series of interconnected triangles (figure 10.6a). These triangles are not static, however, because players constantly adjust their positions based on the changing location of the ball and movement of teammates (figure 10.6b).

Total team support is achieved only when teammates move up and down the field as a single compact unit. As a general rule, there should be no more than 50 yards or so between the last defender in the back line and the foremost attacker at the front of the team.

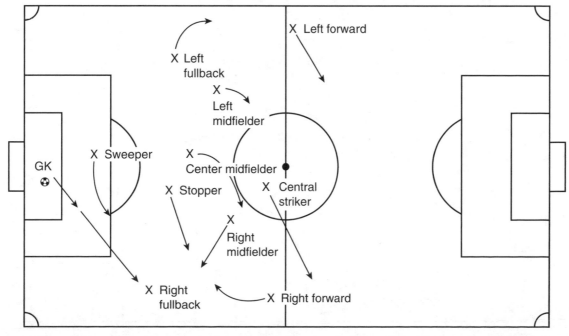

Figure 10.6a Positioning for total team support: players are at proper depth and angle.

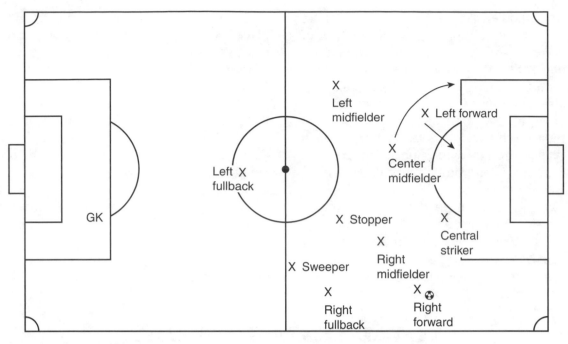

Figure 10.6b Players adjust positions based on the movement of the ball.

CHANGING THE POINT OF ATTACK

Defending players cannot run as fast as the ball can travel, and clever attacking teams will use this fact to their advantage. Playing the ball quickly from one area of the field to another, a tactic commonly referred to as *changing the point of attack,* can unbalance the defense and create

opportunities to penetrate and go to the goal.

It's important to pass the ball quickly using a minimum number of touches, and then switch the play to attack the defense at its most vulnerable area. Two or three short possession-type passes will serve to draw opponents toward the

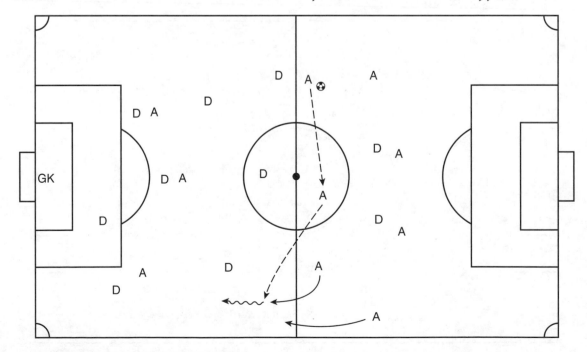

Figure 10.7 Switching the point of attack.

166

ball. At that point, a long cross-field or diagonal pass (figure 10.7) can leave defenders in poor position, unable to recover quickly enough to prevent penetration at the new point of attack.

FINISH WITH A SCORE

Once the team has created gaps of open space within the opposing defense, it must strike quickly before the opportunity is lost. It is to your advantage to create scoring opportunities in central areas that provide a wide shooting angle to goal (figure 10.8). Shots taken front and center of the goal are most likely to find the back of the net, whereas shots taken from the flank where the shooting angle is narrower will rarely beat a competent goalkeeper.

Scoring goals remains the most difficult task in soccer. While sound tactics and coordinated group play will put players in position to score, at the end of the day it is up to the individual to make the final play. On more than one occasion, I've heard coaches say that goal scorers are born, not made. They point to intangible qualities such as anticipation, timing, field vision, composure under pressure, and the ability to be in the right place at the right time, traits that all great goal scorers seem to have. To an extent, I agree with that position although I firmly believe that all players, regardless of inherent strengths and weaknesses, can become more proficient goal scorers through dedicated practice. Develop the ability to shoot with power and accuracy. Learn to release your shot quickly and with either foot. Be able to recognize potential scoring

opportunities, and learn to position yourself to take advantage of those situations. Work on your weaknesses and play to your strengths. If you are willing to commit to that goal, you can become your team's most lethal weapon, the player who can consistently put the finishing touch on a successful attack.

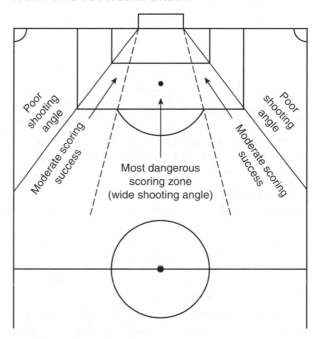

Figure 10.8 Create scoring opportunities with a wide-shooting angle to goal.

Team Attack Drill 1. Check to the Ball and Go

Organize two teams of eight players each, plus goalkeepers. Play on an 80- by 60-yard field with a full-size goal centered on each end line. Each team plays with two forwards in a 3-3-2 alignment. Regular soccer rules apply, except that the two forwards for each team must check back toward their own goal to receive the ball. The checking player is permitted to use one or two touches to pass the ball back to a supporting teammate before spinning and streaking forward to receive a return pass. All attacks on goal must originate off a checking run by one of the forwards. Score

1 point for each successfully executed checking run. Score 2 points for a goal scored. The team scoring more points wins the game.

To Increase Difficulty for Attacking Team

- Add a neutral player who always plays with the defending team.

To Decrease Difficulty for Attacking Team

- Add two neutral players who always join the attacking team.

Success Check

- Check hard to the ball.
- Play firm one- or two-touch passes back to supporting teammate.
- Execute a quick spin turn and streak to goal.
- Finish with a strike on goal.

Team Attack Drill 2. Game With Tactical Dribbling

Organize two teams of six field players and a goalkeeper. Use markers to outline a rectangular field area of 75 by 50 yards with a regulation goal on each end line. Divide the field lengthwise into three equal 25- by 50-yard zones. A goalkeeper gets in position in each goal.

Begin with a kickoff from the center of the field. Each team defends a goal and can score in the opponent's goal. Regular soccer rules apply except for the following restrictions: Players are restricted to three touches of the ball or fewer when within the defending zone nearest their goal. There are no touch restrictions in the middle zone, although players are permitted to dribble the ball forward into open space only; they are not permitted to take on and beat opponents on the dribble. In the front third of the field, players must dribble past an opponent before they can shoot on goal. A player who violates a zone restriction is assessed 1 penalty point for each violation and 1 point for each loss of possession. Individual players keep track of their penalty points. Play for 25 minutes.

To Increase Difficulty for Attacking Team

- Add two neutral players who join the defending team to create a numbers advantage.

To Decrease Difficulty for Attacking Team

- Add two neutral players who join the attacking team to create a numbers advantage.

Success Check

- Advance the ball quickly with limited touches through the defending third of the field.
- Advance the ball through the middle zone by passing or dribbling forward into open space.
- Create one-on-one situations in the attacking third of the field.
- Dribble to penetrate in the attacking third.

Team Attack Drill 3. Penetrate by Dribbling Only

Organize two equal teams of six to eight players each. Do not use goalkeepers. Play within a 60- by 50-yard area. Each team defends an end line and can score by dribbling the ball over the opponent's end line. Regular soccer rules are in effect except for the method of scoring and the following restriction: Players may not pass the ball forward. Square or back passes are used to set up opportunities to advance the ball by dribbling. Award 1 team point each time a player dribbles the ball over the opponent's end line. Play for 20 minutes. The team scoring more points wins.

To Increase Difficulty for Attacking Team

- Decrease the width of field to reduce available space.

To Decrease Difficulty for Attacking Team

- Add three neutral players who play only with the attacking team.

Success Check

- Position for width and depth in attack.

- Pass the ball quickly with limited touches.
- Unbalance the defense to create openings.

Score Your Success

Member of losing team = 1 point

Member of winning team = 3 points

Your score ___

Team Attack Drill 4. Change the Point of Attack

Organize two equal teams of five to seven players each. Use markers to outline a 70- by 50-yard field area. Position flags to represent three 4-yard-wide goals on each end line. Place one goal at each corner and one in the center. Each team defends the three goals on its end line and can score in its opponent's goals. Do not use goalkeepers.

Begin the game with a kickoff from the center of the area. The team in possession should move the ball quickly and attack the goal least defended by changing the point of attack at the appropriate moment. Teams score by kicking the ball through a goal below waist height. Regular soccer rules apply except that the offside law is waived. Play for 20 minutes and keep track of the goals scored.

To Increase Difficulty for Attacking Team

- Limit players to three touches to pass, receive, and shoot the ball.
- Add two neutral players to the game who play with the defending team to create a two-player advantage.

To Decrease Difficulty for Attacking Team

- Enlarge the goals.
- Add two neutral players who play with the attacking team to create a two-player advantage.

Success Check

- Position for width and depth in attack to stretch the defense.
- Draw defenders to ball with short passes and then quickly change point of attack.
- Stress quick transition from defense to attack.

Score Your Success

Member of losing team = 1 point

Member of winning team = 3 points

Your score ___

Team Attack Drill 5. Game With Flank Zones

Organize two teams of five field players and a goalkeeper. Designate two additional players as neutrals who play as wingers with the team in possession. Use markers to outline a field area 75 by 65 yards with a regulation-size goal at the center of each end line. Mark a zone 10 yards wide extending the length of the field on each flank. Station one neutral player (winger) in each flank

zone and a goalkeeper in each goal. Begin the game with a kickoff from the center of the field.

Teams play five-on-five in the central zone. The neutral wingers join the team with the ball to create a two-player advantage for the attack. Wingers may move up and down the length of the field but only within their flank zones. Goals can be scored directly from the central zone or from balls crossed into the goal area by the wingers. When a winger receives a pass from a central player or the goalkeeper, he or she must dribble into the defending team's half of the field and cross the ball into the goal area. Otherwise, regular soccer rules apply. Play for 25 minutes. Award 2 points for a goal scored off a cross and 1 point for a goal scored from a shot originating within the central zone. Each team keeps track of points scored.

To Increase Difficulty for Attacking Team

- Restrict players to three touches or fewer to pass, receive, or shoot the ball.
- Station a neutral defending player in each flank zone to create a one-on-one situation on the flank.

To Decrease Difficulty for Attacking Team

- Station two additional neutrals in the cen-

tral zone who join the attacking team to create a 7v5-player advantage in the central zone.

Success Check

- Position players to ensure width and depth in attack.
- Create scoring opportunities in central areas.
- Execute timed runs into goal area to score off crosses.

Score Your Success

Member of losing team = 1 point

Member of winning team = 3 points

Your score ____

Team Attack Drill 6.   Early Entry Pass

Organize two teams of eight players each. Play on a regulation field with a full-size goal centered on each end line. Position a goalkeeper in each regulation goal. Use flags to represent three 6-yard-wide entry goals on the front edge of each penalty area. Position one entry goal at each corner of the penalty area and one in the center. Do not use goalkeepers in the entry goals.

Teams play 8v8 between the two penalty areas. Attacking players are not permitted to enter the opposing team's penalty area until the ball has been entered (passed) through one of the entry goals. Once the ball is entered into the penalty area, three players from the attacking team sprint into the area to finish the attack. Defending players are not permitted to enter their own penalty area. Once the ball has entered, the attacking team must generate a shot on goal with three passes or fewer. Award 1 point for each entry pass into the opponent's penalty area, and 1 additional point for a goal scored. Play for 25 minutes and keep track of points scored.

To Increase Difficulty for Attacking Team

- Require three touches or fewer to receive and pass the ball.
- Reduce width of entry goals.

To Decrease Difficulty for Attacking Team

- Add three neutral players who play with the team in possession to create a numbers-up situation.

Success Check

- Play the ball quickly and with limited touches to change the point of attack.
- Use square passes to set up penetrating passes.
- Try to enter the ball into the scoring area as early as possible.

Score Your Success

Member of losing team = 1 point

Member of winning team = 3 points

Your score ____

Team Attack Drill 7. Three-Zone Transition Game

Organize three teams (A, B, C) of four players each. In addition, designate one neutral player and two goalkeepers. Use markers to outline a playing area of 75 by 50 yards with a regulation goal on each end line. Divide the field lengthwise into three equal 50- by 25-yard zones. Teams A and C begin in the end zones; team B begins in the middle zone. A goalkeeper takes position in each goal. Team B in the middle zone begins with the ball. The neutral player joins with the team in possession of the ball.

Team B, assisted by the neutral player, advances and attempts to score against team A. Team A gains possession when they tackle the ball or intercept a pass, after the goalkeeper makes a save, after a goal is scored, or when the ball travels over the end line last touched by a player from team B.

After winning the ball, team A players and the neutral player move forward from their end zone into the middle zone. Team B players remain in the end zone to play as defenders on the next round. Team A players quickly organize in the middle zone before advancing into the opposite end zone to attack team C. Regular soccer rules apply. Play for 25 minutes. The team scoring the most goals wins the game.

To Increase Difficulty for Attacking Team

- Limit attacking players to three touches or fewer to pass, receive, and shoot the ball.
- Add one additional player to each team to decrease the available space.

To Decrease Difficulty for Attacking Team

- Add two additional neutral players who join the attacking team.

Success Check

- Make a quick transition from defense to attack.
- Position players for width and depth in attack.
- Move the ball quickly and with limited touches.
- Create quality scoring opportunities in central areas.

Score Your Success

Member of losing team = 1 point

Member of winning team = 3 points

Your score ____

Team Attack Drill 8. Game With End-Line and Sideline Neutrals

Use markers to outline a 50- by 60-yard field area with a full-size goal centered on each end line. Organize three teams (A, B, C) of six field players each. Teams A and B take positions within the field area; each defends a goal. A goalkeeper gets in position in each goal. Team C players stand along the perimeter lines of the field, one on each sideline and two along each end line (one on either side of the goal), to function as support players.

Teams A and B compete within the area. Players can use the sideline and end-line support players (team C) as passing options, creating a 12v6-player advantage for the attacking team. Sideline and end-line support players are not permitted to enter the field area, although they can move laterally along the perimeter lines. Sideline players have a two-touch restriction; end-line players have a one-touch restriction. Play for 10 minutes or two goals scored, whichever occurs first, after which one of the middle teams (A or B) switches positions with team C players to become the sideline and end-line support players. Play a minitournament so that each team plays every other team once. Award 1 point for a goal scored. The team scoring the most goals wins the competition.

To Increase Difficulty for Attacking Team

- Reduce size of field to limit time and space available to players.

- Restrict central players to two touches to receive and pass the ball.

To Decrease Difficulty for Attacking Team

- Permit unlimited touches for the sideline and end-line support players.

Success Check

- Use passing combinations for width and depth.

- Play quickly, with few touches of the ball.
- Change the point of attack to unbalance the defense.

Score Your Success

Member of third-place team = 1 point
Member of second-place team = 3 points
Member of winning team = 5 points
Your score ___

Team Attack Drill 9. Pass, Dribble, or Shoot to Score

Organize two equal teams of six to eight players each, plus goalkeepers. Use markers to outline a playing area of 50 by 70 yards divided in half by a midline. Position a full-size goal at the center of each end line. Place cones or flags to represent a 2-yard-wide goal on each flank, along the midline, and near the touchline. Teams take positions in opposite halves of the field. A goalkeeper stands in each full-size goal. Begin with a kickoff from the center of the field.

Regular soccer rules apply except for the methods of scoring. Award 2 team points for a goal scored in a regulation goal, 1 point for a pass completed to a teammate through a small goal on the midline, 1 point for beating an opponent on the dribble in the attacking half of the field, and 1 point for a shot on goal saved by the goalkeeper. Play for 25 minutes and keep track of the points scored. The team scoring more points wins the game.

To Increase Difficulty for Attacking Team

- Add two neutral defenders to provide the defending team with a numerical advantage.

- Require all shots to be first-time shots, without settling the ball.

To Decrease Difficulty for Attacking Team

- Position four small goals on the midline to provide additional scoring options.
- Add two neutral attackers to the game to provide the attacking team with a numerical advantage.

Success Check

- Position for width and depth in attack.
- Choose the most appropriate scoring option in a given situation.
- Change the point of attack to attack the defense at its most vulnerable spots.
- Create scoring opportunities in the most dangerous scoring zones.

Score Your Success

Member of losing team = 1 point
Member of winning team = 3 points
Your score ___

Team Attack Drill 10. Total Team Support

Organize two teams of seven players each, plus goalkeepers. Play on a 50- by 80-yard area divided by a midline with a full-size goal centered on each end line. Each team defends the goal on its end line and can score in the opponent's goal. Regular soccer rules are in effect except for the following restriction: All seven members of the attacking team must move forward into the opponent's half of the field before the team can attempt a shot on goal. This rule is in effect to ensure team compactness while moving forward in the attack. A score is disallowed if any attacking player is in his or her own half of the field when the shot is taken. Award 1 point for a shot on goal saved by the keeper; award 2 points for a goal scored. Play for 20 minutes and keep track of points scored.

To Increase Difficulty for Attacking Team

- Restrict players to three touches or fewer to receive, pass, and shoot the ball.

To Decrease Difficulty for Attacking Team

- Permit two members of the attacking team to remain in their own half when a shot is taken.

Success Check

- Maintain team shape for width and depth.
- Limit dribbling in defending half of field.
- Encourage dribbling to beat an opponent in attacking half.
- Team moves forward in a compact unit.
- Provide support at proper angle and distance.
- Create scoring opportunities with wide angle to goal.

Score Your Success

Member of losing team = 1 point

Member of winning team = 3 points

Your score ____

Team Attack
Drill 11. Seven Attackers Versus Five Defenders

Designate a five-player team, a seven-player team, and one goalkeeper. Play on one-half of a regulation field with a full-size goal centered on the end line. Use cones or flags to represent two 3 yard wide goals positioned 20 yards apart on the midline of the regulation field. The goalkeeper plays in the full-size goal; do not use goalkeepers in the small goals. The seven-player team attempts to score in the full-size goal and defends the two small goals. The five-player team defends the large goal and can score by passing the ball through either of the small goals. Award the seven-player team possession of the ball to begin the game. The coach serves as the official scorekeeper. The seven-player team can earn points as follows:

- 1 point for eight passes in succession without loss of possession
- 1 point for a successful give-and-go (wall) pass
- 1 point each time an attacker penetrates past a defender on the dribble
- 1 point for a shot on goal saved by the goalkeeper

- 2 points for each goal scored off a shot taken within the penalty area
- 2 points for each goal scored off a ball crossed from the flank
- 3 points for each goal scored from a shot taken 20 yards or more from the goal

The five-player team can earn 1 point for each of the following actions: tackling the ball, intercepting a pass, or kicking the ball through either of the small goals.

Play for 30 minutes and keep track of team points on the scorecard in figure 10.9.

To Increase Difficulty for Seven-Player Team

- Restrict players to three touches or fewer to receive, pass, and shoot the ball.
- Add a defending player to create a 7v6 situation.
- Reduce width of field to limit available space.

To Decrease Difficulty for Seven-Player Team

- Add an attacking player to create an 8v5 situation.

Attacking Team (Seven Players)

	Points possible	Points earned
Make eight passes in succession	1	
Execute successful give-and-go pass	1	
Penetrate past defender on dribble	1	
Take shot on goal	1	
Score goal from within penalty area	2	
Score goal off cross	2	
Score goal from 20+ yards	3	
Total		

Defending Team (Five Players)

	Points possible	Points earned
Successfully tackle offensive player	1	
Intercept pass	1	
Score goal in small goal	1	
Total		

Figure 10.9 Scorecard for seven attackers versus five defenders drill.

Success Check

- Position for width and depth in attack.
- Change the point of attack to unbalance the defense.
- Create one-on-one situations in attacking third.
- Create scoring opportunities in the most dangerous (central) areas.
- Exploit the flank areas.

Score Your Success

Member of losing team = 3 points

Member of winning team = 5 points

Your score ___

SUCCESS SUMMARY OF TEAM ATTACK

The principles of team attack apply to all systems and styles of play. They are designed to provide a framework on which players can base their decisions and subsequent actions. The teamwork required to create a formidable attacking side will occur only when individual players are willing and able to channel their efforts toward the common (team) good.

It is best to practice team attack tactics in competitive, matchlike situations. The games need not be full-sided (11 players per team), but they must include a sufficient number of players to incorporate all the principles of team attack.

The drills described in step 10 involve large groups of players, so it is difficult to assign individual point scores. Each of the drills has been assigned a point value based on the group (team) performance. In most cases, each player on the winning team receives an identical point score while each player on the losing team receives an identical but lower point score. While this method of scoring may not accurately reflect the performance of a very talented individual on a very weak team, the scores will portray how the group of players worked together to integrate the principles of team attack into their play. In this manner, you can evaluate individual performance as it relates to the group performance. Record scores in the following chart and total the points to get an evaluation of group performance.

Team Attack

1.	Check to the Ball and Go	_____ out of 3
2.	Game With Tactical Dribbling	_____ out of 5
3.	Penetrate by Dribbling Only	_____ out of 3
4.	Change the Point of Attack	_____ out of 3
5.	Game With Flank Zones	_____ out of 3
6.	Early Entry Pass	_____ out of 3
7.	Three-Zone Transition Game	_____ out of 3
8.	Game With End-Line and Sideline Neutrals	_____ out of 5
9.	Pass, Dribble, or Shoot to Score	_____ out of 3
10.	Total Team Support	_____ out of 3
11.	Seven Attackers Versus Five Defenders	_____ out of 5
Total		_____ *out of 39*

A total score of 30 points or more indicates that you have successfully mastered the concepts. A score in the range of 23 to 29 points is considered adequate. Review the principles of team attack once again before moving on to step 11. If you scored fewer than 23 points, you need to review the material again, repeat the drills, and improve your overall performance before moving on to step 11.

Defending As a Team

At this point you understand the responsibilities of the first, second, and third defenders. The next step in the team-building process is to incorporate these strategies into an overall plan for team defense. My years of experience as a player and coach have made me well aware of the fact that a group of talented individuals does not necessarily form a cohesive defensive unit. Effective team defense, even more so than team attack, requires teammates to work together in an organized, disciplined manner. Players must be physically fit. They must play with commitment and determination. They must be able to compete successfully in one-on-one situations. They must be able to outjump opponents to win air balls. They must understand the important roles of the pressuring (first), covering (second), and balancing (third) defenders. Above all, they

must accept their roles in the team's defensive scheme and understand how those roles relate to the group as a whole.

Successful team defense is predicated in large part on the decisions players make in response to changing situations during play. Poor decisions will eventually translate into goals scored against the team. You can improve your decision-making skills by developing a clear understanding of what your team is trying to accomplish when the opponent has the ball. The following principles of team defense provide a general framework on which to base your decisions and subsequent actions. These principles are universal to all systems of play and progress through a logical sequence from the moment the team loses the ball until the instant it regains possession and goes on the attack.

APPLY IMMEDIATE PRESSURE AT THE POINT OF ATTACK

A team is most vulnerable to counterattack during the few seconds immediately after loss of possession. Even experienced players can lose focus and become disorganized as they make the

transition between attack and defense.

To prevent the opponent from mounting a swift counterattack, the defending player nearest the ball (first defender) must initiate immediate pressure at the point of attack. The challenge should not be a reckless attempt to tackle the ball, but rather calculated and controlled pressure designed to delay penetration via the pass or dribble. If the pressuring defender can force the first attacker to play the ball backward, or at least square across the field, defending teammates will have extra time in which to regroup and organize behind the ball.

RECOVER GOAL SIDE OF THE BALL

While pressure is applied at the point of attack, defenders away from the ball quickly withdraw to positions behind the ball, referred to as *goal-side position* (figure 11.1). From a goal-side position, you will be able to keep the ball and the opponent you are responsible for marking in view. Also, you will be in position to provide cover for your teammates. As defending players relocate behind the ball, they can compress areas of open space between the ball and their goal, making it more difficult for the attacking team to penetrate and create scoring opportunities.

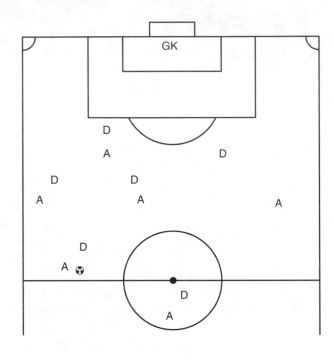

Figure 11.1 Goal-side position.

CONCENTRATE THE DEFENDERS

The defending team's highest priority is to deny opponents space and time in the areas from which goals are most often scored. Toward that aim, consolidating players in the most dangerous (central) scoring zones has become an accepted tactic. As players retreat to a position goal side of the ball, they funnel inward toward the center of the field (figure 11.2). This pinching inward of players behind the ball is designed to eliminate gaps of open space within the center of the defense, thereby preventing opponents from slotting passes through the most vital scoring zones.

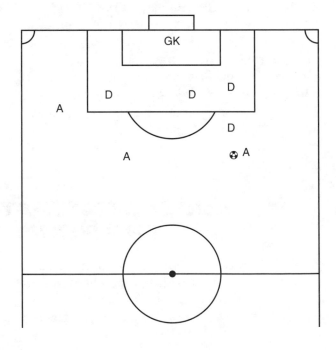

Figure 11.2 Concentration of defenders. Defenders pinch inward to protect the most dangerous attacking space.

COMPACT THE TEAM

The typical soccer field is approximately 120 yards long and 75 yards wide, significantly larger than an American football field. That is an extremely large area for 10 field players to cover when the opponent has the ball. The principle of team compactness is designed to compress the field vertically by reducing the distance between the defending team's back players and front players (figure 11.3). Team compactness eliminates gaps of open space within the defense to make it more difficult for the attacking team to penetrate through the defense. To achieve compactness, defending players must press toward the ball as one compact group. Defending players near the ball must apply immediate pressure on the first attacker to deny that player the opportunity to serve an early long ball behind a compact defense.

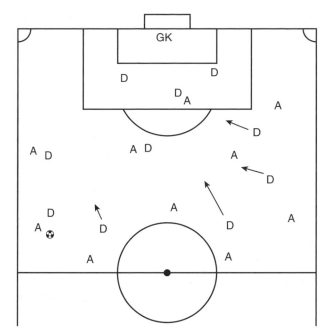

Figure 11.3 Team compactness. Defending teammates are positioned to provide tight cover for one another.

PROTECT SPACE BEHIND THE DEFENSE

As players get in position to reduce the open space within the defense, they must also take measures to protect the space between the deepest (last) defender and the goalkeeper. This is achieved through the principle of *defensive balance*. As discussed previously, balance in defense is provided by players away from the ball as they get in position along an imaginary diagonal line that begins at the ball and travels toward the far goalpost. From a position along the line of balance, defending players can keep the ball in view and also cut off passes directed into the space behind the defense. As a general rule, the farther a player is from the ball, the deeper his or her position along the line of balance should be (figure 11.4).

The goalkeeper can also help protect the vulnerable space behind the defense. He or she must be prepared to move forward to intercept passes that enter the space behind the last defender. When the goalkeeper leaves the penalty area, he or she must play the ball with his or her feet.

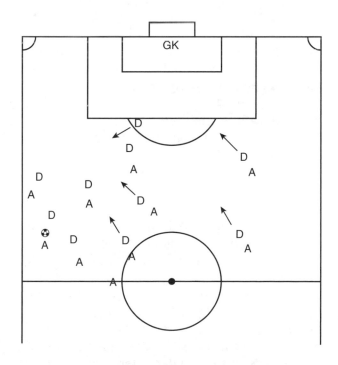

Figure 11.4 Line of balance. Players away from the ball positioned along the line of balance can cut off opponents' passes played behind or through the defense.

MAKE PLAY PREDICTABLE

A primary goal of team attack tactics is to create as many options as possible for the player on the ball to make it difficult for the defending team to anticipate what that player will do. Conversely, defending tactics are designed to limit options through pressure at the point of attack coupled with tight marking of support attackers in the vicinity of the ball (figure 11.5). Immediate pressure on the ball will force the first attacker to play quickly and, since there are no short passing options available, possibly attempt a longer pass with greater risk of losing possession.

Defending players can also eliminate passing options by getting in position to block the passing lanes between attackers, thereby forcing the player on the ball to play the ball through the air or back to a supporting teammate. In either case, the advantage shifts to the defense. Lofted passes are generally less accurate than ground passes and, from a defensive perspective, square and back passes provide additional time for defending players to organize and get in position goal side of the ball.

Finally, defending players can make play more predictable by funneling the first attacker into an area where the space is restricted. For example, when you force a flank attacker to dribble toward the sideline, you effectively reduce the space through which he or she can pass the ball forward (figure 11.6). In that sense, you have limited his or her passing options and made play more predictable. You can achieve the same results by funneling the dribbler into the space occupied by a covering teammate.

The principles of team defense can be listed in a step-by-step progression, but actual implementation of these principles must occur swiftly and simultaneously. At this point, the defending team should be in excellent position to win the ball. There is pressure at the point of attack, defending players are in position to provide cover and balance for one another, the most dangerous scoring zones are protected, and the play of the attacking team has been made as predictable as possible. The final step in the sequence is for the first defender to challenge for and win the ball or force the opponent to play

the ball into an area where a defending teammate can step forward to intercept the pass.

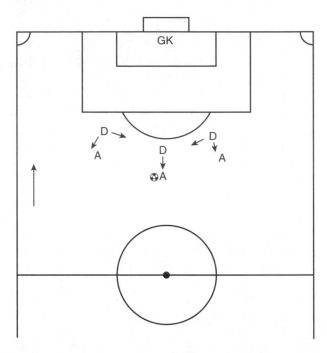

Figure 11.5 Defending players can reduce attacking options by tight marking in the vicinity of the ball.

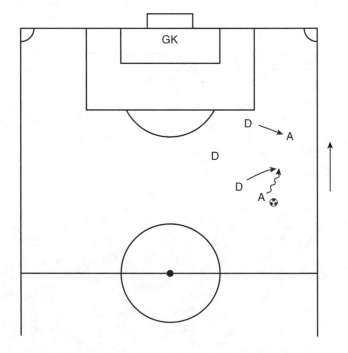

Figure 11.6 Funneling the attacker into tight space along the touchline will reduce his or her passing options.

Team Defense Drill 1. Tight Marking Game

Organize two equal teams of six to eight players each. Use markers to outline a field area of approximately 50 by 75 yards with a 4-yard-wide goal at the midpoint of each end line. Each team defends a goal and can score in the opponent's goal. Do not use goalkeepers.

Begin with a kickoff from the center of the field. Regular soccer rules are in effect. The only restriction is that strict one-on-one marking is required of all players. Shots may be taken from anywhere on the field, so marking must be very tight to prevent long-range scores. Immediate pressure at the point of attack is essential. Change of possession occurs when a defender steals the ball, when the ball goes out of play, or when a goal is scored. Play for 20 minutes and keep tally of goals.

To Increase Difficulty for Defending Team

- Widen the goals to 6 yards.
- Require teams to defend two goals on each end line.

To Decrease Difficulty for Defending Team

- Limit players to three touches or fewer to pass, receive, and shoot the ball.
- Decrease width of goal to 3 yards.

Success Check

- Apply immediate pressure at point of attack.
- Get in position to block passing lanes to goal.
- Provide tight cover for first defender.
- Provide balance away from ball.

Score Your Success

Member of losing team = 3 points

Member of winning team = 5 points

Your score ___

Team Defense Drill 2.
Combination One-on-One and Zonal Marking Game

Organize two teams of six field players and a goalkeeper each. Play on a 50- by 75-yard field with a regulation-size goal centered on each end line. Each team defends a goal and can score in the opponent's goal. Regular soccer rules are in effect with the following restrictions: Four players from each team are assigned a specific opponent to mark and must tackle the ball from that player only. The two remaining field players on each team are assigned zonal marking. These players get in position behind the four markers as the last line of defense on their teams. The zonal defenders provide cover for their teammates and are limited to three touches to control and pass the ball. The three-touch restriction prevents the zonal defenders from advancing the ball by dribbling.

Play for 15 minutes. Every 5 minutes, designate two different players as the zonal defenders so that all players have an opportunity to play in a zonal role and a one-on-one marker role. The team scoring more goals wins the game.

To Increase Difficulty for Defending Team

- Enlarge the area of the field to create more available space for attacking team.
- Add two neutral players who play with the attacking team, forcing the zonal players to mark one-on-one at times.

To Decrease Difficulty for Defending Team

- Reduce length and width of field to limit space and time available to attacking team.

Success Check

- Apply immediate pressure at point of attack.
- Tightly mark second attackers.
- Compact the field.
- Zonal players provide close coverage and balance.

Team Defense
Drill 3. Ball-Oriented (Zonal) Defending

Organize two teams of four players each. Play on a 20-yard-long by 35-yard-wide area. Divide the field widthwise into three zones. The end zones (1 and 3) are 10 yards wide and 20 yards deep; the middle zone (2) is 15 yards wide and 20 yards deep. Place cones or flags to represent a 2-yard-wide goal on opposite sides in each zone. (Note: Goals in each zone are 20 yards apart.) One ball is required per game. Use colored vests to differentiate teams.

Each team is responsible for defending the three goals on its end line (one goal in each zone) and can score in the opponent's three goals. One player from each team takes position in zones 1 and 3. Those players are responsible for defending the team's goal in their respective zones. Two players from each team take position in zone 2 and are responsible for defending the goal in that (the widest) zone. Defending players are restricted to movement within their zone and the adjacent zone. One player in the middle zone can slide sideways into an end zone to provide support (defensive cover) for the teammate in that zone, when appropriate. Likewise, defending players in the end zones can slide laterally into the middle zone to provide cover and balance for the central defenders. There are no restrictions on the team with the ball; attacking players can move between zones and do not have a touch restriction.

Emphasize proper defensive shape and bal-ance. Keep in mind that zonal positioning is based on the location of the ball and the position of defending teammates, not the position of opposing players. Players do not mark a specific opponent. Regular soccer rules apply. Award 1 point for each goal scored.

To Increase Difficulty for Defenders

- Increase width of zones.
- Increase width of goals.

To Decrease Difficulty for Defenders

- Reduce width of zone.
- Restrict attackers to movement within a specific zone.

Success Check

- Defender nearest ball applies pressure.
- Deny penetration via the dribble.
- Defenders in adjacent zone slide toward the ball to provide coverage and balance.
- Play ball-oriented defense—get in position according to location of the ball.

Team Defense
Drill 4. Three Passes in the Defending Half

Organize two teams of six field players and a goalkeeper each. Play on a 50- by 80-yard field divided lengthwise by a midline. Place a regulation goal on each end line. Each team has three players in its defending half and three players in the opponent's half of the field; players are not permitted to cross the midline. Regular soccer rules are in effect except for the following restriction: Once the defending team wins the ball in its half of the field, it is permitted a maximum of three passes to send the ball to a teammate in the opponent's half. This restriction emphasizes the importance of moving the ball quickly and without risk of possession loss when in your own end. Violation of the three-pass restriction is penalized by loss of possession to the opponent. Play for 20 minutes. The team scoring more goals wins.

To Increase Difficulty for Defenders

- Add two neutral players to the game who always join with the attacking team.

To Decrease Difficulty

- Allow five passes in the defending half before entering the ball into the opponent's half of the field.

Success Check

- Defend as a compact unit.
- Deny opponents space and time to develop passing combinations.
- Make swift transition from defense to attack on change of possession.
- Avoid loss of possession in your own half.

Score Your Success

Member of losing team = 3 points
Member of winning team = 5 points
Your score ___

Team Defense Drill 5.   Defend Numbers Down

Organize two teams of seven field players and a goalkeeper. Designate two additional neutral players who join the team in possession to create a 9v7-player advantage for the attacking team. Play on a 60- by 90-yard field with a regulation goal centered on each end line. Each team defends a goal and can score in the opponent's goal. Regular soccer rules apply.

The defending team, being outnumbered, employs zonal marking and implements all principles of team defense. The player nearest the ball applies immediate pressure at the point of attack while the remaining players retreat to a position goal side of the ball. Defending players should compress the field vertically and horizontally so as to limit the time and space available to attackers. Play for 20 minutes. The team conceding fewer goals wins the game.

To Increase Difficulty for Defending Team

- Increase width of field.

- Designate three neutral players who play with the attacking team to create a 10v7 advantage for the attack.

To Decrease Difficulty for Defending Team

- Narrow the field.
- Limit attacking players to three touches or fewer to receive, pass, and shoot the ball.

Success Check

- Apply immediate pressure on the ball.
- Consolidate defenders in central areas.
- Position for coverage and balance.
- Deny shots from central areas.

Score Your Success

Member of losing team = 3 points
Member of winning team = 5 points
Your score ___

Team Defense Drill 6.   Six-on-Four (Plus Four)

Six defenders compete against four attackers within a 30- by 30-yard area. In addition, four neutral players position on the perimeter of the area, one on each sideline. The four attackers attempt

to keep the ball from the defenders and are permitted unlimited touches to control and pass the ball among themselves. The attackers are also permitted to pass the ball to the neutral players on the sidelines Neutral players are restricted to two touches and are not permitted to pass the ball to another neutral player; they must return the ball to one of the attackers within the field area. If the defending team wins the ball, it attempts to keep possession from the four attackers. Defenders are restricted to three touches or fewer to control and pass the ball. The defending team is awarded 1 point for six or more consecutive passes without loss of possession. Play for 15 minutes and keep track of points scored.

To Increase Difficulty for Defenders

- Increase size of field.
- Add an attacker to the game to make it 6v 5(plus 4).

To Reduce Difficulty for Defenders

- Add a defender to the game to make it 7v4 (plus 4).

- Allow defenders four touches to receive and pass the ball.

Success Check

- Apply immediate pressure at point of attack.
- Close distance as the ball is traveling.
- Limit passing options.
- Position for coverage and balance.

Score Your Success

Defending team totals 0 to 5 points = 1 point

Defending team totals 6 to 9 points = 3 points

Defending team totals 10 points or more = 5 points

Your score ___

Team Defense Drill 7.   Pressure to Deny Service

Organize two teams of eight field players and one goalkeeper. Play on a regulation field with a full-size goal centered on each end line. Use markers to designate an offside line 35 yards from each end line. Teams take positions on opposite halves of the field but between the two offside lines. Each team defends the goal on its end line and can score in the opponent's goal.

Begin with a kickoff from the center spot. Regular soccer rules apply, except for the following restrictions: An attacking player beyond the offside line (35 yards or more from goal) is not considered offside even if positioned behind the last defender, and defending players cannot enter the area between the offside line and their goal before the ball enters that area. These rule variations enable the team in possession to play the ball behind the last line of defending players to create breakaway situations. To prevent this, the defending team must deny the opponent the time and space required to serve long balls behind the defense. The emphasis is on immediate pressure at the point of attack coupled with defensive compactness to eliminate open spaces within the defense. Regular scoring is in effect. Play for 25 minutes. The team conceding fewer goals wins the game.

To Increase Difficulty for Defending Team

- Add two neutral players who always join the attacking team to create a 10v8-player advantage for the attack.

To Decrease Difficulty for Defending Team

- Add two neutral players who always join the defending team to create a 10v8-player advantage for the defense.

Success Check

- Maintain proper defensive shape.
- Apply immediate pressure at point of attack to deny long service.
- Tightly cover second defenders.
- Defenders away from ball provide balance.
- Defending players compress the field lengthwise.

Score Your Success

Member of losing team = 3 points

Member of winning team = 5 points

Your score ___

Team Defense Drill 8. Defend the Final Third

Organize one team of five defenders and one goalkeeper and one team of eight attackers. Play on one half of a regulation field with a full-size goal centered on the end line. The game is played within the width of the penalty area (44 yards). Use markers to extend the penalty area to the halfway line. Divide the field vertically into two zones, each 22 yards wide. Position flags to represent two goals four yards wide on the halfway line, one in each zone. The five-player team and goalkeeper defend the full-size goal; the eight-player team defends the two small goals.

Divide the eight-player team into two groups of four, one group within each side zone of the field. A server with a supply of balls stands behind one of the small goals. The server initiates play by distributing a ball to the eight-player attacking team. The attacking team attempts to score in the large goal. Each group of four attackers must stay in their respective side zones of the field, although the ball can cross from one zone into the other.

The five-player team uses a back line of four defenders and a defensive (holding) midfielder who fronts the defense. Members of the defending team are not restricted to movement within a specific zone. The defensive midfielder should be very active, constantly moving to pressure the ball. The back line of defenders provides cover and balance for one another and for the defensive midfielder as needed. Coordinated movement by all five defenders is required to accomplish that objective.

If a defender steals the ball or the goalkeeper makes a save, the five-player team switches to attack and can score in the small goals on the halfway line. The eight-player team defends the small goals. If the ball leaves the field, the server restarts action immediately by playing a ball to the eight-player team. Award the eight-player team 2 points for a goal scored in the full-size goal; award the five-player team 1 point for a goal scored in either of the small goals. Play for 15 minutes. The team scoring more points wins the game. (Note: Repeat this drill a sufficient number of times so that each player has a chance to play on the five-player defending team.)

To Increase Difficulty for Defending Team

- Add two attackers (one in each zone) to create a 10v5 situation.

To Decrease Difficulty for Defending Team

- Narrow the field.
- Add a second defensive midfielder to the five-player team to create an 8v6 situation.

Success Check

- Apply pressure at point of attack.
- Back four defenders are linked in their movements.
- Position to provide coverage and balance.
- Deny the most dangerous attacking space.

Score Your Success

Defending team loses = 0 points for each player on the five-player team

Defending team wins = 2 points for each player on the five-player team

Your score ___

SUCCESS SUMMARY OF TEAM DEFENSE

The principles of team defense apply to all systems and styles of play. They are designed to provide a framework on which individual players can coordinate their actions so that the performance of the group (team) exceeds the abilities of individual players. Establishing a formidable team defense is accomplished by applying immediate pressure at the point of attack, by providing cover (support) for the first defender in the event he or she is beaten on the dribble, by compressing the field vertically and horizontally to limit open spaces between defending teammates, by limiting attacking options, and finally by winning the ball and initiating a counterattack.

The teamwork required for establishing a solid team defense will occur only when individual players are willing and able to fulfill their specific roles within the team's defensive scheme. This is best accomplished through repetitive practice in competitive, large-group situations.

The team defense drills described in step 11 involve large groups of players playing in concert. Each of the drills has been assigned a point value based on the group performance. For example, in most of the drills each player on the winning team receives an identical point score while each player on the losing team receives an identical but lower point score. While this method of evaluation may not accurately reflect the performance of a very talented individual on a very weak team, scores will depict how the group of players worked together to integrate the principles of team defense into their play. In this respect, you can evaluate your individual performance as it relates to the group performance. Your coach can observe the training session and provide specific feedback on the strengths and weaknesses of your overall performance. Record your scores in the following chart and then total the points to get an estimate of the group performance.

Team Defense

1. Tight Marking Game _____ out of 5

2. Combination One-on-One and Zonal Marking Game _____ out of 5

3. Ball-Oriented (Zonal) Defending _____ out of 5

4. Three Passes in the Defending Half _____ out of 5

5. Defend Numbers Down _____ out of 5

6. Six-on-Four (Plus Four) _____ out of 5

7. Pressure to Deny Service _____ out of 5

8. Defend the Final Third _____ out of 2

Total _____ *out of 37*

A combined score of 30 or more points indicates that you have sufficiently mastered the defending concepts discussed in step 11. A score in the range of 23 to 29 points is considered adequate. Rehearse the principles of team defense once again as a group before moving on to step 12. A score of 22 points or fewer indicates that you and your teammates need to review the material again, repeat the drills, and improve both individual and group performance before moving on to step 12, the final step.

Understanding Player Formations, Roles, and Responsibilities

The team's system (formation) of play refers to the organization and positioning of the 10 field players. In my experience, one of the first questions asked by enthusiastic young coaches seeking to expand their knowledge of the game is "What do you think is the best formation to play?" On the surface, that sounds like a reasonable question, but in reality there is no clear-cut answer. The best I can offer is that it all depends—on the players.

At its most fundamental level, the game of soccer is not about formations. Soccer is about players—their strengths, their weaknesses, their personalities, their character. For that reason, the system of play most appropriate for my team may differ from the system that works for your team. The best formation is one that maximizes players' strengths while minimizing or hiding their weaknesses, one that provides the team the best possible opportunity to succeed.

There are no magical formations that can transform ordinary players into great players or change a weak team into a dominant team. No system of play will work effectively if the team is stocked with inferior players, whereas virtually any formation can succeed with superior players. So although the system of play provides

structure and defines a starting point for team tactics, it should never be the primary focus. Individual player development is and always will be the most important ingredient for success on the soccer field.

The individual, group, and team tactics you have learned to this point apply to all systems, although player roles and responsibilities may differ from one formation to another. Within the team's system of play, each player has a clearly defined role. Some roles are narrower than others. In some cases, players listed as playing the same position may be assigned different responsibilities. For example, two players may both be called *midfielders* but fulfill substantially different roles. One may function as a defensive, or holding, midfielder, whose primary responsibility is to anchor the defense and shut down the opposing team's playmaker; the other may be an attacking midfielder, whose primary role is to create scoring opportunities for teammates. To achieve the cohesive play necessary for successful team performance, each player must understand and accept his or her role within the system.

Several different formations were apparent at the 2002 World Cup tournament. Most teams used four defenders spread across the back in zonal coverage. One or sometimes two defensive (holding) midfielders were positioned in front of the four defenders. The defensive midfielder functions as sort of a front sweeper, whose role is to prevent penetration through the center of the defense, to act as a screen for the central defenders, and to initiate the attack through accurate distribution of the ball. One midfielder was stationed on each flank to provide width in attack, and one was usually assigned a central attacking role, playing underneath the forwards. Most teams, including World Cup finalists Brazil and Germany, played with two forwards, although a few, such as France and the Netherlands, played with three front-runners. Virtually all teams played zonal (ball-oriented) defense or a combination of zone and one-on-one marking. I mention such differences in how teams were organized only to emphasize the fact that no system of play is inherently better than any other. They all work if played correctly.

SYSTEM ORGANIZATION

A system of play is composed by 10 field players and a goalkeeper. Field players are designated as defenders, midfielders, and forwards. Variations in how the field players are deployed result in different formations and players' responsibilities. In describing a system of play, the first number refers to the defenders, the second to the midfielders, and the third to the forwards. The goalkeeper is not included in the numbering of players.

The following provides a historical perspective on some of the more popular formations of the latter half of the 20th century. It concludes with a brief discussion of a few newer variations unveiled at the 2002 World Cup and 2003 Confederations Cup.

4-2-4 System

The 4-2-4 system (figure 12.1) was first introduced by the Brazilian national team during the 1958 World Cup. Blessed with several world-class players, including the incomparable Pele, Brazil attracted the attention of soccer enthusiasts throughout the world by winning the world championship. In the aftermath, the 4-2-4 system gained widespread popularity as coaches at all levels of competition tried to emulate Brazil's success.

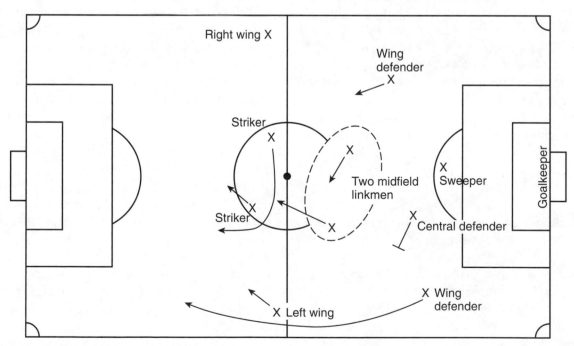

Figure 12.1 4-2-4 system.

The 4-2-4 places an emphasis on an attacking style of soccer with a large number of players in forward positions. The four defenders are organized with a sweeper, one central (stopper) back, and right and left flank defenders. The flank defenders and stopper are generally assigned marking responsibilities, while the sweeper provides cover for the back line. The sweeper functions as a free defender and is not assigned a specific opponent to mark.

Two central midfield players, or linkmen, serve as the connecting thread between the defenders and forwards. The midfielders are responsible for supporting the forwards on attack. They establish the first line of defense when the opposing team has the ball.

The four forwards are organized with two wingers and two central forwards or strikers. One striker usually is stationed high up in the opponent's defense as a target to spearhead the attack. The other often plays underneath the target where he or she can also provide help in the midfield as needed.

The 4-2-4 system places an emphasis on flank play and relies on wingers who have the ability to penetrate on the dribble to open up space for the strikers. The two midfielders must be true workhorses because they have to patrol a large field area. For the most part, the player positions are fairly static with minimal interchanging of roles.

4-4-2 System

From a tactical point of view, the 4-2-4 system places tremendous responsibility on the two midfielders. In an attempt to lighten the load, teams withdraw their wingers into the midfield to create a 4-4-2 alignment (figure 12.2). Theoretically with four players patrolling the midfield, the team should dominate play in that area.

Players' responsibilities in the 4-4-2 are similar in most respects to their responsibilities in the 4-2-4. When the 4-4-2 system first appeared, most teams played with a sweeper positioned behind the three other defenders. Today most teams play a flat back four, with the four defenders playing flat across the field in zonal coverage. Four midfielders get in position ahead of the back line. A wide midfielder patrols each flank, providing width in attack, while two midfielders set up in central positions. The talents of the two inside midfielders should complement one another: One typically occupies a more attacking role, the other a more defensive role. The abilities of the two forwards should also complement one another. Usually one forward plays as more of a target, looking to receive passes from his

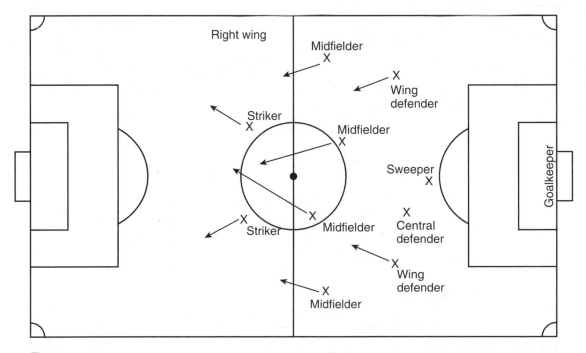

Figure 12.2 4-4-2 system.

or her midfielders or defenders, while the other plays a more active role, darting into open space and playing off the target.

Traditional wingers—players who typically stay high and wide in the attack and rarely withdraw to help on defense—are absent in the 4-4-2. They have been replaced by flank midfielders, players who withdraw into their own end to defend when the opponent has the ball and then move forward quickly into the attack when their team gains possession. If the flank midfielders fail to make the quick transition from defense to attack, then the 4-4-2 can take on a defensive orientation.

Playing the 4-4-2 successfully requires quality midfielders who can control the ball and dictate the tempo of the game. It also requires forwards who can hold the ball under the opponent's pressure until midfielders can move forward in support. Although the four defenders are expected to support the midfielders when the team has possession of the ball, for the most part they function primarily as defenders, and as a general rule they rarely make overlapping runs out of the back. When they do so, it is the flank defenders who move forward. The central defenders are typically big, strong, skilled players who anchor the defense and stay home.

4-3-3 System

The 4-3-3 system (figure 12.3) evolved out of efforts to create a balance between attack and defense while placing greater emphasis on players' mobility and interchanging positions. The four defenders can be organized as a flat back four or with a sweeper playing behind the two flank defenders and stopper back. Three midfielders are responsible for the controlling middle third of the field.

The center midfielder is the key player in this system. He or she must be a creative playmaker, have good passing and dribbling skills, and have the ability to move forward and score goals. On defense the center midfielder must be a strong ball tackler and a dominant player in the air. A wide midfielder is on each flank.

Three forwards spearhead the attack. A deep-lying central striker is flanked on each side by a winger, or flank striker. Some teams play their wingers wide, almost to the touchlines, while others prefer that they pinch in tighter to the central striker, leaving the flank space open for the wing midfielders to fill at opportune times. In either case, the three forwards must exhibit a great deal of movement both with and without the ball. Through intelligent off-the-ball (third-

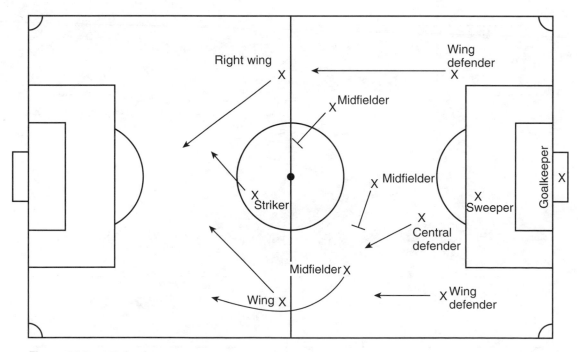

Figure 12.3 4-3-3 system.

player) running and interchanging positions, the front-running players can create space in which midfielders and defenders can move forward.

Playing the 4-3-3 system successfully requires players who are very fit, very skillful, and comfortable playing different roles. Midfield players must be willing and able to push forward into the attack at opportune moments to assume the role of either a striker or winger. Likewise, flank defenders must have the technical ability and level of fitness required for overlapping midfielders to push forward into more attacking roles. The three forwards are expected to interchange positions through diagonal and looping runs and be comfortable playing both as central strikers and as wingers. In short, playing the 4-3-3 effectively requires complete soccer players who are willing to expand their roles as the situation dictates.

3-5-2 System

Germany unveiled the 3-5-2 alignment (figure 12.4) with great success during the 1986 and 1990 World Cups and continued to use it throughout the 1990s. In its original form, the three defenders were organized with a sweeper playing behind two central markers. Teams using this system today generally deploy the defenders in zonal coverage as a flat back three.

One midfielder is stationed directly in front of the back three as the anchor player; his or her primary role is to prevent opponents from penetrating the center of the defense via the pass or dribble. This player also provides coverage for the remaining four midfielders who are deployed across the field in front of the anchor, two centrally and one on each flank. One of the central midfielders is usually assigned an organizer role while the other plays a slightly more attacking role. Two strikers spearhead the attack.

Playing the 3-5-2 successfully requires excellent flank players, people who can patrol the entire length of the touchline from one end of the field to the other. The two strikers must be very mobile and very active, constantly moving into positions where they can receive passes from midfielders and defenders. As a whole, the team must be able to possess the ball for stretches of time in order to dictate the tempo of the game, and to provide flank midfielders with ample time to move into more attacking roles.

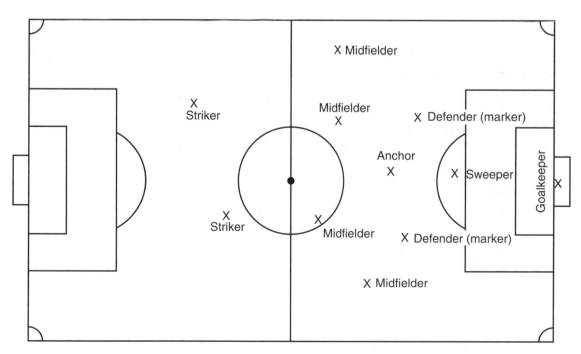

Figure 12.4   3-5-2 system.

RECENT VARIATIONS

Major international competitions such as the World Cup, European Cup, and Confederations Cup often showcase the most up-to-date playing styles and systems of play. A significant observation gleaned from the 2002 World Cup was that all systems of play were based on tactical flexibility, which enabled teams to change their playing style quickly. For example, it was not uncommon to observe teams switching from a 4-3-3 to a 4-4-2 to a 4-5-1, all within the same game (figure 12.5). In addition, most formations were organized with a free player positioned in front of the defense, as opposed to the traditional role of sweeper as the last defender. This tactic has become standard at the highest levels of competition.

The 2003 Confederations Cup, a FIFA tournament involving the champions of the various continental associations, provided a preview of what is to come, especially from the national teams of Brazil, Japan, Turkey, France, the United States, and a few others. The two most commonly played formations were the 4-4-2

and 4-3-3. All teams deployed a flat back four alignment with the defenders playing ball-oriented (zonal) defense. The two central defenders provided coverage for one another depending on who was pressuring the ball at any particular moment. At appropriate times, they would slide sideways in tandem to provide coverage for the flank defenders. Teams played three or four players in the midfield with two or three players up front as targets.

It was clearly apparent that different teams sometimes played the same formation in a different manner. For example, Japan played a 4-4-2 with midfielders aligned in a straight line across the field, similar to the positioning of their back four (figure 12.6a). Turkey, on the other hand, played its four midfielders in the shape of a diamond with one as a central holding (defensive) player, one as an attacking central midfielder, and one on each flank (figure 12.6b).

Similarly, Brazil and France both played a 4-3-3 system but with a slightly different structure. Brazil's midfielders were in the shape of

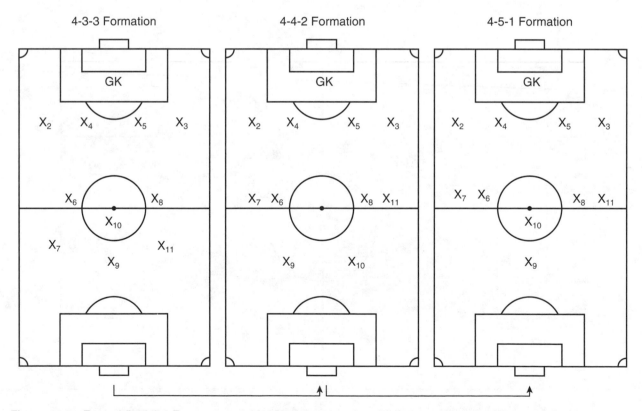

Figure 12.5 Tactical flexibility. Teams can quickly switch from one formation to another during the run of play.

a triangle with one holding midfielder, or front sweeper, playing directly in front of the back four. An attacking midfielder was positioned ahead and to each side of the holding midfielder (figure 12.7*a*). The French midfielders also aligned in the shape of a triangle, but in the reverse direction. France played with two holding midfielders in front of the back four

and one attacking midfielder underneath the forwards (figure 12.7*b*).

The moral of the story is this: Regardless of which system of play a team used, all formations conformed to the principles of attack and defense discussed in steps 10 and 11. All teams were compact on defense, and players moved as one tightly knit unit to follow and pressure

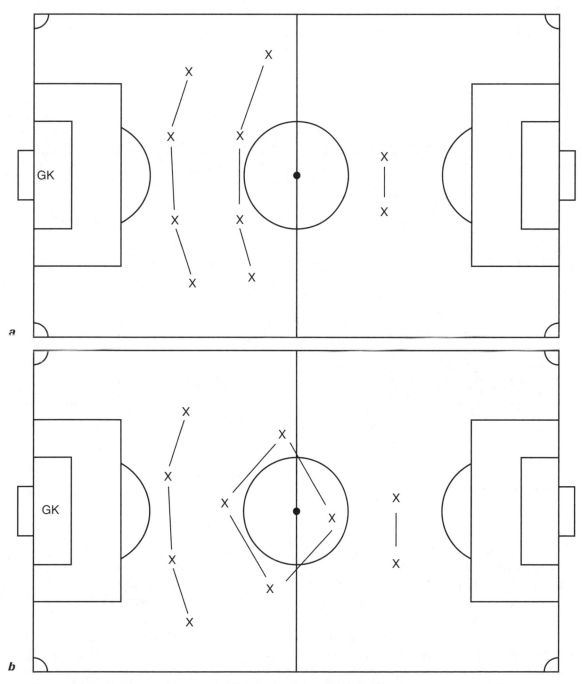

Figure 12.6   Variations of the 4-4-2: *(a)* Japan's version; *(b)* Turkey's version.

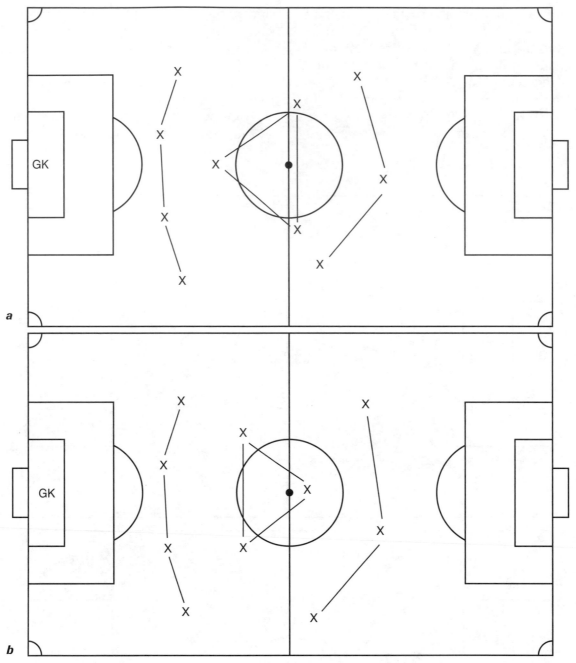

Figure 12.7 Variations of the 4-3-3: *(a)* Brazil's version; *(b)* France's version.

the ball. After loss of possession, defending players immediately withdrew behind the ball and funneled inward to protect the most dangerous attacking space. When on the attack, teams used a mix of long and short passes to alleviate pressure and unbalance the defense. The speed of play was very high as players moved the ball with a minimal number of touches. Defenders constantly moved forward in sup-

port of the front-runners. Dribbling was used only in appropriate situations and appropriate areas of the field. Players constantly changed positions, demonstrating a great deal of mobility with and without the ball. The only real differences between systems were the roles and responsibilities assigned to individual players, and that is one aspect of the game that will never change.

SIGNALING FOR SUCCESS

The soccer field is not a quiet place, nor should it be. It is usually filled with constant chatter as teammates communicate with one another during play. Your verbal commands can provide important information to teammates that will help them make decisions that are in the team's best interests. Follow these general guidelines when verbally communicating with teammates:

- Keep your comments simple and concise.
- Call early to provide teammates sufficient time to respond.
- Call loudly and clearly—you probably won't have time to repeat what you said.

Teams should adopt a standard set of verbal signals to avoid misunderstandings. The following terminology is common in soccer and should be understood by all players.

Use these verbal signals when your team has the ball:

- "Man on" when a teammate is about to be challenged from behind as he or she receives the ball. This will alert the player to protect the ball as he or she receives it and to control the ball into the space away from the defender.
- "Turn" to indicate that a teammate has sufficient space to turn with the ball as he or she receives it.
- "One time" to inform your teammate to pass the ball with his or her first touch.

- "One–two" when you want your teammate to execute a wall pass with you.
- "Hold it" to indicate that your teammate should shield the ball until supporting teammates arrive as passing options.
- "Dummy it" when you want a teammate to let the ball roll past him or her to you.
- "Switch it" to indicate a long cross-field pass to change the point of attack.

Use these verbal signals when the opponents have the ball:

- "Mark up" to instruct a teammate to lock onto an opponent.
- "Step up" to instruct a teammate to reduce the space between himself or herself and the opponent with the ball.
- "Close it up" to instruct teammates to compact the distance (space) between them.
- "Runner" to indicate that an opponent is running diagonally through or behind the defense.

Experienced players often use visual cues in addition to verbal instructions to communicate with teammates. Obvious signals include pointing to where you want the ball to be passed or where you want a teammate to move. You can also communicate with teammates in more subtle ways. A sudden glance in a certain direction or a slight nod of the head can alert teammates that you want the ball.

TEAM ORGANIZATION DRILLS FOR REHEARSING SYSTEMS OF PLAY

The system of play is only a starting point. Once the game begins, the alignment of players is in constant flux. In reality, if players adhere to the principles of team attack and team defense, all systems end up looking very similar during the general run of play. The only real differences are the roles and responsibilities assigned to individual players. Consequently, there are no specific drills or exercises for practicing the individual systems. However, you and your teammates can use the shadow drill to become familiar with the movement patterns of the various alignments.

Team Organization
Drill 1. Shadow Drill for Team Attack

Play on a regulation-size field with goals. Select the system to be used, such as a 4-3-3, and position players accordingly in one-half of the field. The goalkeeper stands in the goal. The coach stands about 30 yards from the goal with a supply of balls. The coach begins the exercise by driving a ball into the goalkeeper, who immediately distributes it to a defender or midfielder. From that point teammates collectively pass the ball down the field unopposed and shoot it into the opposing goal. Do not involve any opponents. Emphasize proper attacking movement of all players in relation to the movement of the ball as the team advances toward the goal. Begin the drill at three-quarter speed and gradually progress to game speed. Players are limited to three touches or fewer to receive, pass, and shoot the ball to keep the play fluid and moving. After each score, players sprint back to their original positions, and the coach serves another ball to the keeper. Repeat the exercise 30 times at game speed. Score 1 point for each shot on goal.

To Increase Difficulty for Attacking Team

- Add six opponents who defend 6v11.

To Decrease Difficulty

- Work the ball down the field at half speed unopposed.

Success Check

- Position to ensure width and depth in attack.
- Provide short passing options for player on the ball.
- Frequently change point of attack.
- Adjust positioning in relation to movement of ball and teammates.

Score Your Success

0 to 19 shots on goal without error = 1 point

20 to 24 shots on goal without error = 3 points

25 to 30 shots on goal without error = 5 points

Your score ___

Team Organization
Drill 2. Shadow Drill for Team Defense

Use the same setup as the shadow drill for team attack, but add an opposing team to the exercise. Your team gets in position to defend a goal. Your opponents take positions in the opposite half of the field.

The opposing goalkeeper has the ball to begin. The goalkeeper initiates play by distributing the ball to one of his or her teammates. Your opponent tries to move the ball down the field to shoot at your goal. Attacking players are limited to three touches or fewer to receive and pass the ball.

Defending players work together to deny penetration, prevent shots with a wide angle to goal, and ultimately gain possession of the ball. Defending players closely shadow their opponents to close space and deny penetration. Defending players are permitted to intercept errant passes, but they are not permitted to tackle the ball.

The attacking team scores 1 point for each shot on goal. After a shot on goal, or if your team wins the ball, immediately return the ball to the opposing goalkeeper and repeat. Repeat 30 times at game speed.

To Increase Difficulty for Defending Team

- Defend with only eight field players (10v8).

To Decrease Difficulty for Defenders

- Attacking team uses only seven players to create a 10v7-player advantage for the defense.

Success Check

- Position to ensure pressure, coverage, and balance.

- Reduce space between players to ensure team compactness.
- Position to deny penetration and block passing lanes.
- Anticipate opponents' movements to intercept passes.

SUCCESS SUMMARY OF TEAM ORGANIZATION

Every system of play has inherent strengths and weaknesses. It is the responsibility of the coach to select a system most appropriate for his or her team, one that will highlight players' strengths and minimize shortcomings. As a player, you are responsible for becoming familiar with the team's system of play, understanding your role within the system, and accepting that role for the overall good of the group. Your opportunities for individual as well as team success will be greatly enhanced if you do assume these responsibilities.

At this point of your development, you are ready to fulfill an important role within the team. The drills described in step 12 involve the entire team playing as one, so it is difficult to determine performance scores for individual players. Each drill has been assigned a point value based on the group (team) performance. All members of the team receive an identical point score. In this way you can get a rough idea of your individual performance as it relates to the group's performance. Your coach can provide more specific feedback with respect to the strengths and weaknesses of your individual performance. Record your scores in the following chart and then total the points to get an estimate of team performance in executing the various systems of play.

Team Organization

   1. Shadow Drill for Team Attack   _____ out of 5

   2. Shadow Drill for Team Defense   _____ out of 5

Total   _____ *out of 10*

Your total score will depend on how many different systems your team rehearses in the shadow drills. As a general rule, the team should average at least 3 points per drill per system of play. Scoring fewer than 3 points indicates that the team does not fully comprehend the system and how it should be executed on attack or defense. Decide how your team wants to play and then rehearse that system, or systems, until the movements become routine. As the saying goes, "Perfect practice makes perfect performance."

About the Author

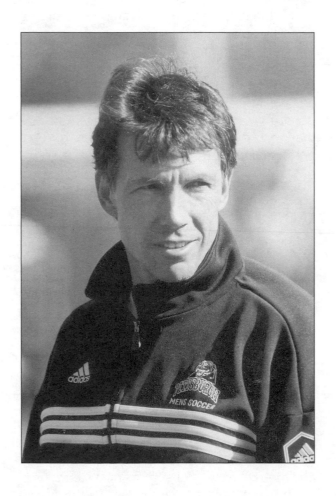

Dr. Joseph Luxbacher has been involved in the sport of soccer for more than 30 years as both a player and a coach. A former professional player in the North American Soccer League (NASL), American Soccer League (ASL), and Major Indoor Soccer League (MISL), Luxbacher has been the head men's soccer coach at the University of Pittsburgh since 1984 where he was twice named Big East Athletic Conference Soccer Coach of the Year.

Luxbacher earned his PhD in 1985 from the University of Pittsburgh with a specialization in the administration and management of physical education and athletics. He has published extensively in the areas of sport and physical fitness. He was inducted into the Beadling Sports Club Hall of Fame in 1995 and into the Upper St. Clair High School Athletic Hall of Fame in 2002. Luxbacher was honored as a Letterman of Distinction by the University of Pittsburgh in 2003. Joe Luxbacher is the author of *Soccer Practice Games, Second Edition; Attacking Soccer;* and *The Soccer Goalkeeper, Third Edition.* He lives outside of Pittsburgh, Pennsylvania, with his wife, Gail; daughter, Eliza; and son, Travis.